Sandra

Thanks for coming

Best,

Chelsea Rose

Enjoy,

Victor Helfand

PRAISE FOR *MOBILE ADVERTISING*

"This necessary book is the kind of road map we all wish we had back in 2001. It will guide you to success in mobile advertising and help you cross the chasm from unproven to proven success for your brand. It will help technologists think about what they can bring to the table, and help investors think about where to invest." (Foreword, *Mobile Advertising*, p. xii)

Greg Stuart
Former CEO, IAB
Coauthor, *What Sticks*

"This book is a critical contribution to defining the biggest opportunity in the wireless industry today—mobile advertising. And more importantly, it provides a blueprint to exploit that opportunity! Brilliant insights, clearly written—a must-read."

Paul Palmieri
President and CEO, Millennial Media

"The authors provide unique insights into the emerging world of mobile advertising in light of the distinct features—and challenges—of mobile media, and their perspectives will help operators and marketers grow mobile advertising and ensure the delivery of benefits to users, providers, and advertisers alike."

Dr. Robert Roche
Vice President, CTIA, The Wireless Association

MOBILE ADVERTISING

MOBILE ADVERTISING

Supercharge Your Brand in the Exploding Wireless Market

CHETAN SHARMA

JOE HERZOG

VICTOR MELFI

WILEY

John Wiley & Sons, Inc.

*To the two ladies in my life—my wife, Sarla, and my
daughter, Maya—who inspire me, endure me, teach me,
and make it all worthwhile.*

—Chetan

*For my wife, Laurie, an inspiration, life partner, and very best friend,
who made this book possible; to my children, Hailey and Charlie,
with the wish that they pursue their passions and become the
best at them; to my dad, Dr. Joe, who amazed me through
the years with his incredibly patient guidance; and to the
memory of my mom, Lou Anne, and brother John,
who constantly remind me that each day
really, really counts.*

—Joe

*To my wife, who urged me to write this book, but will never read
it; and to my two favorite research data points, Laura and
Julia. Not much else matters.*

—Victor

Contents

Foreword

"How do we not make the same mistakes the Internet guys made" is the most common question I get from each of the newer media channels, whether it be digital out-of-home media, IPTV (Internet Protocol TV) or mobile.

Looking back at my experience as the CEO of the Interactive Advertising Bureau during the initial growth of the industry from $6 billion to $17 billion in online ad spending between 2001 and 2006, it is clear that success was not easily won. That's hindsight, of course, for the online ad spending, but it's *opportunity* for mobile advertising. No one wants to make the same mistakes and everyone wants to get there quicker.

I am offering the perspectives I gathered from that experience because they are relevant this time around.

A key obstacle was the degree to which marketers and agencies resisted the Internet as a viable ad medium despite facts to the contrary. They would explain away their disinterest with several reasons, including "Internet is not a mass medium" (false), or my favorite, "I don't look at online ads myself" (which is equally not true). As a result, the vast majority missed the opportunity to build their company; their brands, and even their own careers.

So what is my prognosis for mobile medium on this score?

The good news is that that, like the Internet, mobile already is a mass medium. With over one billion handsets sold worldwide every year and a mobile broadband network infrastructure that can transmit those ads, mobile is at a basic level, ready for prime-time advertising. Equally important is that mobile has unique attributes versus other media choices including the locality, or geographic specificity, it can attain; and the potential personalization of the medium because each consumer has a handset. Both factors are major differentiators and are of major value to many marketers, thereby giving mobile the opportunity to capture some of the nearly $500 billion spent worldwide in advertising annually.

But what about the challenges to growth in mobile marketing and advertising? First and foremost, they are up against the same thing we were—marketers and inertia. As progressive as the advertising industry supposedly is, in my experience, it is painfully slow to change. Research we did at the IAB indicated that two-thirds of marketers describe themselves as "tried and true." This is not a leading indicator of innovation, particularly when a key part of your job is to chase consumer eyeballs as they get continually bombarded with new attractions.

But why don't marketers adopt new media easily? There are many reasons but a big part of it is that they don't recognize the value and they are uncomfortable with the new and, at least to them directly, unproven.

On some level, this is human nature and understandable. Mobile advertising, just like the early days of online advertising, is emerging, complex, and filled with techno-speak. It would have been helpful back in 2001 to at least have a road map: How does the medium fit into what we've seen before? And what are its unique capabilities? What is the necessary technology? What is the existing and evolving industry value chain and potential business models? What are the current challenges, and what is our best thinking on how they will be overcome?

This necessary book is the kind of road map we all wish we had back in 2001. It will guide you to success in mobile advertising and help you cross the chasm from unproven to proven success for your brand. It will help technologists think about what they can bring to the table, and help investors think about where to invest.

Mobile Advertising: Supercharge Your Brand in the Exploding Wireless Market does more than just teach you a new and strange vocabulary, although that is often half the battle.

It is also a framework for understanding how to be successful in mobile. It leverages the collective wisdom today for all of mobile advertising so that you don't have start at the bottom of the learning curve.

Let's return to the other point raised around the value of the mobile medium and the opportunity within that.

Seminal research we conducted while I was leading the IAB indicated that when online advertising was added to a media plan in the 10 to 15 percent of total media mix range, the overall campaign results would increase around 20 percent to 30 percent. This increase was in part a result of adding any new medium to a mix but also because the demand was low relative to the supply. Pricing made online advertising the so-called deal of the century. There is no reason to believe that mobile will not have a similar economics.

For that reason alone, marketers should consider mobile as part of the mix. While many marketers are slow to respond, the early adopters have a chance to capture immediate value while locking in long-term benefits by gaining valuable experience. The marketing manager at Ford, with whom we worked on one of the research studies, put it best: "We will use what we learned here [using the insights from online campaigns] to kick the competition's ass."

Additionally, the value of that unique knowledge to your brand also adds value to your career. Many people that I worked with in the early days of the Internet industry, whether they were at the agency, the client, or the media company, witnessed their careers rocketing forward. Sure, the excitement of the business attracted the talented, just as mobile is doing now, but it went well beyond that. They generally could distinguish themselves from their peers in both learning something new and then in delivering big value back to their brands and companies. Basically, they leapfrogged normal career paths.

I urge those of you in marketing and advertising to get a road map for success in mobile. Learn from this book and then from your own experience. And leverage that experience to capture competitive advantage for your brand, your company, and your career.

Peter Drucker, the father of modern management, put it best, "Today knowledge has power. It controls access to opportunity and advancement." This book is knowledge.

Greg Stuart
CEO of Project Rialto, a stealth company
Former CEO of the Interactive Advertising Bureau
Coauthor of *What Sticks: Why Most Advertising Fails and How to Guarantee Yours Succeeds* (Chicago: Kaplan Business, 2006).

Preface

Mobile advertising is the stuff of which great cocktail party conversations are made. Some research houses are telling us to expect a $12 billion market by 2011. Online advertising has grown to look like a business to print money, so it's only natural for there to be a little envy among us all. But that shouldn't cause us to forget that online advertising didn't exactly happen overnight—it was tough sledding. And while there are obvious winners today, we all tend to forget the carnage left in the wake of unrealistic expectations.

This book is about assessing the market opportunity and understanding its challenges and issues so as to make money and create long-term value with mobile advertising. We're convinced there's a market here but developing it to its full potential won't be easy. It never is.

Mobile Advertising: Supercharge Your Brand in the Exploding Wireless Market is the first comprehensive book on the business of mobile advertising, and we hope it is useful to anyone involved in the Web or wireless industries, from either the technology or marketing/advertising side.

Because the market is nascent, we focus on the unique advertising capabilities of this emerging medium. And we evaluate the structural obstacles currently in the way of this potential and evaluate possible remedies and solutions.

Figuring out what mobile advertising means at this early stage and what you may want to do about it is best served by incorporating several distinct perspectives—the conceptual, the analytic, and the practical. This is why the three of us decided to collaborate on this initiative.

Because we all have a passionate interest in going from buzz to biz, we've interviewed many prominent and relevant thought leaders to round out our perspectives.

For the purposes of our discussion, we use the term *mobile advertising* broadly. By mobile advertising we mean any way to message a person while they're mobile through any mobile device, so as to influence their behavior. This includes space advertising such as a mobile banner in an application, promotional treatments such as an SMS "coupon," or even a mobile search model.

Mobile technology has the opportunity to turn a lot of image advertising into direct response treatments. It can provide remarkably valuable targeting capabilities and the kind of interactivity required to get people's attention. Because of these inherent capabilities, the traditional lines between marketing, direct response marketing, database marketing, and promotion converge in creative ways.

So in this book, we use the term mobile advertising as meaning the systematic planning and implementation of a mix of activities designed to bring together mobile consumers and sellers. Given this definition, we discuss and include:

- Direct response, including promotions requiring a consumer response.
- Search advertising and marketing and its derivatives around pricing and auction types.
- Brand campaigns and all the implementation possibilities regardless of mobile technology.

Our basic thesis is that mobile advertising shows great potential due to the compelling nature of the medium and the fact that advertisers want to see this happen. Once any new advertising medium is established, such as the Internet, it's always easy to forget how long it took and that its success was not guaranteed. There are significant obstacles to overcome for mobile advertising to become meaningful. We want to offer a detailed and honest analysis of those hurdles and offer a perspective on how they can be managed.

Learning lessons from the past is important—hence *Chapter 1*. As new technologies have driven new media, it has always taken a while for the technologists and advertisers to understand each other. In putting mobile advertising into a basic historical framework, we hope to show that the basic objective of getting people's attention and trying to influence their behavior has not changed. All that ever changes is the *way* the objective can be reached.

In *Chapter 2*, we look at the powerful dynamics that the Internet drove around digital advertising and consumer control, and their overall impacts on the world of media and advertising. There were critical tipping points on the Internet that helped large-scale digital advertising become possible. The advent of a true digital age, as defined and driven by the Internet, is a powerful, positive undercurrent for the eventual success of mobile media and advertising. We begin to lay out a baseline of how mobile advertising is affected by these dynamics and how we can leverage them.

Once the world moves to digital media, a whole new set of metrics can be applied. In *Chapter 3*, we cover the measurement effects of the powerful new baseline shift toward digital that was put in place by the Internet advertising ecosystems. With this powerful paradigm shift comes media audience fragmentation. And new media rock stars, the analytics geeks. We have a new benefit of mobile interactivity being rolled out and combined with the new consumer paradigms of engagement and viral media sharing and have come up with a five-points measurement paradigm for reach, targeting, engagement, viral effects, and transactions.

In *Chapter 4*, we discuss the basics of mobile advertising and dive into what is working today in the world of mobile advertising. Mobile has some unique aspects and differentiators as a media platform versus other media. Mobile phones are high volume, personal fashion statements. They are always carried and always on, unlike computers. They enable unique user input experiences of cameras and voice, and they have built-in payment mechanisms. In theory, these have powerful enabling effects for mobile media and advertising, but we are not yet fully realizing them. Throughout this chapter, we begin to lay out a fabric of underlying issues as well.

The major structural issues and mobile market accelerators are discussed in *Chapter 5*. All is not the glossy, hype-happy smiley picture painted in many analyst or industry media reports around mobile advertising. There are some major, perhaps irreversible, structural flaws in the way of campaigns getting from experimental budgets of $50,000 to over a million and running many of those in parallel. The potential is huge, and the mobile-specific accelerators are massive, but the realities are complex, confusing, and sometimes involve head-popping implementation and measurements or metrics problems. Despite these issues, mobile presents some amazing accelerators. To get to these accelerators, we need to remove major barriers and hurdles.

In *Chapter 6,* we cover the various business model shifts that have to happen in mobile media to get to massive consumer usage scales. These eyeballs will then be the base for attractive advertising to major brands. When it all comes in right as a model, a consumer value proposition, and a revenue generator—it can be massive in its impact.

Mobile advertising is geographically complex and looks very different in many regions of the world. In *Chapter 7,* we provide several case studies discussing facets of mobile advertising such as user experience, and off- and on-deck. The studies include companies from around the world. We hope these examples give you a good sense of the potential and creative and technical elements of various campaigns.

Technology is the lifeblood of digital advertising. In *Chapter 8,* we delve deep into the technology issues that need to be resolved and the processes that will need to be put in place to kick-start the industry. We discuss the opportunities available to entrepreneurs, operators, and other players in the industry who will innovate and solve some of the thorny technical problems.

In *Chapter 9,* we take a look at "a day in the life of" consumers—what will their advertising experience be like in the future? We also discuss the major trends that will have a significant impact on the business of mobile advertising. The convergence of "three screens" and the "always-on" era is upon us and their role in changing the user experience will be profound. A focus on youth will continue to drive advertisers to use the new mediums creatively. We also discuss the tensions in the ecosystem and how they might evolve in the next few years.

Over the course of this project, we had the good fortune to confer with the key movers and shakers in the industry. Some top-notch executives also contributed to the project. *Chapter 10* complements our work with 13 thought-provoking pieces from some of the most brilliant minds in this emerging industry. The reader can gain insights from executives at Ogilvy, Microsoft, Nokia, Qualcomm, Rhythm New Media, Reliance Infocomm, Yahoo, NTT DoCoMo, Nielsen Mobile, Diageo, Vodafone, Mobile Marketing Association (MMA), Disney, and MTV Networks.

This book is about the journey of the mobile advertising industry from the phase of *cautious optimism* to the transcendental state of *contextual nirvana.* This medium provides context, immediacy, and personalization like no other. In *Chapter 11,* we summarize our thoughts with a review of the text as well as offer recommendations for key constituents of the value chain.

In Gratitude

This project began in earnest two years ago when the three of us were brainstorming about new opportunities in mobile. We instinctively knew that mobile advertising was coming down the line, but a lot of work needed to be done before it became a viable revenue channel. At that time, the young industry was still trying to find its way in the very complex, often confusing, ecosystem of technologies, companies, and competing visions. Fast forward to January 2007. We met at coffee shops to catch up and started discussing the subject and how the market had evolved. We felt that things had improved tremendously but there still was a lack of complete understanding of the opportunity, the space, and a cohesive vision. Thus the seedlings of our humble endeavor were sown.

First, we want to thank Emily Conway and the great team at John Wiley & Sons for seeing the value in our proposal. Emily got it at first sight when others were scratching their heads. Thanks also to Miriam Palmer-Sherman and Charlotte Saikia for seeing the project through editing and production.

We were blessed with generous help from scores of individuals. It is difficult to acknowledge everyone who touched this project, but we would like to express our gratitude to folks who made a significant difference to the outcome. Our work was influenced by some of the pioneers in Internet advertising and in the mobile industry. We had great support and received many valuable market insights and strategic validation from some of the best minds in the mobile media, mobile advertising, and advertising worlds. They provided invaluable guidance, inspiration, feedback, and important introductions along the way. We would like to thank Alana Muller, Andreas Manguel, Anne Baker, Anurag Mehta, Brian Cowley, Brian Lent, David Weiden, Ed Sarausad, Eric Hertz, Federico

Pisani Massamormile, Gene Keenan, Greg Sterling, Harry Kargman, Ian Foley, Jeremy Lockhorn, Jim Cooley, John Hadl, John SanGiovanni, Julie Ask, Kevin Stone, Larry Shapiro, Mark Logan, Martin Cheng, Mike Baker, Neil Strother, Nihal Mehta, Nitin Shah, Omar Takawol, Patrick Moorehead, Paul Reddick, Peter Miles, Ron Elgin, Russell Buckley, Scott Dunlap, Scott Ferris, Scott Shorter, Shawn Conahan, Tim Jemison, Tom Burgess, Tomi T. Ahonen, Tony Fish, and Webster Lewin for taking the time out of their busy schedules to challenge our suppositions and let us bounce ideas.

As the pieces started to come together, Greg Gilles provided invaluable initial editing on the chapters. He made us think about the reader, flow, and themes in a fundamentally better way.

Many more people helped during the course of the project by providing additional input and feedback, and many more introductions. Our heartfelt thanks go out to Aaron McKee, Aaron Santell, Andy Shields, Ben Hosken, Brian Bowman, Brian McGarvey, Cindy Spodek Dickey, David Rittenhouse, Dennis Glavin, DevKumar Gandhi, Elliott Hamilton, Erin Fors, Gary Lee, Ganesh Pattabiraman, Greg Badros, Hadley Quish, Ike Lee, Jamie Minney, Jason Spero, Jeff Hasen, Jeff Kunins, Jeff Torgerson, Jim Cook, Josh Blackwell, Kartik Raghavan, Katie Thompson, Kelly Weston, Kieran Barr, Liz Croker, Manik Khanna, Maria Bumatay, Markus Munkler, May Petry, Mike Galgon, Minh Tran, Peggy Jacobson, Peter Cranstone, Ron Pessner, Rowena Wong, Ryan Mackle, Satoshi Nakajima, Scott Alderman, Stephanie Grossman, Stephanie Myers, Steve Wood, Susan Brazer, and Yoshikazu Kumagai for their assistance.

The industry thought leaders and key contributors of Chapter 10 not only took time out of their incredibly busy schedules to pen their valuable thoughts but also provided incredible insights and feedback throughout the course of this project. Their time and insights are deeply appreciated. Our sincere thanks to Harry Santamaki (VP, Nokia), Ian Stewart (SVP, Viacom [MTV] Asia), Joe Duran (GM, Microsoft),

Kanishka Agarwal (VP, Nielsen Mobile), Laura Marriott (President, MMA), Mahesh Prasad (President, Reliance Infocomm), Marco Boerries (SVP, Yahoo!), Maria Mandel (Executive Director, Ogilvy), Marianne Marck (VP, Walt Disney Internet Group), Omar Javaid (VP, QUALCOMM/ MediaFLO), Richard Saggers (Head of Mobile Advertising, Vodafone), Syl Saller (Executive Director, Diageo), and Ujjal Kohli (CEO, Rhythm New Media). Without their help, this project wouldn't have been complete. We are tremendously grateful for their contributions and their respective organizations for working with our tight deadlines and constant pestering.

Several executives patiently read through the manuscript and provided us their valuable feedback. We are indebted to Bob Roche (VP, CTIA), Chamath Palihapitiya (VP, Facebook), Larry Weber (Chairman, W2 Group), Om Malik (Founder, GigaOM), Paul Palmieri (President & CEO, Millennial Media), Ron Elgin (Chairman & CEO, DDB Worldwide), Dr. Yasuhisa Nakamura (Executive Director, NTT DoCoMo), and Dr. Young-Chu Cho (President & CEO, KTF).

Some friends and colleagues went out of their way to help us out and they deserve special mention. Dave Smiddy, Laura Marriott, Paul Schaut, and Sunil Jain provided assistance whenever we needed them. Many thanks to Greg Stuart who readily agreed to help us with the project and wrote the Foreword for this book.

Chetan would like to thank clients, friends, and colleagues of Chetan Sharma Consulting who have helped shape his thinking over the years and had a profound impact on the outcome of this book. You know who you are.

We owe the most to our families. No book project can be successful without the selfless sacrifice of our loved ones. Chetan would like to thank his parents Dr. C. L. Sharma, Prem Lata Sharma, and Dropadi Sharma, brother-in-law Aditya, and brother Rahul for their support and encouragement of whatever he pursues. He is probably among the very few authors who have subjected his wife through the pain of five books in as many years. Sarla has supported every single one of his projects with the same unwavering dedication, patience, intensity, love, and foresight. In addition to being his reviewer-in-chief, the encouragement and help he receives from her is priceless and he is forever indebted for the privilege of spending their lives together. And finally, Chetan would like to thank Maya, his three-and-a-half-year-old angel, who sympathized with dad's long hours around the clock for six straight months. The glimpse of her fills him with joy and keeps reminding him what's important. This historical document is dedicated to you, Maya.

Joe would like to thank his wife Laurie for her amazing support watching Hailey and Charlie in the early morning hours while he wrote. He would also like to thank his young son Charlie for smashing the keyboard of his Windows laptop and forcing him to think about switching to a Mac in the middle of the book. It was a great decision to switch! He would also like to thank his young daughter Hailey, who demonstrated repeatedly that young kids will never know a mobile phone as only a phone and who kept Charlie busy so Dad could write. Thanks also to MacSpeech, the makers of iListen—it is a lot easier to speak than to type! Finally, Joe is grateful to have had the opportunities over the years to help guide the product management of a key mobile platform and many mobile applications, while working in the world of Internet search. This has been an invaluable experience combination and provided the strategic context for this book.

Victor would like to thank his wife Liz and daughters Julia and Laura, who inspire him to get up in the morning let alone write a book. He would also like to thank his coauthors, who had to shoulder a lot during the time of an unfortunate life event.

In closing, our final gratitude is reserved for our readers—you—for picking up this book. We hope you find it useful and that we can carry the conversation forward.

Chetan, Joe, and Victor
Seattle, December 2007

About the Authors

Chetan Sharma, President, Chetan Sharma Consulting, is one of the leading strategists in the mobile industry. Executives from wireless companies around the world seek his accurate predictions, independent insights, and actionable recommendations. He has served as an advisor to the senior executive management of several Fortune 100 companies in the wireless space. Chetan has helped several players in the ecosystem develop their mobile advertising strategy. Some of his clients include NTT DoCoMo, Disney, KTF, Sony, Samsung, Alcatel Lucent, KDDI, Virgin Mobile, Sprint Nextel, AT&T Wireless, Reuters, Qualcomm, Reliance Infocomm, SAP, Merrill Lynch, American Express, InfoSpace, BEA Systems, and Hewlett-Packard.

Chetan is the author of four other books on the mobile industry. He has patents in wireless communications, is regularly invited to speak at conferences worldwide, and is an active member in industry bodies and committees. Chetan is interviewed frequently by leading international media publications such as *Time* magazine, the *New York Times*, the *Wall Street Journal, BusinessWeek, Japan Media Review, Mobile Communications International*, and *GigaOM*, and has appeared on NPR, WBBN, and CNBC as a wireless data technology expert. He frequently addresses several telecommunications industry trade delegations to the United States, such as executive teams from Japan, Korea, and Finland. He served on the U.S. advisory committee of the Korea-Pacific U.S. States Joint Conference on wireless and multimedia. Chetan has published several articles and industry reports on a wide variety of topics.

Chetan is a sought-after strategist on IP matters in the wireless industry. He has advised clients with some of the biggest patent portfolios in the world and has worked with players across the wireless value chain. He has been retained as an expert witness and advisor for some of the most prominent legal matters in front of the International Trade Commission (ITC) including *Qualcomm vs. Broadcom* and *Ericsson vs. Samsung.*

Chetan is an advisor to CEOs and CTOs of some of the leading wireless technology companies on product strategy and IP development, and serves on the advisory board of several companies. Chetan is a member of IEEE, IEEE Communications Society, and IEEE Computers Society. Chetan has Master of Science degree in Electrical and Computer Engineering from Kansas State University and Bachelor of Science degree from the Indian Institute of Technology, Roorkee.

Joe Herzog, Senior Director, Search Products, Info-Space, has more than 12 years of experience in mobile data and media product management and marketing. An accomplished leader of new product launches, he helped conceive and launch a significant mobile platform and many breakthrough new consumer mobile products, including; InfoSpace's first mobile local search ads, voice interfaces, consumer GPS applications, iPhone application, and 411 maps application. At InfoSpace, Joe is responsible for developing new search strategies and products for the Web; he currently directs the product management of the metasearch product line, interfacing with Google, Yahoo, Microsoft/ Live, and IAC/Ask. In 2006 and 2007, he led the InfoSpace local search Web and mobile product lines and product teams, which were subsequently sold to Idearc in October 2007 for $225 million. He also led the teams that launched InfoSpace's mobile search offerings in 2005.

Prior to joining InfoSpace, Joe held product leadership positions at two mobile software start-ups: ViAir for wireless e-mail and CTS for mobile fraud prevention. Before entering the world of mobile data, Joe worked for Microsoft cofounder, Paul Allen, at his multimedia software company Asymetrix. In his position as National OEM Sales Manager, he helped launch a series of market-leading Windows Multimedia software products with major PC OEMs such as IBM, Dell, Compaq, Toshiba, and Gateway.

Joe's areas of expertise include overall go-to-market planning, strategic planning and positioning, and product management team building. He has a Master of Business Administration degree from the University of Montana and is an active member of Montana Academy of Distinguished Entrepreneurs (MADE) and also has a Bachelor of Science degree from Montana State University in Marketing.

Victor Melfi, Chief Strategy Officer and Senior Vice President, VoiceBox Technologies, has extensive professional expertise in technology strategy, direct marketing, and advertising. He was in the Strategy and Media practice in the New York office of Booz-Allen and Hamilton where his client work included IBM, AT&T, MCI, McGraw-Hill, and the Omnicom Group, after which he oversaw the reengineering of the Global Promotion, Selection and Analytics business and systems at Reader's Digest, Inc. He led a successful 1997 IPO of Multiple Zones as CEO, and subsequently led and sold two other technology companies. Recently, Victor served as Chief Strategy Officer of InfoSpace and now holds the same title at VoiceBox Technologies in Bellevue, Washington.

Victor has done extensive technology strategy consulting for the CEOs of many of the world's leading technology companies. Victor was educated at Shimer College, Oxford University, and Yale University, where he received his Master of Business Administration degree and was named the Jesse Morrow Johns Scholar in Advertising. Victor has served on the board of several technology companies and professional associations including the Mobile Marketing Association. He has published articles on a variety of technology topics.

1

A Brief History of Advertising

ADVERTISING AS A MARKET

The world of advertising is a market through which advertisers can send messages to influence consumers' behavior.

The good news from researchers is that the market for mobile advertising will exceed a gazillion dollars by 2010. So all we have to do is figure out where we are on the value chain, what portion of the economics it will receive, and what share we'll command. Add a few numbers, and voilà, we can figure out how much of that gazillion dollars is ours. Right?

The challenge is that the market is too nascent to make simple linear projections and assumptions. We must be mindful of the difference between *emerging* and *steady state* markets when building our business strategies.

A quick look at the basics of any stable market provides a useful context for reviewing the history of media advertising because it clarifies the basic participants in any market as well as the implicit needs and contract between them.

Markets emerged in history as soon as people wanted goods that other people had. When a particular need became common enough that it didn't make sense for any one person to knock on doors looking for the item, markets emerged. It began to make more sense for buyers and sellers to get together at a given place and time. This setup is what the ancient Greeks called the *agra*, although certainly markets existed before then (see Figure 1.1).

A market is a *place* and/or *method* in which buyers and sellers transact.

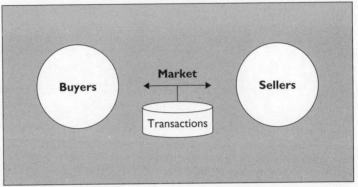

Figure 1.1   The Agra 101

The Agra

Let's say we live in an old fishing village and are getting tired of eating fish. We know edibles grow in the more fertile soil inland, so we pack up some flounder and go for a walk. Sure enough, we find a village of farmers who appear to be sick of vegetables. Ah, room for a deal!

So now we're carrying some flounder and a mess of fennel and luckily come upon a village of basket weavers. The rest of the walk suddenly becomes less cumbersome, and we arrive home pretty excited.

The next day, our neighbors take the same walk, and the following day a basket weaver shows up at our fishing village. A week later, someone proposes that we all meet Saturday at noon, somewhere in between our villages.

Soon enough, lots of other villages show up with all kinds of stuff—so many that finding what we want is getting tedious. So someone recommends organizing the stalls into categories of sorts: tools down aisle one; households on aisle three. The following week someone shows up selling gyros. Some things never change.

At some point, a seller notices that a lot of people who show up at the market are posting messages on a board. It was an effective way to circulate, expose, or advertise stuff—like the next time Socrates would be in town (see Figure 1.2).

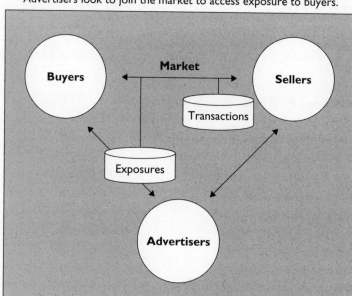

Figure 1.2   The Agra 102

At a basic level, marketing is still pretty much the same. The modern-day supermarket exhibits many characteristics that are the same as those seen in the *agra*. They both share the same goal—organizing goods to facilitate the transaction for both the store owners and the shoppers. And since a lot of people are walking through, it is also an opportunity to communicate information.

Think about the elegance of the modern food market and the way it organizes thousands of products. If we want to run in and get eggs, we know where to go. If we don't know what to cook for dinner, products are arranged to encourage browsing and discovering. Our needs are satisfied.

And it works for store owners, too. People want a huge variety of things at attractive prices. The store owners need to influence customers to buy many items to maximize the profit of each visit. By controlling the shopping experience effectively, store owners can maintain profits with low product margins.

And because so many people are schlepping through the store, the owners can sell advertisers exposure to the customers.

In a stable market, everyone wins. Their needs are met.

Markets Are Made

Markets weren't thrown out of the Big Bang. The market for abdominal exercise machines did not always exist, as hard as that is to imagine. It was made.

We need to appreciate that it is our job to build and maintain markets. There can be people who want hats and people who want to sell them, but if the mechanism for the transaction is a single store up in the Gaspé Peninsula of east Quebec, well there won't be much of a market, will there?

When an emerging market is surrounded by lots of hype, it's easy to fall into the psychological trap of feeling entitled to extracting its inherent value. We technologists fall into this one easily, particularly those of us who lived through the recent bubble economy.

Let's talk about ring tones. Worldwide sales topped $4 billion in 2004, with over $300 million in the United States.[1] Who would have thought?

In 2007, analysts expected an 8 to 10 percent decrease in U.S. ring tone sales. And margins were tanking. What happened?

Well, it could be that ring tones were a bit of a fad, but it is equally important to acknowledge that no one has been minding the basic store to create an effective market. Have you ever tried buying a ring tone, or accessing any content on your cell phone for that matter? It is not exactly easy. And now you want to add advertisements onto the purchase experience! Oh my: It takes us (hold on, let us check . . .) nine taps to find the place to get a ring tone, and (wait . . . hold it, there are a few "stores" here apparently . . . um . . .). Now hold it: You now want to push us an ad? I don't think so.

Demand can be there. Supply can be there. But if the market doesn't make it easy to buy, then the market doesn't clear. And we can blow opportunities to bring advertising into our business models if we don't satisfy the basic needs of the core participants trying to buy and sell.

All steady state markets share basic characteristics:

- A market brings together buyers and sellers.
- A market is organized to facilitate a transaction between them.
- When *and only when* a market meets the needs of the participants, it can be an effective forum for communication.

Buyers or sellers form the fundamental nucleus of any market, and if their needs are not met, the market will unlikely be able to sustain an advertising model.

We evaluate the mobile market against these basic requirements in Chapters 3 and 4.

HISTORICAL BACKGROUND

Advertising is complex and various, so it makes sense to base our strategic thinking on a good grasp of basic concepts. It's helpful to take a quick look at the history of advertising, as it plumbs some important themes that will help us develop our mobile strategies.

A Short History of Media Advertising

Come, buy of me; come buy, come buy, buy, lads,
or else your lasses cry.

—A Winter's Tale, Shakespeare

Very early ads were probably as simple as shouts in the agra—peddlers announcing their goods to the crowds. All the essential elements were there: buyers looking to buy and sellers looking to sell; a market facilitating the transaction; a format for the messages to buyers.

But in time, technology offered alternatives to shouting the message. The printing press and paper are early examples. It has never taken long for advertising to find its way onto any medium that technology has come up with.

As consumerism became more formalized in seventeenth-century Europe, newspaper ads emerged in the great centers of Paris and London. They were quite popular, and as early as the 1680s, ad-only shopping guides appeared in London. Outdoor advertising became so prevalent that King Charles II stepped in with likely the first gesture of government regulation. Apparently, he outlawed any banners that blocked the all-too-scarce London sunlight.

Although we love European history, we want to focus on the development of advertising in the United States. After all, where better to learn than from a place where the cultural mantra is, "I advertise, therefore I am."

In 1704, a wealthy plantation owner wanted to sell his estate in Oyster Bay, along the Gold Coast of Long Island, New York. To sell it, he had to let people know it was for sale—simple enough. But this seller was shrewd enough to realize that the bigger the market, the better his chances were of getting a good price. So, he bought some space in the *Boston News-Letter* and announced that his house was for sale. As far as we know, this may be when it all began here in what is now the United States:

> *At Oyster-bay on Long-Island in the Province of N. York, There is a very good Fulling-Mill, to be Let or Sold, as also a Plantation, having on it a large new Brick house, and another good house by it for a Kitchin and work house, with a Barn, Stable, and so on, a young Orchard, and 20 Acres clear Land. The Mill is to be Let with or without the Plantation: Enquire of Mr. William Bradford Printer in N. York, and know further.*[2]

There were a lot of implicit considerations, but he likely didn't sweat the analysis in any formal way:

- Are the people who read the *Boston News-Letter* the sort who might be interested and capable of buying my property?
- Will they be receptive to my message?
  - Will they notice?
  - Will it annoy them as a distraction from their basic reason for buying the newspaper?
- Is it worth spending the money for the newspaper ad versus other options?

So: Mr. Printer printed a print ad with print on paper to purchase Printer's place.

Twenty-five years later, Benjamin Franklin began publishing the *Pennsylvania Gazette,* which included pages of "new advertisements" (see Figure 1.3). Very quickly, printers and advertisers began to experiment with new devices and treatments such as headlines, illustrations, and advertising placed next to related editorial material.

These new advertisements apparently caught on like wildfire. Franklin's *Gazette* even included ads for Paul Revere brand dentures. And personal ads showed up as well, including this gem from the "I Saw You" genre:

> *A tall, well-fashioned, handsome young woman, about 18 with a fine bloom in her countenance, a cast in one of her eyes, scarcely discernible; a well-turned nose, and dark-brown uncurled hair flowing about her neck, which seemed to be newly cut; walked last new years day about 3 o'clock in the afternoon, pretty fast through Long acre . . . and near the turn into Drury Lane met a young gentleman, wrapped up in a blue roccelo cloak, who she look'd at steadfastly. He believes he had formerly the pleasure of her acquaintance: If she will send a line direct to H.S. Esq., to be left at the*

Figure 1.3 *Pennsylvania Gazette* advertisement.
Source: Ben Franklin, *Pennsylvania Gazette* (January 2, 1750), www.earlyamerica.com.

> *bar of the Prince of Orange coffee house, the corner of Pall
> Mall, intimating where she can be spoken with, she will be
> informed of something greatly to her advantage.*[3]

True to his industrious reputation, Franklin began printing the first American magazine ads in the publication,

General Media, in 1794. We guess the concept of new media isn't as new as we might have believed.

Soon many publications were selling access to their readership. Advertisers, the buyers in this market, now had to make more decisions: Where should I put my money to optimize getting my message across? How should I design my message to be most effective?

The needs of both buyers and sellers here aren't as simple as they seem. If the *Pennsylvania Gazette* reached 400 homes and was the only game in town, advertisers would just go to Ben's office. But if the circulation started getting really big and other newspapers and magazines started popping up, should poor Ben have started knocking door-to-door to see who might want to advertise?

And if we were looking to advertise snuffboxes in Philly, my decision making would also have gotten a lot tougher with all that new market and media activity. If there is only so much money to spend, we have to think about where to spend it.

Thanks to the industrial revolution, printing presses became capable of printing ten thousand pages per hour. The 1850 U.S. Census listed 2,526 newspapers and more than 600 magazines, and both increased nearly fivefold 30 years later. Which ones were read by users of snuff? Don't ask us.

In any market, there comes a point when things get complex enough to warrant having a service provider. And in many cases that takes the form of an intermediary whose expertise helps keep the transactions flowing.

Such was the case in Philadelphia, where in 1843, the first advertising agency was established. Agencies got business from advertisers, wrote ad copy, and decided where to place the ads. Many of today's largest agencies (e.g., J. Walter Thompson) were there from the beginning.

Advertising Becomes a Business Model

We can thank Frank Munsey, or blame him, for packaging all this into what today we'd call an "advertising business model." He dropped the price of *Munsey's Magazine* to ten cents and the cost of yearly subscriptions to one dollar, driving the business with advertising revenue instead of with newsstand sales.

The innovation here is a subtle but a true milestone. What Munsey did in 1893 was expand the view of advertising from supplemental revenue to a fundamental role in the business model. He appears to have been the first person to look at circulation as a core business asset: how many exposures the ad vehicle generates. In fact, before the end of the 1800s, magazines weren't really seen as businesses in the modern sense: "A publisher started a magazine because he had something to say."[4]

Munsey's gamble worked, so many magazines followed. The great race for circulation ("eyeballs" if you lived through the recent Internet bubble) began. *Ladies' Home Journal,* nearly 50 pages per issue (impressive, with all due respect to Martha and Oprah), reached a circulation of one million by 1900.[5] Heck, there were only 16 million households in the whole country back then.

The advertising business model became entrenched in that first decade of the twentieth century. In 1909, advertising made up over two-thirds of total magazine revenue, and media companies became focused on growing their circulations.[6]

Advertising as a Formal, Dynamic Industry

Advertising had gotten to be serious business by the close of the century. In 1882, Procter & Gamble Company spent a stunning $11,000 advertising Ivory soap—which, by the way, is so pure it floats.[7]

If a market emerges between the sellers of the circulation exposures and the buyers interested in messaging to those exposures, then it becomes critical to define and track the currency being traded. Thus in 1914, the Audit Bureau of Circulations formed to standardize the auditing procedures and definitions of paid circulation.

Beyond Print: Media Becomes Virtual

And in this period, technology once again spurred the development of a new, *radically* new medium. At about the same time that Munsey dropped the price of his magazine to invest in circulation, Guglielmo Marconi validated James Maxwell's electro-magnetic wave theory by creating a device that actually created and received the waves. The following year, in 1844, Samuel Morse transmitted the first telegraph message, "What hath God wrought!" In our minds, the answer to that famous question is obvious: a new advertising medium, essentially the first virtual medium.

Less than 30 years later, a Long Island real estate firm bought the first radio ads in history—15 spots for $50 apiece, thus dispensing with the oft-touted theory that pornography historically drives new media technology. It appears Long Island real estate led the charge for both newspaper and magazines. Those first radio ads were famously effective and word spread.

Total advertising spending reached $2.1 billion in 1929, not a good year for most industries.[8] That's around $25 billion in today's dollars and an amazing amount when you consider the total U.S. gross national product (GNP) was $104 billion, according to the U.S. Department of Commerce.

Only $10 million was spent for radio advertising at that point, but the new media was here to stay.[9] And while radio was finding its stride, technology was in the background stirring the pot once again.

Back in 1927, Philo Farnsworth essentially invented video, as one of the first offshoots of the new relativistic science. Prior to that, the Newtonian engineers were creating moving images by spinning disks and mirrors, which was likely pretty cool, although we wouldn't want the likes of a Baird Falkirk in our media-entertainment center (see Figure 1.4).

Farnsworth's innovation soon became television as we know it today. Initial experimental broadcasting began in the late 1920s, albeit thwarted by the Depression and then

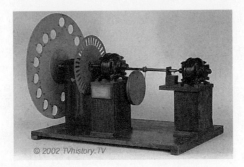

Figure 1.4   1926 Baird Falkirk—a new medium emerges.
Note: This 1926 Baird Falkirk is, believe it or not, an early television.
Source: www.tvhistory.tv, *courtesy:* Steve McVoy Collection.

World War II. In 1929, the first television broadcast—2 inches tall and 2 hours long—was pulled off on one of these contraptions by RCA in New York City. Well, okay, the action was about as compelling as Andy Warhol's infamous film, *Sleep,* but how about that character development (see Figure 1.5)?

After the end of World War II, television exploded in the late 1940s, likely in part because the American psyche was focused on reversing the feeling of wartime deprivation.

Figure 1.5   Felix the Cat—the first commercial TV broadcast. The first public television broadcast took place in 1929. This two-inch image of Felix the Cat ran for two hours.
Courtesy: David Sarnoff Library.

The first TV advertisement aired in 1941 before a baseball game. A Bulova watch spanned a map of the United States: "America runs on Bulova time!" The spot cost $9 ($125 in today's dollars) for 20 seconds.[10] Although that certainly seems like a good deal, it's important to remember that this wasn't Super Bowl 2007. New media needs to prove itself.

But the promise of the medium was clear—television was gaining consumer attention, and it allowed for great creativity in the messaging format. And this is the magic combination. While the 1941 Bulova commercial may seem a bit lame by today's standards, it was radical in its integration of multiple design elements—image, copy, voice, music.

Advertisers were attracted not only to the reach of the medium but also to its very nature. After all, it's more about attracting attention than gaining mere exposure. And again, as soon as advertisers became comfortable with the new medium and started to invest steadily in TV ads, the need for measurement became clear. Accordingly, in 1953, the Advertising Research Foundation officially accepted ACNielsen's machine-based ratings system for TV.

Television penetrated U.S. households faster than any prior technology. To expand that reach deeper into tertiary markets that often had problems receiving a broadcast signal, cable TV technology was developed as early as the 1950s.

So at this point, advertisers could spend money to communicate their message in many different ways—through newspapers, magazines, radio, and television. It got complicated. So the value of agency services became more evident, and together with the postwar explosion of TV came the emergence of the modern superagency.

And this coincided with the development of the social sciences. So, while the basic objective of advertising is simple—to persuade people toward a specific behavior, such as purchase—we began to see the application of rigor to that objective.

The *art* of persuasion evolved quickly to become the *science* of persuasion. This development really picked up speed after World War II. Social psychologists investigated how to persuade people without making them feel manipulated. As Dr. Ernest Dichter, president of the Institute for Motivational Research put it in the late 1950s, the agency "manipulate(s) human motivations and desires and develops a need for goods with which the public has at one time been un-familiar—perhaps even undesirous of purchasing."[11]

The next innovation in the history of media advertising was cable television. Although cable had been around since the 1940s and 1950s, it did not reach its stride until quite a bit later. In the 1960s, cable became more than expanded reach with the introduction of alternative programming content. Because the cable signal was direct into each home and not uniformly broadcast, it was possible to offer selective programming by interest—movie channels, sports channels, and so on. People could choose and subscribe to whatever interested them. And cable became a hot advertising medium in the 1970s.

But once again, concurrent with a new media establishing itself by figuring out what it was distinctively good at, technology was in the background getting ready to rear its head once again. The impact of the Internet was seminal in many ways. We focus on this radical transition in the history of advertising in Chapter 2.

Other Emerging Media

At this stage in the history of advertising, we are all transfixed and infatuated with the phenomenon of paid Web search advertising. But other interesting stuff is going on from which we might learn something.

Fairly recently, film studios have come to see their reach as a monetizable asset of interest to advertisers. The classic example is Steven Spielberg's 1982 movie *ET.* The movie was a huge success, and the product placement of Reese's Pieces as ET's favorite candy significantly increased sales for the Hershey Company.

By 2001, products started essentially *starring* in movies such as *The Fast and the Furious* together with humans. Blog comment-reviews are telling:

OMG!! I now have a new favourite movie.

*that was the best movie i have ever seen. . . . and it has the car
that i would like to one day own for myself, the mitsubishi evo.*

*THAT MOVIE WUZ OFF THE CHAIN . . . THE CAR
I LIKED WUZ HAN'S EVO.*

Great movie and Love the music and Cars

It's hard not to LOL . . . A plot summary from Wikipedia
is equally telling:

> *After O'Conner loses his **Mitsubishi Eclipse** to Toretto
> in a race for "pink slips" and then loses it again when they
> are confronted by Tran, O'Conner tries to gain the trust of
> Toretto by working on repairing and upgrading a burned
> out **Toyota Supra** to hand over to him.*[12]

Product placement has also entered the world of video
games. And why not? Nielsen recently reported a 12 percent
shift away from TV viewing in young males. So, advertisers aren't supposed to notice? It is their job to follow the
eyeballs. Accordingly, it is hard to miss signs for Best Buy,
Burger King, AT&T, and, yes, Old Spice when playing *Need
for Speed Underground 2.*
    And so here we are, for better or worse. . . . Anything con-
sumers see is a potential advertisement, from race cars to the
human body (see Figure 1.6).

Database Direct Marketing: The Emergence of Engagement

While traditional media have been competing for the attention of American consumers in the face of economic progress,
women in the workforce, and increasingly busy lives, an often
overlooked parallel trend has developed in advertising—
direct marketing. It represents the refinement of the art of
persuasion to the concept of *engaging* the consumer.

Figure 1.6   Advertising takes many shapes and forms.

As the mother-in-law says, "Every generation thinks it invented sex and Coca-Cola." Although technology has surely accelerated the possibilities of engagement, it is useful to look at what has already been done before we reinvent wheels and start spinning them.

In Venice, in the year 1498, Aldus Manutius printed the "Earth's biggest selection" of books. A lot of companies followed. We don't know about your mailbox but ours are stuffed—both the one outside our house and the one inside our computer. The basic idea is not to wait for people to notice an ad in any particular media but to go directly to them with the message, and in a more interactive way.

In fairness, it wasn't until 1961 that the legendary Lester Wunderman coined the term *direct marketing*. He later described the essential quality of the craft as "where the advertising and buying become a single action."[13]

So, you just don't message people through media and hope they will come. You hit them where they live (e.g., via the mailbox) and go right in for the kill with a call to action: "ORDER NOW and we'll send you a second auto-eject melon baller for free!"

Another key innovation here, compared with prior media advertising, was to create a direct, traceable link to the cause (the message treatment) and the effect (the sale). Direct marketing is measurable.

Mass mailings started in the 1940s, but a whole slew of creative promotional and direct response techniques really blossomed over the ensuing decades. The enhanced objective of the message format, the *treatment*, was seen as being less passive than other advertising media. This idea of active engagement evolved from advances in the science of human memory.

After all, you just don't call someone you don't know and offer your hand in marriage. You go out to dinner together and try to *engage* the person before proposing.

The mathematical science of segmentation jumped in around the 1960s, catalyzed by improving computer resources. This advancement allowed advertisers to develop treatments specific to groups with similar characteristics instead of using the same piece for everyone on the mailing list.

Reader's Digest, a genuine trailblazer here, had already developed its unified customer database well before we started using fashionable terms like customer relationship management (CRM). Their huge flat file contained a single view of a customer, including not only demographics but also a running history of every contact between the customer and the company. Providing the marketing function with easy access to this information was a profound technical database innovation. Fed into an analytics system, this information (literally billions of bread crumbs tracing the customer contact history) helps marketers figure out how best to *engage* the customer and close the sale.

Technology provided another boost with the advent of the modern database in the 1980s. The more information you can store and easily retrieve, the better you can target your message.

The Dynamic Evolution of Competing Media

In discussing the historical roots of interactivity and engagement, we have mentioned the development of newspapers, magazines, radio, television, cable, and the Internet, as well as the insertion of advertising into video games and onto our cars and bodies. And we have discussed direct marketing in this context.

But to understand the fundamental dynamics of advertising media, it's important to look at why new media emerged and how they have competed for advertising dollars. The moral of this story is that a new medium competes with established formats based on its *distinctive* characteristics and how they help advertisers reach and message consumers.

Technology is often the initial trigger, but why exactly does a medium resonate with consumers to the extent that advertisers want to jump in? It seems that all successful advertising media evolve beyond a mere technology when creativity not only grabs people's attention but also aligns with some functional or psychological consumer need.

Anyone who was ever forced to take an introductory psychology course (or forced to listen to those who have) has surely heard of *Maslow's Hierarchy of Needs*. This seminal conceptual framework laid out a pyramid of human needs, from basic food and shelter up to self-actualization and beyond—stuff like being among the first to see Paris Hilton's post prison haircut.

We can look at the evolution of media content similarly: Media have climbed the pyramid from being sources of practical information to serving as entertainment. In fact, the distinction between news and entertainment is becoming increasingly blurred.

Newspapers Inform

Newspapers had their roots in the basic sociopolitical need to communicate during formative periods in history. There are newspapers of sorts dating back to the 1400s, with basic information of real importance to people—like what warlords were expected to be passing their way. This was a pretty low readership on Maslow's pyramid, more concerned with head cuts than haircuts.

Newspapers played a central role in the early, turbulent period of American history. The purpose of newspaper content was aligned with the American spirit: freedom of the press.

> *Were it left to me to decide whether we should have a government without newspapers, or newspapers without a government, I should not hesitate a moment to prefer the latter.*

Thomas Jefferson, 1787[14]

So the purpose of newspapers was to inform, and the role of the medium was always catalyzed during social and political transitions. Advertisements were there, but they never intruded on the objective to inform. The content was serious and its cause often noble.

Then came the first new medium—magazines. Why did it evolve to the point of interesting advertisers?

Magazines Entertain

Newspapers and magazines are both printed media, but the first obvious difference is the focus of their content. Magazines addressed a need a step or two up Maslow's pyramid of needs. In fact, this was a quantum leap, popping us to the level in the step curve we're still riding today—the human need for entertainment.

As Western culture began to stabilize politically, people began to be less consumed with basic survival (we're not referring to the leisure class, who—being on top—had the time to be entertained; they could always call their court jester or pay someone to paint pictures on their ceilings).

For the rest of the populace, magazines provided mass entertainment. Before then, yes, people might go to a play or a witch-burning, but magazines redefined or expanded the previous notion of *editorial content* more toward entertainment than for pure information.

Early magazines explored new content formats such as serials written by the likes of Charles Dickens. And images became content in their own right, beyond the informational sketches in newspapers.

From fiction to photography, the content of magazines had a wider editorial palette capable of expressing and evoking a wide range of emotions. This paralleled the emergence of brand marketing, and the parallel was not coincidental.

So magazines came along with a new range of capabilities to help support a business model focused more on making a profit than on the noble cause of informing society. And this had an important social context: Media, together with society in general, were becoming more commercial.

The impact on newspapers from the new medium was initially low. Advertising was new and growing at a rate such that cannibalism wasn't an issue. Demand from advertisers was higher than supply, and there was more of a focus on how each medium could be used distinctively.

Since newspaper content was initially local, it makes sense that the circulation would be good for "classifieds" and local announcements like the one advertising the Long Island estate for sale. But for selling an Amana (every housewife's dream), it made sense to use colorful, less serious, and more entertaining magazines.

Radio Sings

In the 1920s, radio emerged and competition between media for advertising dollars really started to heat up. American life had gotten very busy by the time radio came along. So now media not only had to differentiate its format, but also had to compete for consumer time. And radio brilliantly *created* incremental time for consumers.

When we are reading, we are typically singularly focused. But we can listen to radio while doing other things. Housewives (as they were called in the 1940s) could listen while mopping the floor. And when radios showed up in cars, even more free time was created. Radio was the first mobile, eyes-free, hands-free medium. Was it the birth of multitasking?

In terms of content, newspapers gave us written information; magazines added visuals, color, and entertainment. Radio added yet another vehicle to get a message across—sound.

The human voice can achieve a level of emotional pull that the written word can't quite match.

Newspapers and magazines are both printed media. But radio relies on intangible waves, not ink on paper. Radio is there when you turn it on. You don't have to go out, purchase it, and bring it into your home. And once you pay for the device, the content is free. Radio was, indeed, a very innovative medium.

And with the advent of radio, the role of the advertiser became more powerful through the new concept of sponsorship. Radio content was a lot more expensive to produce than print. And in stepping up to cover that cost through sponsorships of radio shows, advertisers gained unprecedented influence. This allowed for a lot of creative opportunity to blend messaging into editorial content to heighten the impact of the ad. No pretense of journalistic objectivity here!

Advertisers were no longer merely riding on a medium's exposure to consumers through its reach, they were shaping the very nature of the medium. And here the lines between content and advertisement were beginning to blur.

The commercial capabilities of radio scared the heck out of the established media and advertising world. There were 5 million radios in 1925, with around 20 million listeners in over 19 percent of U.S. homes. Radio advertising jumped from $4 million in 1927 to $19 million in 1929. Overall household penetration jumped to 35 percent, with 75 percent presence in cities and wealthy suburbs.[15] And beyond the burbs, radio reached out in a vital way to previously isolated rural areas, creating a greater sense of community.

How did the established print media defend themselves? The reaction was more aggressive than when magazines began to compete with newspapers. Although there was competitive tension between the newspaper and magazine communities, at least they were the same basic medium—the printed word. And initially, printing technology restrictions kept them pretty much at parity with respect to visual qualities.

The print world used its reach to discredit radio—there was lots of mudslinging. Advertising was just finding its stride, and the pie likely didn't seem big enough for three media to share. And radio caused additional anxiety because it was a very different format.

It is certainly not random choice that determined the print editorial mix at the time. Magazines, in particular, focused a lot on movies and theater, neither of which competed for its advertising dollars. It was hard to find any coverage about radio in newspapers or magazines; many newspapers refused to print radio programming schedules.

As a technology, radio was downplayed by many. Jack Woodward, in *Forum for July 1929*, attacked it as primitive, citing everything from breakdowns and static to bad programming. He predicted (and you get a sense that he hoped) it would never cut it as a consumer device.

In the same year (June 11, 1929), *Christian Science Monitor* published the editorial, "Whither Advertising." There's a definite alarmist tone to the article. It cast the radio industry, including manufacturers, in a bit of a subversive light, pointing to its plethora of advertising.

Technology helped magazines defend against radio with the advent of full-color photographic reproduction in the early 1930s. *Vogue* published the first color photo cover for a magazine on its November 15, 1931, issue. Perhaps print couldn't make sound, but it could certainly catch your eye.

So the 1930s was the great age of the picture magazine. In 1936, the venerable *Life* sold more than one million magazines in its first few weeks.[16] By the 1940s, magazines were an important part of any brand advertising strategy and maintained over 12 percent advertising market share throughout that decade.

Print and radio eventually learned to coexist by finding their distinctive "sweet spots"—magazines are visual; radio is audio. And peaceful coexistence was easy because advertising budgets were steadily increasing. Competition was not yet that intense.

TV Seems to Have It All; Competition Heats Up

The 1950s saw the impact of television. Like a bat out of hell, it flew into over 70 percent U.S. households around the middle of the decade.[17] It was a medium rich in entertainment potential, combining the sound of radio with the imagery of the picture magazine improved with motion. Just when media had started to settle down by focusing on what each did best, television upended advertising with its compelling capabilities.

The proliferation of the medium was extraordinary. World War II was no one's idea of a good time, and Americans' appetite to kick back and be entertained was high. The war had given everyone a feel for what life would be like a step lower on Maslow's pyramid. And there'd be none of that: It was time to party.

National radio advertising sales felt it first. It reacted by leveraging what radio did distinctively compared with the upstart. While compelling, television was only capable of uniform broadcasting. Radio could be broadcast selectively, and it leveraged that capability by focusing on regional and local content and advertising.

Initially, magazines were less affected. The format of the print medium differed more from television than radio. And they had perfected the use of color. Magazines also were portable—you couldn't drag your TV set to the dentist's office.

Magazines' resilience gave way going into the 1960s. The cost of color television declined, and household penetration had reached 97 percent. But more importantly, television was winning the battle for consumer time. It was genuinely changing the American lifestyle. Reading lost ground to vegging—sitting back and being entertained without effort.

As early as 1956, television grabbed 12.2 percent of the advertising dollars, leaving magazines with 8 percent.[18] Magazines reacted by becoming increasingly focused on specialty interests, including the emerging TV star cult.

But soon television faced competition from new media. Cable, which originally was just a way to reach out to areas that couldn't get a broadcast signal, came into its own as a medium, It became a "content play" in the 1960s with the introduction of target programming. Network content started looking like one-size-fits-all.

The established networks exercised political influence, demanding that the Federal Communications Commission (FCC) regulate the industry. Regulation served as a thumb in the hole of the dike throughout the decade.

Cable TV dislodged the thumb in the 1970s, and the advertising world sat back to watch the ensuing flood of change. In 1978, the big three networks enjoyed over 90 percent prime time share, but by 1986 it dropped to 75 percent, further dwindling to 61 percent in 1993.[19]

The next competitive entry into the media game was the Internet. It is fair to say that media have not seen such a fundamentally different contender for ad dollars since television. And like television, the Internet has threatened to fundamentally change the way Americans live.

The Internet not only chased the exposure game with traditional space/banner ads but essentially invented another advertising technique by free-riding on a new form of exposure: the online search. It soon became clear how distinctive the Internet really was.

In its current state of maturity—and it is still a young medium—the Internet combines text, images, motion, and sound. It entertains, informs and is a channel for commerce. And most distinctively, it was the first medium that handed the steering wheel over to the consumer, making the experience much more interactive. And advertisers don't have to infer consumers' interests because they declare them in their Internet usage and search behavior.

Early competitive response included a fair share of mudslinging reminiscent of early radio days. Internet safety and security issues, stories of click fraud and child predators still get a lot of media attention.

But the bottom line that can't be hid from advertisers is the basic data on how we all spend our time. In 2006, we spent over an hour a day on the Internet versus 23 minutes reading.[20] The Internet has seeped into the fabric of American life, impacting our culture in a way the history of media hasn't seen since the entrance of the boob-tube.

What we have seen from Internet advertising is impressive, particularly for a medium that is barely out of its first half-decade. Yet it is important to appreciate how nascent the medium really is. In absolute size, online advertising isn't expected to surpass even radio spending until 2010, when Forrester and the like predict online advertising to hit around $26 billion. And while consumers now spend three times more hours on the Internet than on reading, advertisers are still spending six times more of their budget on newspapers and magazines.[21] New media takes time to establish itself, even if it seems sizzling hot.

Although different media have competed to be noticed throughout the history of advertising, direct marketing took a different approach. It didn't wait to be noticed, but instead interrupted our attention by going into our mailboxes. And by tracking our responses and sending additional mailings based on it, direct database marketing planted the seeds of interactivity and engagement we now see blooming in Internet advertising.

How Media Compete

History shows us that, just like people, media compete best based on things they are good at. And the winners have always competed on attributes of meaning to consumers. The dimensions on which media have competed over the past two hundred years are telling:

- The unique characteristics of the medium in terms of its potential to attract and engage customers:
  - Type of content and its creative capabilities
    - The written word; images; sound; video; direct mail pieces; user-generated stuff: how well the content type grabs consumer attention
  - A unique usage characteristic
    - The portability of magazines; the eyes-free, hands-free nature of radio that allows people to participate while doing other things; the user

> *control* and *flexibility* of searching for stuff on the
> Internet
> - Segmentation and specialization
>   - Affinity programming of cable; specialty
>   magazines
> - Mudslinging—government intervention
>   - Network's influence over the FCC combating
>   against cable; the printed word's attack on radio

New media will likely continue to emerge. Any successful
medium will compete based on its distinctive characteristics.
So, when developing mobile advertising business strategies, we want to be very clear about what the medium can
uniquely do for advertisers.

In Chapters 3 and 4, we explore the unique characteristics that generate excitement for the future of mobile
advertising.

THE BASIC CONCEPTS AS THEY APPLY TO MOBILE ADVERTISING

We have presented basic concepts and a short history of
advertising media because while we believe there is money
to be made here, we believe it must be earned through hard
work. *Markets are made, and that process can fail.* The window
of opportunity never stays open forever, and there is no time
to waste reinventing the wheel here.

What can we take away from our review of the basics
and history? How can it help us get through the window of
opportunity before it closes?

Summary: Basic Concepts and Media History

Markets emerge and sustain themselves by meeting the needs
of their constituencies. It may only take two to tango—buyers
and sellers—but advertisers often increase the value generated from the market. Advertising can be seen as a market for
exposures to consumers on which to send a message.

At its most basic, advertising aims to expose its message to the market toward the end of influencing the behavior of the participants. The first gating item for ad effectiveness is to not intrude on the core transaction that generates the exposure on which the message rides. In a market, the needs of every constituency must be met. If any group—buyers, sellers, advertisers—leaves the market relationship because its needs aren't satisfied, the market as it is known will fall apart or at least morph into something else.

So, mobile advertising must be mindful of the basic rules of the game. We can blow it and be asked to leave the market.

Advertisers have a variety of ways to send their message to the marketplace. At its most basic, the advertisement must get exposed, so advertisers have to find out where consumers are spending their time. The history of advertising shows that technology affects where consumers' eyeballs go. Thus, advertising is constantly in flux.

Advertisers, then, are always watching consumers' media consumption. And they are also looking for new creative techniques because they want their message to be memorable. The better the impact of the message, the more effective the ad investment. So they'll also spend money testing different treatment techniques offered by the medium.

They can increase hit rate by targeting the message to be meaningful, and thus memorable to the consumer. So, advertisers invest in research and data that help clarify different consumer segments and tailor their messaging accordingly.

And, if all these variables are the same, advertisers want to reach as many people as possible, as inexpensively as possible.

New media has an inherent initial edge, at least theoretically, because its newness helps it get noticed and remembered. But this does not mean that every new medium is guaranteed budget and good times. Sellers of media are responsible to prove its effectiveness in being seen and influencing behavior.

We have seen lots of media emerge, from shouting to print to audio to electronic. Each has competed on the basis of what it does best. At a certain point, the size of the advertising budget doesn't grow as fast as new media emerge, so they eventually fight for share. The reality is that once advertisers have tested you out using marketing development or research funds, you must compete for budget with all the other established media.

In proving itself meaningful, new media have always been mindful of a few basic questions:

- What is *distinctive* about my medium, my device, or my treatment?
- Do consumers use it in any *distinctive ways?*
- How do these characteristics allow advertisers to craft and deliver compelling messages?
- How can it be used to enhance the effectiveness of other media?

We evaluate these core questions in Chapters 3, 5, 7, 8, and 9. But even at a gut level, when we look at mobile advertising from this perspective, we find good news and bad news.

The Good News

Advertisers are always looking for new places to message consumers. There are around 3 billion worldwide cell phone subscribers, and they stare at their phones a lot.

Advertisers look for targeted reach. We know a lot of demographic and behavior data about mobile subscribers. Adequate analytic software is out there to make good use of that information. If mobile search can be made compelling to users, we will know a lot more about consumers because they will declare their interest in the query.

Advertisers look for the creative capabilities of a new medium in terms of the capability to produce memorable messages. Cell phones combine sound, image, video, communication with others, and soon enough, location information.

Advertisers want to measure effectiveness to help them allocate their media budget. As we discuss later, there's progress here in mobile.

Without question, the cell phone resonates with the lifestyle, interests, and behavior of young consumers. Increasingly younger consumers own phones and are using them with great frequency.

The Bad News

Consumers aren't using their cell phones for reasons other than phone calls as much as we all hoped. And unless someone proves that consumers are willing to have their basic phone call experience interrupted with messages in exchange for lower cost or free access, then that is a problem. Research and experience suggest that the "this phone call is brought to you by . . . " advertising model resonates with only a few segments. And those are typically lower-value consumers from an advertising perspective.

But advertising messages can also ride on the device and application interface, and here is where we've seen a lot of early activity. And we'll be blunt on this one: It's the interface, stupid. People can't even find out how to turn on their speaker phone, let alone search for and download a video clip.

The current interface is a vestige of the personal computer/ graphical user interface (PC/GUI) and is based on nested menus from *somebody's* (not ours!) categorization scheme. Drilling down using a small keyboard (even if it's a pretty graphical one like the iPhone) is tedious, if not frustrating, particularly when you're mobile or multitasking.

So we run right into the fundamental need of any market to satisfy consumers and vendors. We fail miserably on the basic experience of finding and using: How can we expect people to accept advertisements? We discuss the critical problem of the interface in more detail in Chapter 5.

And even if we clean up the interface, are we delivering the kind of reach advertisers are looking for? The structure of today's industry is understandable—major carriers

(we will be using the terms carriers and operators inter-
changeably throughout the book) need to protect and leverage their investment in their network—splitting consumer
reach into several mutually exclusive buckets makes it hard
to hit the critical mass of reach. And the huge potential reach
of mobile devices is one of the key assets we have to offer
advertisers.

And have we yet made a convincing case to advertisers
that cell phones allow for creativity in messaging? Have we
answered the basic question: What's distinctive about the
device and what can it mean to advertisers?

Ready . . . Aim . . . Fire?

It's intuitively clear that mobile advertising has some distinctive attributes and capabilities that can help advertisers get their message exposed. As we speak, advertisers are
kicking the tires.

So, we know we're *ready*—but have we adequately *aimed*,
and are we ready to *fire* and win? Not entirely.

Like any new medium, there's work to be done. Riding
on the coattails of a bubble economy, it's easy to have a sense
of entitlement to success, especially when venture capital is
flowing into mobile advertising and we are writing books on
the subject.

But remember: The bubble popped.

So while the trigger may be cocked, it's smart to go on to
the next chapter before shooting. The road ahead is not an
easy one, so bring a map with you. This is a particularly complex ecosystem, and you want to look at it carefully before
you load the kids up in the car for the journey. We take a
closer look at the complexities of the business environment
in Chapter 6.

But the pain will be worth the gain: The reward shows
promise of being valuable indeed. In Chapter 2, we argue that
the Internet has combined nearly all the attributes of value
to advertisers that have emerged in the history of advertising to date, with increased targeting, direct response, and

engagement capabilities. And the new age of digital media has been highly disruptive to the old guard silos of traditional media. Mobile advertising will continue to build on this digital media momentum and bring both further value and disruption to the advertising world.

NOTES

1. Baker Braiker, "Dial a Song," *Newsweek* (March 4, 2005).
2. *New York Times* (January 12, 1896): 29.
3. David Wallechinsky and Irving Wallace, *People's Almanac* (New York: Doubleday, 1975–1981).
4. Bart, "Giants on Uneasy Footing," *Columbia Journalism Review* (1962): 32–33.
5. See note 3.
6. See note 3.
7. P&G Company, "Ivory Soap Donates Historic Advertising Material to Smithsonian" (press release, October 24, 2001).
8. David M. Blank, "A Note on the Golden Age of Advertising," *Journal of Business* 36, no. 1 (1983): 33–38.
9. T. Peterson, "Successive Threats Peril Magazines: Editorial Values Keep Medium Vital," *Advertising Age* 51 (April 30, 1980): 166–170.
10. "The History of Bulova," www.bulova.com.
11. See note 3.
12. www.wikipedia.com.
13. Lester Wunderman (speech given at the Massachusetts Institute of Technology, November 29, 1967).
14. Julian P. Boyd et al., eds., *Papers of Thomas Jefferson* (Princeton, NJ: Princeton University Press, 1958).
15. Coolidge-Consumerism Collection, "Interactive Historical Introduction," Library of Congress, www.lcwebw.loc.gov.
16. T. Peterson, *Magazines in the Twentieth Century*, 2nd ed. (Urbana: University of Illinois Press, 1964).
17. A. J. van Zuilen, *The Life Cycle of Magazines: A Historical Study of the Decline and Fall of the General Interest Mass Audience Magazine in the United States during the Period 1946–1972* (Uithoorn, The Netherlands: Graduate Press, 1977).
18. Cobbett S. Steinberg, *TV Facts* (New York: Facts on File, 1980).
19. See note 18.
20. James Belcher, report in *eMarketer* (September 2006).
21. TNS Media Intelligence report (September 2006).

2

A Digital Revolution

As described in Chapter 1, print was the initial format of mass media and advertising, primarily in newspapers and magazines. In the 1920s, the advent of radio led to the second mass media type. It had, for the first time, a captive audience. Broadcast media included AM, FM, and eventually digital and satellite versions. Using broadcast media, advertising models realized major new revenue streams. Although recorded music can be considered the third mass media type, it has not been supported effectively by advertising, even in today's digital arena. Despite digital downloads, recorded music is primarily associated with purchase or subscription models, although this may change to rental models over time.

Movies, the fourth mass media type, introduced multimedia. Sight, sound, and motion were incredible additions to the world of advertising although it took years for advertisers to nail that value in ads. Movies represented the first pay-per-view models to the world. The advertising before the main features in movies produced large-scale revenue and brand-new video formats. As movies evolved from silent films to sound, they provided a solid development of advertising types for the fifth generation of mass media—television—in the 1950s. This included a rapid change from black and white to color television and from a major broadcast network model to an explosion of channels and advertising opportunities on cable networks. New advertising revenue streams were generated with targeted TV shows such as sports, sitcoms, talk shows, music videos, and reality. These productions represented a strong magnet for the passive attention of a large percentage of audiences and therefore enabled higher impact advertising.

While cable was being initially implemented in the 1970s, ready for the industry to apply some creativity to its inherent capabilities, the Internet was being conceptualized. Based on the networking of universities to research data through leased, private network lines among them, pioneers like Vannevar Bush and J. C. R. Licklider imagined what has become today's "connected world":

> *A network of such [computers], connected to one another by wide-band communication lines [that provided] the functions of present-day libraries together with anticipated advances in information storage and retrieval and [other] symbiotic functions.*[1]

When Licklider's concept of a ubiquitous connected network beyond academic institutions started becoming a reality, the outrage from academia was overwhelmed by the formation of the for-profit band of Internet service providers of the 1990s.

Internet entered as the sixth medium and as the broadest platform of digital-enabling media that consumers had ever seen. Today, TV attention time is eroding in most markets around the world, but there is an explosion of new media choices along with surging consumer media activity, including mobile media. Media slicing and multitasking define a new generation of consumers who graze the digital media. Fragmentation of former audience segments has already happened and will accelerate.

Digital advertising, spurred by the advent of the Internet, has irrevocably changed the old-guard silos of video, audio graphics, and text advertising. The earlier approach of successful brands aiming an expensive major national campaign at a few consolidated audiences in one silo, such as TV, is getting scarce. Instead, a successful campaign now involves text, graphics, video, and audio across many media types and seeks out an audience segment that would have been far too expensive to target in mass media prime time in the past. A campaign might include user-generated content for TV, web banner ads, permission-based e-mail, web video clips, web search, mobile banners, and now, the new mobile advertising video format of mobisodes.

Although it is sometimes hard to remember, Internet advertising—just like other new media—had to find its way. And importantly, its eventual success was not exactly a slam dunk. That is a critical point: Nothing ever *guaranteed* the success of Internet advertising, or of any new medium or market for that matter.

In the words of Dr. Stephen J. Fredericks:

> *In this digital dreaming future, content is defined not by its old media name, but by its core property: text, video, and audio. All content, clarified and freed, can be distributed via any converged technology. Consumers will control this content. They will decide what they see, how they see it, when they see it, and where they see it. Households will have a hardware distribution service that will deliver this content on the consumers' demand, on the consumers' terms.*[2]

In time, the world moved from mass market, interruption-based advertising to a more relevant engagement. The legacy of the old media (print, music, radio, and television) is being affected fundamentally by consumers who are in control with myriad remote gadgets. Thus the stage is set for digital and analytics to replace the old guard with new data-driven rock stars. The Internet has all the characteristics that an advertiser seeks. Lots of people are generating lots of exposures and transactions, but perhaps more importantly, their interests are self-declared. When people are on a paintball accessories site, chances are they're interested in paintball; no need for too much subscriber analysis there. And where people go and what they do is all tracked—a quantitative marketer's dream.

In this scenario, audience targeting will be based on user intent rather than on abstract theory, especially when it comes to search. The return on investments (ROIs) will have more immediate visibility. The many variations of mobile media will be a key part of this explosion, yet the campaigns will span all digital networks at once, including mobile. To accommodate these changes, the old advertising agency is now part software company, part analytics shop, and part emerging technologies practice. And there are very few three-martini lunches.

OLD MEDIA MODELS FLIPPED UPSIDE DOWN

How did the stable world of TV-driven advertising suddenly land upside down? Until the world of the Internet, the paths from the advertiser to the consumer were generally controlled by a few powerful companies and advertising agencies. The old structure looked something like this: At the top were the brands and the advertisers. Close to the top were the advertising agencies that were responsible for crafting the messages. The media buyers then took the messages and determined the best campaigns and channels to reach the targeted consumers. Those channels included classic broadcast television, newspapers, magazines, and radio stations. At the bottom were targeted consumers.

Most advertising campaigns were run across silos of print, TV, and radio. Each was considered somewhat separately in the advertising budgets. Text and graphics campaigns were built for print, video was built for TV, and audio was built for radio.

In the late 1960s, a television advertiser could spend as little as $5 million and reach an audience of over 40 million viewers. By running similar ads sustained consistently over a few years, it was possible to attain incredible message penetrations into the targeted audience. Advertisers chose the time and spots to present their stories to a passive and relatively captive audience. The three networks that effectively reached the majority of their audiences now reach minority percentages at best. Scarcity of televisions, television spectrum, and channels forced viewers to huddle around a few shows and channels, mostly at the same time.

There is no longer a stronghold on audience attention span. Even before the Internet hit with massive consumer scale, the audience broadly spread out across the new channelscape when four television channels exploded into 50 cable channels. This fractured viewership meant that putting a large audience back together for a unified campaign suddenly became very expensive.

Advertisers no longer had control over the channels or the unified audience reach they once had. The old top-down hierarchy and message flow was forever and inevitably changed. What remained were the relative silos of audio campaigns that ran on radio, video campaigns that ran on TV, and text with graphics in print. But these also were about to undergo a radical transformation.

By the late 1980s, the Internet started to leak out of the closets of geeks and technologists. The number of Internet hosts rose above 100,000 for the first time. Very few people, especially in the old-guard media of TV, radio, or print advertising, predicted that this would permanently change their worlds. After all, the Internet was the purview of academic pinheads, geeks, and outspoken champions of free and noncommercial usage. Advertising was forbidden, or so they thought. The early mantra for the Internet was "free." It turns out they were right that the Internet was always to be free to consumers. But this brigade totally misunderstood the strength of digital relevancy and advertising. That force simply was powerful enough to change the media forever.

The old guard of media executives, who stood on the sidelines for much of the dot-com boom and bust, were affected on a massive scale. Driven by the Internet and empowered by new devices that access massive networks of distributed media, the media grazers will collaborate, control, and contribute to advertising. In addition, advertisers will be held accountable for unheard of transparency and audience engagement. But we are getting too far ahead of ourselves. How do we get there and what role does mobile media and advertising play in that game?

The Mosaic Age

Once the number of hosts on the Internet exceeded 100,000 or so, it started to become difficult for people to find things. The world of search was invented to solve a navigation problem, which seemed innocent enough, but eventually had the most profound impact on advertising ever known.

In 1990, McGill University student Alan Emtage created a file transfer protocol (FTP) indexing tool called *Archie*. One year later, Mark McCahill introduced an alternative called *Gopher*. *Veronica*, the grandmother of all search engines, appeared on the scene in 1992, spidering Gopher text; but the web interface, as we know it today, was not there.[3] With the introduction of search, the key ingredient for mass consumer adoption was right around the corner. However, all these early attempts at search technology lacked any sort of semantic capability, meaning that you had to know exact terms to get the search right and find what you were looking for.

In the early 1990s, around the time that everyone decided the Internet was an all-text medium with e-mail, file transfers, chat, and Usenet, the Web came along. In December, 1991, a demonstration by World Wide Web creator Tim Berners-Lee in San Antonio at Hypertext '91 was a key step in revealing the potential of the Web with the new linking language called hypertext markup language (HTML).[4] As a result, The 1991 CERN (the world's largest particle physics laboratory) release about this demonstration attracted masses of developers worldwide, who began to build new hyperlinked and interconnected applications that ran on massive distributed networks. This irrevocably changed the media and advertising landscapes.

Early Web Experiences

In 1993, the first really popular web browser, known as *Mosaic*, took the world by storm. The first web robot, created by Matthew Gray and called the World Wide Web

Wanderer, also took off.[5] Initially, Wanderer was designed to track the explosive growth of Internet servers, but it was soon updated to track uniform resource locaters (URLs). It was controversial for the traffic it created. Wanderer development work also spawned more advanced spiders that tracked the links on the start pages.

By the end of 1993, the basic but critical groundwork for today's search engines was in place. In addition, the web site volumes that would eventually create a brand-new breed of advertising and media models were also unleashed. *Search* became the most powerful disruptive factor the advertising world had ever seen because consumers told a search engine their intent; it was a marketer's dream.

The basic Internet service provider (ISP) services were expensive, slow, and still unreliable. They were suitable for e-mail, which came into prominence early, but they were not very usable for graphics and even basic media. Consequently, most consumers in 1993 did not perceive that this new medium could do everything that the previous five mass media types did.

The first Internet advertising probably appeared in 1993. The pioneering web portal Global Network Navigator (GNN) had to get special dispensation from the National Science Foundation for what became a banner ad. The first banner placement was probably sold to Heller, Ehrman, White and McAuliffe, a law firm. In the original press release that introduced GNN, the Online Whole Internet Catalog was described this way: " . . . subscribers can not only read about these subjects, they can actually connect to them with the click of a button." GNN described itself as "a new experiment in online publishing."[6] What was considered experimental and seemed big enough to require special approvals from the National Science Foundation triggered a decade-long avalanche of disruptive change in the media and advertising businesses. The field was disordered, but we didn't quite understand that yet. The progress was rapid from this point forward.

Mobile Data during the Early Web Era

The old guard at the helm of most of the carrier organizations didn't really believe in data, as voice continued to be the main focus and they didn't think data could generate serious revenues for their businesses. But there were signs of mobile data being birthed in this time frame.

Like the Internet, the early clear winners in mobile data delivery were text and messaging based. Short Message Service (SMS) was originally defined as part of the Global System for Mobile or GSM series of standards in 1985, but it took a full seven years before the first commercial SMS message was sent. In December 1992, Neil Papworth of the Sema Group used a PC to send an SMS message or TXT to Richard Jarvis over the Vodafone UK GSM network.[7] That first TXT was "Merry Christmas."[8] The first SMS message or TXT typed on a GSM phone is claimed to have been sent by Riku Pihkonen, an engineer student at Nokia, in 1993.

In 1994, the Mobile Data Association (MDA) was established to increase awareness of mobile data among consumers and member companies. In June 1997, the Wireless Application Protocol (WAP) forum was founded by Ericsson, Motorola, Nokia, and Unwired Planet (now Openwave).[9] WAP was inherently problem ridden because, unlike the Internet, mobile networks such as General Packet Radio Service (GPRS) or code division multiple access (CDMA) are not IP based and therefore do not support the standard protocols of the Internet. When WAP was first released, it was also throttled by severe device limitations, usability issues, and advocates who hyped it beyond all reason.

The initial WAP user experiences were also hampered by misguided design principles from traditional web design. For example, four screens were often used to present two screens' worth of data. In addition, early WAP applications often had heavyweight, web-based, splash screens. Essentially, web technology was being plopped onto mobile phones and it didn't work. Furthermore, web user experience design was still in its brochureware phase so the mobile implementations of quality user experiences were still far off.

AT&T took a shot at mobile data in 1997. It failed because the devices were severely limited and the data rates were so slow. If you asked for something today, you would get it next Tuesday, or maybe later. But they persevered and relaunched PocketNet in 1999.[10] It failed again. In November 2000, NTT DoCoMo and AT&T[11] formed a long-term partnership to develop wireless multimedia applications. The alliance's goal was to enable users to access HTML applications and content on mobile wireless terminals and allow the two companies to promote common global standards. AT&T Wireless launched mMode, an i-mode like service, but never could adopt the same market strategy of giving content providers a larger share of the revenue pie. As such, the strategy floundered. As described in Chapter 8, this is a critical area to model correctly to enable a truly massive mobile media ecosystem.

Short Message Service (SMS) based TXT was launched commercially for the first time in the United Kingdom in 1995. It didn't really take off until 1998, when consumers could send TXT messages between O2, Orange, Vodafone, and T-Mobile U.K. carriers or devices. By December 2002, one billion TXT global messages were being sent every day.[12]

Around 1998, the first crude forms of mobile advertising were small carrier logos that showed on the splash screens when consumers turned their phones on. Sometimes these logos could be replaced by a person's name or a small character, but not always.

In 1998, a Finnish company, the Jippii Group, introduced a radical innovation for mobile phones. They invented the downloadable ring tone. Another early player in the ring tone field explained his motivations:

> It was a gloomy December morning in Helsinki in 1997 when 26-year-old Vesku Paananen woke up with a hangover after a night of Koskenkorva vodka and beer. Paananen, a chief technology officer with new-media company Yomi

Group, was jolted out of bed by the annoying ring of his Nokia 6110 mobile phone. "I didn't want to hear 'de de de de deeeee' ever again," Paananen recalls. "I wanted to hear Van Halen's 'Jump', and I was willing to pay for it." The technology was there to program mobile phones to play pop tunes rather than electronic bleeps. The biggest resistance was from the operators, who said, "Ring tones, what's that?"[13]

They were almost lost on the public as bleeps masquerading as music. But they were going to radically change mobile media. Gartner forecasted mobile music, including ring tones, ring-back tones, real tones, and music would top $15 billion in revenues in 2007 and grow to $32 billion in 2010.[14] Quite a spark was created to cure a hangover and to hear Van Halen's "Jump" instead of just plain old "de de de de deeeee."

In the early days of the Web, mobile data was, for the most part, still in the labs and brains of engineers. Mobile media were almost inconceivable in those days because mobile data networks were simply too slow and far away to support true media. But these early experiments would turn into something unique and massive.

Data: The Seeds of Disruption Are Planted

Mass media reached a significant milestone in 1996 when Procter & Gamble convinced Yahoo that it would only pay for ads on a cost-per-click basis. This meant no more payments for mere eyeballs on the banner ads; this kicked off web advertising accountability and transparency.[15]

This approach and metric held the Internet advertising world to a higher standard than other advertising media. Eventually it became a major factor in attracting advertising budgets that formerly went to TV and other legacy media. This led to breakthrough levels of advertising spending in 1997 and beyond. Further, metrics, audience measurement approaches, and tools began to appear that were unique to Web advertising.

In June 1996, a new company called WebConnect offered the first generation of web measurement tools to advertisers. They created private URLs to track user impressions and clicks. This drove new web advertising management technologies that supported animated Graphic Interchange Formats (GIFs), banner rotations, and common gateway interface (CGI)/Pearl scripting to get ads onto web sites.

Some ISP measurement tools for audience size accountability were appearing as well. Nielsen Media Research broke new ground by signing up major ISPs like UUNET in July 1996. UUNET agreed to provide support for Nielsen's full range of site traffic measurement and analysis tools to all their web-hosting customers.[16] Many other hosting agreements like this happened in 1996 and 1997.

By the end of 1997, the key audience measurement vehicles and standards were almost in place. They would evolve and winners would emerge by the end of the decade, but audience measurement could now be verified. Consumer currency for clicks on banner ads and clicks on paid search links would rapidly follow. The new and rapidly evolving combination of audience tracking at the hosting level and advertising ROI analysis tools for consumer clicks had not been seen in any previous generation of media. Breakthrough advertising accountability was starting to occur. It was early, but the seeds planted here eventually transformed the old guard of legacy advertising silos and media buying. The disruption would not really occur until 2007 . . . a full 10 years later, but it would be massive.

The growth of Internet advertising since its birth in 1994 has been phenomenal. What started out with bland, tentative banners that were as common as roadside billboards has morphed into a search-driven, media-rich explosion of revenues, the likes of which was never been seen before.

More importantly, the famous "threes" of TV media buying from the 1980s became risky behavior, although it is unlikely that anyone involved in them noticed that in 1996. In the old TV media-driven advertising ecosystem, almost everyone was comfortable and content with the way things were. After all, the system worked. The old media habits of making three phone calls to three networks to arrange a three-martini, three-hour lunch that ended in time to tipsy-trail home to Connecticut on the three o'clock train was going to end—and hard. It was over, but few professionals involved in this TV media-derived landscape of threes noticed the data-driven seedling planted right smack in the middle of their comfortable territory.

Digital advertising driven by the Internet and measured by new forms of consumer and ROI data made the silos of threes obsolete by 2007. Going forward, data ownership will determine who owns this new advertising world. Clear boundaries of the former TV-driven media and advertising are blurred. Companies that dominate this new landscape will stake their claims on data ownership, analytics, and with whom they share or do not share their data. The seeds of this paradigm were planted in 1993, and they will turn the advertising arena upside down once again as data drives consumer interruptions into engagement-based advertising.

THE DOT-COM SHAKEDOWN

Web sites that had no assets and burned too much cash with lavish parties, marketing run amuck, and zero revenues spelled trouble for businesses that had Internet advertisers at the core of their revenues. A major source of the problems was totally unsustainable advertising spends by dot-com companies. Those companies were spending more than one dollar to make one dollar, and substantially more in most cases, for the classic upside down, dot-com advertising spend splurges of the late 1990s as shown in Figure 2.1.[17]

PointCast was perhaps a highlight of mistaken hype around useless-to-consumers new technology and poor broadband timing. In 1996, PointCast launched push technology, which was a hot press concept at the time. It was promptly banned by many corporate networks for clogging precious bandwidth. However, that did not stop the press from lavishing heaps of praise on the product. Consumers' opinion did not really matter, and those who tried to use it

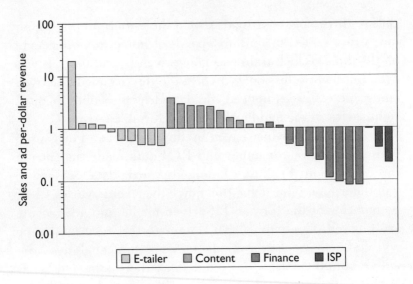

Figure 2.1   Upside down ad spends.

on dial-up networks were sorely disappointed and found it utterly unusable. Those tenacious few that got it to work were inundated with ads.

But this was just the beginning. Useless services and sites were proliferating. Fringe ideas based on zero-sum games that ignored consumers and didn't have even a fraction of a percentage chance of succeeding, captured $50 million in funding. This occurred virtually overnight, in frantic bidding wars between trigger-happy, reactive venture capital (VC) firms.

Then it all came crashing down—thud.

Casualties included the infamous web brands Webvan, Pets.com, CDnow, Peapod, DrKoop, Value America, Bingo.com, Kozmo, Flooz, eToys, Boo, and MVP—and the list goes on and on.

British fashion retailer Boo.com ran through $120 million in investor money in roughly six months and then promptly folded.[18] Boo's immersive retail site had its own online guide, Miss Boo, as well as its own online magazine, *Boom*. It was wildly overdesigned, the user experience was horrible, and it was completely out of touch with most retailers' vision of quick shopping and ease of use. When they hired KPMG to liquidate, the technology was hawked for a paltry $368,000 and eventually folded into Fashionmall.com, never to be seen again. Boo.com is just one example; most dot-coms just folded. What happened to the Boo.com founders? In 2003, they were paid $187,500 for talking about their misadventures in the book *Boo Hoo: A Dot Com Story.*"[19]

Some of these dot-com companies were simply too early for broadband capabilities, yet their products were built for big broadband. They found out that free is a folly. Building the chicken and the egg at the same time is a monumental and often oxymoronic task, since one or the other has to be first. Also, the codependencies between massive egos of young start-up CEOs and third-tier VCs looking to place $80 million bets was an experiment in grandiosity that finally imploded. The chart[20] shown in Figure 2.2 represents the funding rush.

Nothing changes overnight, and the zero-sum games of the first wave of Internet start-ups were unreasonable. New things don't replace old things overnight, especially across

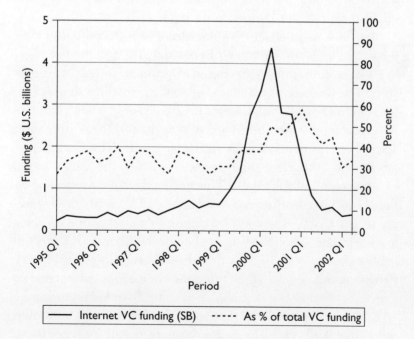

Figure 2.2   Venture capital funding for the U.S. Internet industry.

an entire consumer base that is comfortable with what they know already. But the 2001–2002 blowout laid the critical foundation for an explosion in dynamic new web companies and products after 2003. Getting the dot-com system cleansed was critical for a fresh perspective and portended a second, far more impactful, creative rush.

Mobile Gets Its Own Mini Shakedown

Mobile media is by no means isolated from the world of hype and overzealous funding, especially with respect to mobile advertising and the numerous failures of companies trying to distribute media off of the main carrier decks that simply run out of money before carriers run out of patience. The end of the dot-com era also brought a rush of mobile funding as the next major wave of the Internet. But most of the companies funded in this era are gone now. Mobile is not the Internet. And it took new forms of mobile-specific media and technology, such as ring tones and TXT, for it to take off. But that didn't happen until later.

In 2001, as handset manufacturers introduced better ring tones, personalizing mobile phones quickly became the rage. Web sites containing ring tones of popular songs and tunes started appearing, with many of them providing the service free of charge and with little or no advertising. Their popularity grew mainly through word of mouth, and these sites soon started charging a small fee for the upgrade. The next step—advertising the ring tone services—drove the early forms of advertising mobile data. This early advertising was not on the phone but on other mass media, (e.g., TV), and urged viewers to get a new ring tone by typing in a short code on their mobile phone. Then the first big backlashes to mobile advertisers hit. Jamba! (known for their Sweety the Chick and Crazy Frog ring tones) and other ring tone companies, advertised so aggressively that the British Advertising Standards Authority (ASA) ruled in late 2005 that advertisements could be shown only after 9:00 PM.[21] The primary intent was to prevent these companies from targeting youth audiences in their campaigns.

Yet Crazy Frog still permanently changed mobile media by introducing a new mobile media format to the masses and driving aggressive new mobile advertising that had a major consumer and financial impact.

Mobile ads were born in Japan in June 2001, when the country's largest mobile operator NTT DoCoMo got together with the country's largest ad agency Dentsu and formed D2C.[22] This was the world's first major advertising agency specializing in mobile. Also in 2001, AT&T trialed WAP banner ads on PocketNet for a brief period. They failed. They annoyed consumers, primarily because they had to pay packet fees for the ad bits. Plus the relatively bulky ads clogged an already very slow data network.

In July 2001, Ericsson, Motorola, Nokia, and Siemens founded the Mobile Games Interoperability Forum (MGIF) to set standards for games. In April 2001, the first Mobile Entertainment Forum (MEF) meeting was held in Paris.[23] In November 2002, MGIF was absorbed into the Open Mobile Alliance, the technical standards body of the mobile industry. MEF was to go on to be a major standards force in mobile media and advertising.

Other experiments in mobile advertising that began in the 2003 time frame quickly folded. The handsets were just becoming useful and colorful. The browsers were improving, but were not fully capable of graphics across a broad handset base and the networks were slow. Downloads had not taken off yet, except for ring tones at $0.99 and up per download. Mobile usage, excluding Asia and TXT messaging, was simply not extensive enough to drive advertisers to a critical mass of consumer eyeballs.

BUILDING A HUNDRED-BILLION-DOLLAR ADVERTISING EMPIRE AT FIVE CENTS A CLICK

The combined atrocities that afflicted users—ad-laden paid inclusion search results, spam-filled keyword indexes, and pop-ups assaulting user eyeballs on every click—created a brilliant opening for a relevant search engine that redefined the user experience. The traffic that resulted from highly relevant searches was fundamental to creating strong consumer reach for advertising via text keywords. First Overtureand then Google took advantage of these dynamics and changed the search and advertising worlds as we knew them.[24]

The media business has always been based on predicting consumer behavior, where consumer eyeballs will land, or what they intend to purchase. Advertising then gets positioned in the media where the consumers will be. Whether people are sitting at home watching *American Idol* on Tuesday evenings or perusing *Cosmopolitan* for clothing ads, advertising's track record demonstrates a long history of planning and buying based on perceiving where people are and predicting what might appeal to them. The same rationale has come to apply to search as well. Search behavior—whether it is related to someone buying an air conditioner when temperatures rise in the late spring, or the buzz around whether a certain *American Idol* contestant has been voted off—has already made a huge impact on the way all advertising is planned and bought.

The high penetration of broadband access was the precursor to a rapid adoption of web search. High usage, driven by broadband and combined with the advent of performance-based advertising models, has rapidly evolved search to become the most important part of the online media and advertising landscape. This spawned a whole industry of search engine marketing and paid search specialists that literally did not exist 10 years ago.

In 1998, Bill Gross at Overture launched the idea of pay-per-click ads, enabling a search engine to sell targeted traffic to advertisers on a per-click basis. His breakthrough idea was to arbitrage traffic streams and sell them by auction with a very high level of cost transparency.[25] Typically, pay-per-click ads are keyword targeted. Search engine advertising platforms are now incorporating simple text-based links with local, geographic, behavioral, and demographic targeting. One of the oldest forms of commercial market enablers, the lowly auction, was brought back in full force to the world of search and advertising. The simple standardizations of the text-based ads also enabled massive advertiser adoption in short periods of time. This magical combination of the auction, transparency, text-based simplicity, and user intent was to have the single biggest effect on advertising to date.

It was clear that the previous generation of search engines had been throwing too many paid inclusion ads at consumer expectations. In the original paper Sergey Brin and Larry Page wrote, they took a dim view toward this practice:

> *Since it is very difficult even for experts to evaluate search engines, search engine bias is particularly insidious. A good example was OpenText, which was reported to be selling companies the right to be listed at the top of the search results for particular queries. This type of bias is much more insidious than advertising, because it is not clear who "deserves" to be there, and who is willing to pay money to be listed. This business model resulted in an uproar, and OpenText has ceased to be a viable search engine.*[26]

How right they were. Google changed the game by creating an amazing, fresh, and highly relevant search product and released it into a very crowded market. With lots of word of mouth and little formal marketing outside of solid public relations (PR) and amazing consumer buzz, it soon attracted millions of users. Google then leveraged that amazing search volume to attract hundreds of thousands of web advertisers.

Google did not start off to create an advertising empire. There were a few stumbles before the media experts got AdWords right, early in 2002. AdSense, the second major prong in their advertising quiver, came later in that year. AdWords, AdSense, and Search Engine Optimization (SEO) combined to form a powerful three-pronged arsenal that any media campaign could choose from. It took a while to integrate an ad model into their search engine, and there were at least two less-than-successful iterations.

But by 2003, they had it pretty well nailed. The press release announcing Google's AdSense says it all, utterly perfectly:

> ### *Google Expands Advertising Monetization Program for Websites*
>
> *Google AdSense Enables Sites to Maximize Revenue Potential While Enhancing User Experience*
>
> —MOUNTAIN VIEW, California—June 18, 2003 [27]

Look at the subtitle of that press release. We have a succinct statement of a market's requirement to meet the needs of its various constituencies. In this case, the web sites, suppliers of the content of interest, maximize revenue potential; those looking for relevant results, searchers, get an enhanced user experience. And Google, the broker facilitating the market transaction, gets its cut.

To develop winning mobile advertising approaches, it would be brilliantly comforting if we could describe our market that cleanly.

At first, advertisers balked at the lowly text ads that Google proposed. Nevertheless, Google eventually became an advertising empire because it matched the advertisers' content to consumer search intent—but without the baggage of paid inclusion listings. The ads were clearly marked and put off to the side, outside the core listings. Also, advertisers paid only when the ads were clicked.

These pay-per-click ads are sold in "second price auctions" where the highest bidder gets the highest presentation rank for that keyword. But the winner ends up paying only a penny over the second bid. Click-through rates are also a factor in the ranking of the pay-per-click ad being auctioned, which ensures that the ads consumers feel are the most relevant get the best placement. The result is a highly transparent, highly targeted, performance-based advertising medium that is heavily influenced by consumer intent and click behavior. Superefficient market results for a merchant who writes a compelling ad and gets a very high click-through rate will mean that the merchant pays less per click for their traffic.

Paid search is now so important that even in 2005, it was almost 45 percent of the total online ad spend. It should stabilize around that percentage overall moving forward. Figure 2.3 shows the percentage growth slowing or dropping over time. But it has already had a major impact on advertising.

As noted in Figure 2.4, pay-per-click (PPC) ad spends dominate in the overall search spends. Paid Inclusion still exists, but for the most part has been relegated to shopping engines. In this chart, paid search is the amount spent on search engines. Paid inclusion is the amount spent to get placed in shopping sites, and agency fees are the amounts spent on overall support to place all these ads.

Paid search has truly dominated and made a major impact on all these areas and budgets. It will be a long time before we see the same scale in mobile advertising. But there is no doubt that Google, Yahoo, Microsoft, and others see a

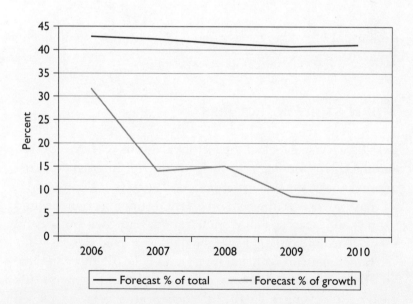

Figure 2.3   U.S. paid search as a percentage of online ad spend.
Source: eMarketer (September 2006), using U.S. online spending benchmarks against the IAB/PWC full year 2005 data.

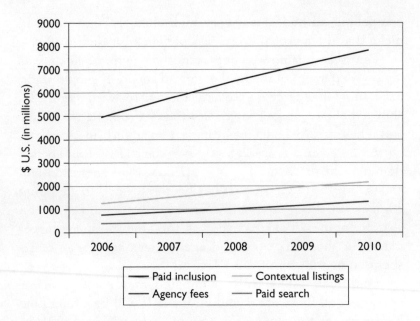

Figure 2.4   U.S. search marketing spend to 2010.
Source: Charlene Li and Shar VanBoskirk, "US Online Marketing Forecast 2005
to 2010,"*Forrester Report* (May 2005): 14.

similar pot of gold in mobile and will be heading to mobile in
a massive way very soon.

THE HISTORY IN PICTURES

Let's take a visual look at the historical events we have covered
and the corresponding revenue growth with Internet advertising revenues over that same period of time (see Figure 2.5).[28]
We have covered in the text some definite tipping points around
banner ads, search, online penetration, and then broadband
usage. The dot-com dip is notable in the graphic view as well.

In comparison with Internet views over roughly the same
time frames, mobile data have moved far slower to generate the
meaningful revenues that the Internet advertising base achieved
(see Figure 2.6). Notice the time frames between the $1,000
campaign of ipsh! and the first time it crossed $1 million—six

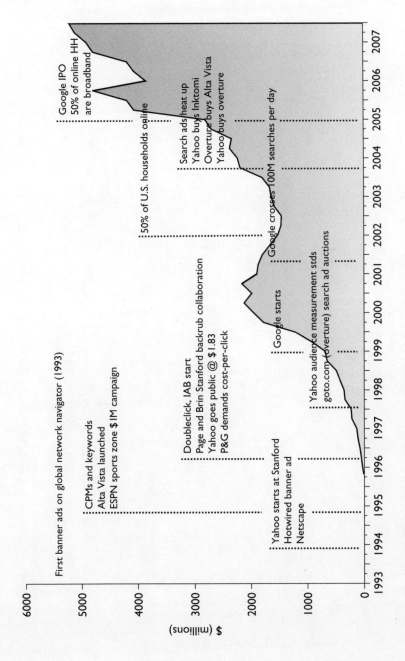

Figure 2.5 Internet advertising history and revenues.
Note: Revenue numbers from IAB

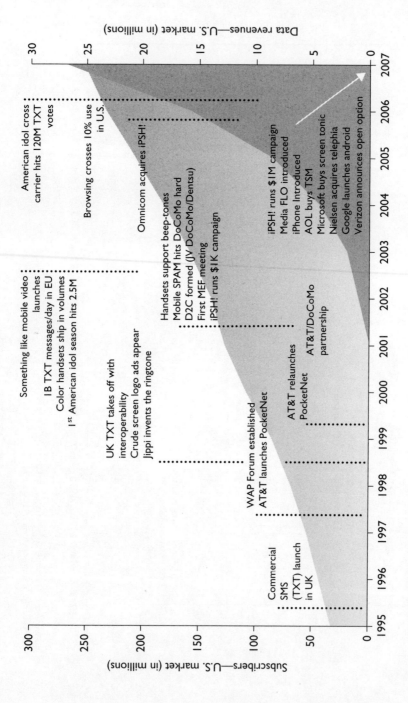

Figure 2.6 Mobile data history revenues.

Note: Subscribers up to 2006 are from the CTIA. Subscribers in 2007 are estimates. Revenues are estimated from Chetan Sharma Consulting.

years. Also note that we do not have total mobile advertising revenues broken out yet. They are not tracked by an equivalent to the Interactive Advertising Board/PricewaterhouseCoopers group. But we do have more than a few $11 billion forecasts that we chose to ignore for this chart.

For mobile media, we are underway finally. But we have a road to travel to get to the same advertising revenue we see on the Web. Before we dive into what the mobile opportunities are, here are some hard hitting dynamics that will affect the future of media in general, web advertising, and eventually mobile media.

IMPLODING ATTENTION SPANS ON OLD MEDIA

The average consumer watches over 30 hours of television a week. On the average, consumers are engaged in some sort of media for over 8 hours a day, making for an obsession with it. We are bombarded with an estimated 3,000 ads (or more) per day. They are everywhere . . . and nowhere. We try to ignore them or block them out, but we live in the age of interruption where unwanted advertisements prevail. However, a media earthquake is changing this paradigm.

The Internet, search, and more recently—user-generated content—are ripping apart the highly structured, mostly one-way, top-down media and advertising paradigms. Today's consumers have far greater control and influence in the outcome of a successful, or unsuccessful, media or advertising campaign. The elimination of the old structure of information flow from the top to the bottom is well underway. Heck, a consumer may have even produced the ad for one of the biggest media events in the world, the Superbowl, on legacy TV. To augment this massive transformation, the World Wide Web is being connected to mobile media phones that are capable of video, music, blogging, taking pictures, and messaging. Audiences that were once somewhat passive are now bouncing all over the mediascape, and they have far more control over what they see, when they see it, and what they respond to. Old media eyeball and audience-reach metrics are gradually being replaced by engagement metrics in this new fragmented world.

In Figure 2.7, a modified chart from Piper Jaffray & Company, an investment firm, shows the impact of this media fragmentation from 1986 through 2007. Audiences as well as their time became incredibly fragmented. All the forms of digital mobile media, with devices connected everywhere, will only accelerate this process.

The old arrangement of a solo video silo for TV, an audio silo for radio, and a print or graphics silo for print is also being ripped apart and repurposed. Today, audio, video, text, and graphics are being used in single campaigns across a dynamic mix of digital and legacy media.

The main factor driving diminished attention spans is that media are no longer scarce. Consumers currently have a tremendous set of options available to them for media consumption. As a result, they are consuming traditional media far less than even five years ago,[29] as related by the graph in Figure 2.8.

The Internet has jumped up tremendously in daily reach. In 10 years, it has leaped from novelty status to competing with the time consumers spend listening to the radio, as illustrated in Figure 2.9. TV is still ahead and will be so for a while longer, but all other media are fading from daily reach.[30]

The combined effect of these dynamics is to push digital advertising on the Internet into the mainstream of advertising. The combination of broadband, truer advertising accountability, search, and highly distributed communities of user-generated media can create the greatest disruption ever seen by major media outlets, the music and video industries, and the advertising arena.

TELEVISION IS A WHEEL WITH DIGITAL SPOKES

Existing advertising models that were derived in the heyday of broadcast television are being challenged. We are witnessing the disruption of these models through aggressive, and

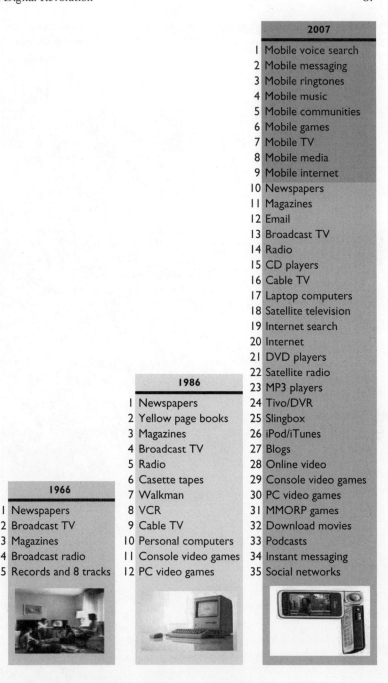

2007

1 Mobile voice search
2 Mobile messaging
3 Mobile ringtones
4 Mobile music
5 Mobile communities
6 Mobile games
7 Mobile TV
8 Mobile media
9 Mobile internet
10 Newspapers
11 Magazines
12 Email
13 Broadcast TV
14 Radio
15 CD players
16 Cable TV
17 Laptop computers
18 Satellite television
19 Internet search
20 Internet
21 DVD players
22 Satellite radio
23 MP3 players
24 Tivo/DVR
25 Slingbox
26 iPod/iTunes
27 Blogs
28 Online video
29 Console video games
30 PC video games
31 MMORP games
32 Download movies
33 Podcasts
34 Instant messaging
35 Social networks

1986

1 Newspapers
2 Yellow page books
3 Magazines
4 Broadcast TV
5 Radio
6 Casette tapes
7 Walkman
8 VCR
9 Cable TV
10 Personal computers
11 Console video games
12 PC video games

1966

1 Newspapers
2 Broadcast TV
3 Magazines
4 Broadcast radio
5 Records and 8 tracks

Figure 2.7   Fragmentation of media consumption.
Note: Based on Piper Jaffray, "The User Revolution: The New Advertiser Ecosystem" (February 2007): 16.

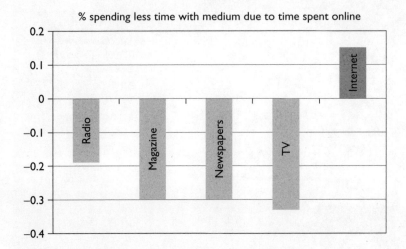

Figure 2.8   Diminishing attention on traditional media.
Sources: Arbitron/Edison Media Research Internet and Multimedia 2006:
On-Demand Media Explodes and comScore Networks. Also used in Piper Jaffray,
"The User Revolution: The New Advertiser Ecosystem" (February 2007).

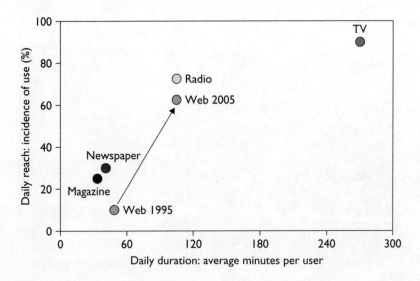

Figure 2.9   Daily reach and duration for various media.

opportunistic digital media that are working their way into the media buying and advertising process that buyers and sellers call "the wheel." You don't buy just television advertising time anymore, especially network television. The television networks are becoming the hub rather than the whole wheel. Television ad spends still represent over two-thirds of average national media plan spending, but it is shrinking. Digital, search, and other emerging advertising platform opportunities like mobile are becoming the spokes of the wheel, and they are eating into the TV spends typical of the past.

The new spokes will mix up the old silos of text, video, audio, and graphics. The digital spokes will demand creative efforts in all areas—text on search, video on mobisodes and YouTube, audio on 411 calls, and graphics on mobile and web advertising networks around the globe, all simultaneously. Further, they can be dynamically adjusted based on near real-time analytics for the performance of the campaign with the audience segment identified.

These new spokes originated on the Internet in 1993 and are rapidly expanding into mobile and other digital media. This is a transformation from the post dot-com shakeout models, in which most advertising networks were digital dabblers that offered online and other digital components as add-ons, mostly on an ad hoc basis.

SOFTWARE OFFICIALLY INVADES ADVERTISING

After over a decade of rapid growth in Internet advertising and more specifically an explosion in search advertising, the domain of the advertising agency has been forever changed by torrid acquisitions. The impact of digital is deep and the pace of change is furious. The resulting infrastructure will make it easier for mobile advertising to achieve scale, and to do so in a shorter time frame than it took the Internet. Chief marketing officers (CMOs) are beginning to lose faith in traditional advertising agencies. They believe that those agencies are ill-suited to meet online marketing needs and have difficulty thinking beyond traditional print and TV media models. With the advent of digital media in the Internet and soon in mobile and interactive television, the old ways are no longer effective to engage consumers.

Many agencies are struggling to adapt to changing consumer behavior and incredibly fast-paced marketing changes wrought by the Internet with its digital implementations. This trend has only just begun with the advent of consumer-generated content, mobile media, and other changes not even felt yet. There has been a massive consolidation of the online advertising industry. The race to extend advertising networks into digital is on between the big web power-houses like Google and the biggest advertising and media holding companies, such as WPP. This consolidation trend also includes emerging mobile advertising companies such as Third Screen Media and Screen Tonic, although on a far smaller scale.

ANOTHER DAY, ANOTHER BILLION-DOLLAR ACQUISITION

The three biggest online advertising players—Google, Microsoft, and Yahoo—have snapped up the three biggest independent online advertising agencies. Large portions of revenues at the acquired companies are digital advertising networks and digital advertising serving technologies.

Consolidation accelerated in a big rush forward during early 2007, when Google announced its intention to buy Doubleclick for a whopping $3.1 billion cash for their targeted display ad serving expertise, search engine marketing (SEM) capabilities, and digital advertising affiliate network. In April, right on the heels of the Google acquisition, Yahoo announced it would buy Right Media for $680 million in cash and stock. And Microsoft then announced it would buy ScreenTonic for an undisclosed amount, to acquire its mobile ad serving capabilities.

In May 2007, AOL acquired the mobile advertising company Third Screen Media, which brought them a mobile advertising network and a mobile advertising management platform. Also in May, the WPP Group, the world's second-largest marketing conglomerate, announced the acquisition of 24/7 Real Media for $649 million to plunge much further into the advertising world of the Internet.[31] However, by far the biggest news in May was Microsoft's announcement of its intention to acquire aQuantive for an estimated $6 billion. Microsoft clearly thinks digitally driven advertising is significant. With aQuantive, Microsoft can now manage far more campaigns, maximize ad inventory across advertising networks, and design ads. In other words, Microsoft's online division just became an online advertising firm.

With a few exceptions, such as the WPP Group, this new trend also puts the legacy advertising agencies at risk of not having enough in-house critical mass of search marketing and online campaign management expertise. The best summary of this trend was penned by Aaron Goldman, a VP of Resolution Media (an Omnicom Company), in June 2007. Note that Aaron did not change the words here, he just inserted some excellent analogies:

Little Miss Muffet

Little Miss Muffet (read: media agencies and content publishers)
Sat on her tuffet (read: keister)
Eating her curds and whey (read: making money)
Along came a spider (read: Google)
Who sat down beside her (read: disintermediated)
And frightened Miss Muffet away (read: the sky is falling, the sky is falling!) [32]

Still, most major media agencies could be accused of not adapting fast enough to incorporate search as part of their core talent and expertise set. This digital advertising world is fundamentally different from the offline world, where it takes a long time to measure whether an individual advertisement was effective and usually the measurement is only directionally accurate. Agencies, for the most part, were set up for media buying and planning in a nondigital world. Search is about execution. With solid analytic-based solutions built on the search platform, it is now possible to draw a clear connection between the advertising purchased and the results obtained. Conclusions can be made tomorrow on today's campaign and adjustments can be made faster than ever before.

The acquisition firestorm of 2007 was partially mobile. Mobile valuations were tiny compared with the major premiums paid for companies like aQuantive. However, mobile is being pursued by all the major acquirers listed previously— Google, Yahoo, AOL, Microsoft, WPP, and others. The critical mass lent by the horsepower that is pursuing mobile advertising will drive its adoption at a faster pace. The digital impact on the old media guards will also accelerate the adoption of mobile advertising, while breaking down the barriers and data silos that are obstacles today.

AND THE WINNER IS . . .

Digital Advertising! The market growth in advertising has shifted from the old guard of television, print, and radio to digitally driven models. The Internet has been a massive ground-shaking event in the world of media and advertising. The old guard advertising offices may still be on Madison Avenue, but the power centers of this world are largely located on the West Coast of the United States. Let's look at the Q2, 2007 scorecard:

U.S. advertising revenue at four big online media companies—Google, Yahoo, AOL, and Microsoft grew by $1.3 billion in Q2, or 42 percent. U.S. advertising revenue at 15 big television, newspaper, magazine, radio, and outdoor companies (Time Warner, Viacom, CBS, etc.) shrank by $280 million in Q2, or 3 percent. The online portion of this pie grew from $3 billion to $4.2 billion or from a 23 percent share to a 30 percent share. The offline portion, meanwhile, shrank from \$9.9 billion to \$9.6 billion, or from a 77 percent share to a 70 percent share. The online companies, in other words, picked up *7 percentage points of market share in a single year.*[33]

These changes are truly massive and most likely are irreversible. The old guard media executives have simply lost the advertising market momentum to digital upstarts. Although one of these upstarts could screw up and lose a position in the market, it would quickly be replaced by the next big digital advertising paradigm and solution.

The province of media and advertising has forever changed. The years from 1998 through 2007 represent quite a decade! There are many history lessons, analogies, and tipping points from the Web to apply to mobile advertising. The transition of advertising to a digitally driven world will have profound effects on mobile advertising. The heavy lifting of measurement and metrics; of banner ad standards; of search keyword auctions; of advertising cost models and the new, digital ad networks that support them have been built. The groundwork for digital advertising in mobile is largely in place. We have learned some key lessons that can be applied to mobile advertising at a faster pace than was possible on the Internet because these basic rules do not need to be reinvented. Mobile will leverage this foundation and look a lot like Internet advertising out of the gate, but it will evolve into something very different over the next few years. In 2008, a critical crossover will find more users accessing the Web from mobile phones than from PCs. The most critical consumer on ramp to mobile media, mobile search, is still highly fragmented. Yet it will radically improve over the next few years—making mobile media more discoverable for consumers and attractive to advertisers. Some aspects of interactive web phenomena are not affecting mobile media yet, but eventually, most will have large-scale impacts. For all the hype in mobile interactivity, users still can't cut and paste in mobile today. Or cross-link mobile sites. Those basic phenomena are still lacking in mobile. But there are tremendous strengths as well, one of the greatest being the highly connected, younger consumers who are rising up and will influence this new world of media and advertising in a big way. This new generation is not playing by the rules of the old-guard media executives.

The next few chapters focus on the forms that mobile will take, the successes evident in the market today, and the relevant issues. If some of the industry structural issues specific to mobile can be addressed in a timely manner, the pace of mobile advertising growth will be torrid.

Notes

1. J. C. R. Licklider, *Libraries of the Future* (Cambridge, MA: MIT Press, 1965), 177.
2. Stephen J. Fredericks, *StrADegy: Advertising in the Digital Age* (New York: TNS Media Intelligence, 2007), 47.
3. Wes Sonnenreich, A *History of Search Engines* (Hoboken, NJ: John Wiley & Sons, 1997).
4. www.w3.org/Conferences/HT91/Denoers.html, accessed November 20, 2007.
5. See note 3.
6. Tim O'Reilly, "Ten—No, Eleven—Years of Internet Advertising" (blog entry in O'Reilly Radar, April 30, 2005), http://radar.oreilly.com/archives/2005/04/tenno_elevenyea.html, accessed November 20, 2007.
7. For this book, we use TXT for SMS Text or for Mobile Originate-SMS or MO-SMS.
8. http://en.wikipedia.org/wiki/Short_message_service, accessed November 26, 2007.
9. www.w3.org/Mobile/1998/Workshop/Papers/WAPForum, accessed November 28, 2007
10. Kelly Carroll, "A PocketNet Full o' Services: AT&T Relaunches CDPD," *Telephony Magazine* (November 22, 1999), http://telephonyonline.com.
11. NTT DoCoMo's investment in AT&T Wireless is a classic case study showing why big investments (or mergers) like this don't work. These two companies came into the agreement with different mindsets and goals and were never on the same page. Another example of failed forced-fitting strategy was Vodafone's adventure into Japan, where the company tried to apply their European strategy in Japan

and failed to adapt. Telefonica has done a better job in reading the markets in South America and investing appropriately.

12. TEXT.IT, United Kingdom, www.text.it/mediacentre/facts_figures.cfm, accessed November 29, 2007.

13. Mark Halper, "The Sweet Sound of Success," *Time* magazine (August 2004), www.time.com.

14. Gartner Group, "Consumer Spending on Mobile Music Will Surpass $32 Billion in 2010" (January 2007).

15. *AdAge*, 1996 archives.

16. UUNET and Nielsen Media (press release, July 1996).

17. "How They Pared: An Advertising Age/Pegasus Research Ranking of Business-to-Consumer Dot-Com Spending," *Advertising Age* (May 21, 2001): 32–35.

18. Salon.com, May 2000.

19. www.weht.net/WEHT/the_Boo.com_founders.html, accessed November 28, 2007.

20. "An Economic Map of the Internet," MIT Program on Internet and Telecoms Convergence, Fletcher School of Law Diplomacy, Tufts University, September 2002; TPRC 30th Research Conference of Communications, Information and Internet Policy, Alexandria, Virginia.

21. John Oates, "ASA Stamps on Crazy Frog Ads: No Amphibians before 9:00," *Register* (September 21, 2005), www.theregister.co.uk/.

22. NTT DoCoMo, "NTT DoCoMo, Dentsu, NTT AD to Jointly Launch" (press release, June 1, 2000).

23. Mobile Entertainment Forum, www.m-e-f.org/index.php?id=307, accessed November 21, 2007.

24. Derived from John Battelle's work in *The Search* (New York: Penguin Group, 2005).

25. See note 24 and www.searchenginehistory.com.

26. Larry Page and Sergey Brin, section 8, appendix A, of *The Anatomy of a Large-Scale Hypertextual Web Search Engine: Advertising and Mixed Motives* (Stanford University, Palo Alto, CA, Computer Science Department, 1998).

27. Google (press release, June 18, 2003).

28. Interactive Advertising Bureau/Pricewaterhouse Coopers data through Q2, 2007.

29. Piper Jaffray, "The User Revolution: The New Advertiser Ecosystem" (February 2007): 19.

30. See note 29. Sourced from *A Day in the Life: An Ethnographic Study of Media Consumption* (Ball State University, Muncie, IN, Center for Media Design), 20.

31. Internet Outsider blog, "M&A in the Digital Ad Sector Is Smoking Hot; Here's Your Handy Future-Take-Out List" (May 2007),

www.internetoutsider.com/2007/05/ma_in_the_digit.html, accessed November 28, 2007.

32. Aaron Goldman, vice president at Resolution Media, an Omnicom Media Group Company, June 13, 2007. MediaPost Communications blog, "Search Insider."

33. Henry Blodget, "The Great Ad Share Shift: Google Sucks Life out of Old Media," *Silicon Alley Insider* (August 15, 2007), www.alleyinsider.com.

3

A Five-Points Framework

From the beginning, digital advertising on the Internet was subjected to broadcast media metrics. The cost per mille (CPM; Roman numeral "M" refers to the French word *mille* meaning "thousand") impressions was based on established print metrics that were the accepted norm for reach and frequency. Cost per action (CPA) is a derivative of CPM and primarily drives response-based approaches to advertising. Way back when, web sites were mostly brochureware, and the early advertising was about brand building. Reach and frequency drove CPMs, which was normal at that time. Then the dot-com bubble burst, and the effectiveness of advertising on the Internet beyond branding fell apart. The advances in search and the power of narrowcasting keywords for user intent shifted the industry to pay-per-click (PPC) metrics, based on the rationale that an advertisement was effective if it drove the consumer a step further toward a transaction.

All the older established models and measurements work fine when well-defined entities, such as a brand or a company, are the only influence on consumer behavior. But what about the exchanges that take place in the user-generated content and community sites? The conversations have a heavy influence on consumer attention, are highly engaging, and can lead to viral effects on a brand or sale. To accommodate this new user-generated content, the media must be sufficiently contagious, making it critical for mobile advocates to understand the viral nature of mobile media. That it might take off in viral form with 200 people influencing 100,000 is an incredible new possibility.

In this chapter, we consider the new digitally driven metrics and measurements and apply them to the brand-new world of mobile media and advertising.

THE CHALLENGE OF ADVERTISING MEASUREMENT

Nicholas Negroponte first described the digital footprint as "the slug trail" in *Being Digital* on the Web in 1996.[1] More than any other device on any other media, mobile devices can capture the daily activity stream. Turning the mobile digital footprint into a consumer's "declared intent" may be more achievable in mobile than in almost any other media, except for interactive TV. Reaching the full power of this declared intent has been the holy grail of advertising for decades. As John Wanamaker, considered the father of modern advertising by many, famously stated, *"I know that half of my advertising dollars are wasted . . . I just don't know which half."*[2] Measurement of advertising effectiveness has been an issue since the early days of advertising. The quote speaks to the reality that many marketing programs are not easily justified on basic return-on-investment (ROI) measures, and that advertising in particular ends up being a leap of faith because it is expensive and its direct benefits are difficult to quantify. Measuring the actual impact of a campaign has been a constant challenge, as stated by John Coulson, Vice President of Research at Leo Burnett Company: *"As I see it, this is where we stand. We measure the sales effectiveness of ads or commercials on their ability to attract attention and communicate, or on their ability to affect attitudes, or on some combination of these and we hope, and have some evidence to indicate, that we are really measuring the sales effects of the advertising."*[3]

With the advent of Internet advertising, things have become more transparent and, we dare to say, measurable. Indeed, search advertising is all about results, and the ad dollars only get spent when there is some measurable user action. Yes, there are still issues with the model because of click fraud and lack of openness on the part of some players, but Internet advertising has been a big improvement over past media. Indeed, a new generation of advertising pioneers and thinkers is promoting the new medium that gives some control to the consumers. Chris Anderson, editor of *WIRED* and author of *The Long Tail*, said in an interview: *"Television advertising is pretty ridiculous, when you think about it: It interrupts the programming and irritates people, and it's only relevant to a tiny fraction of the audience. You're basically annoying a lot of people for very little benefit. And the networks charge more and more for it each year. The only reason it exists at all is that we don't have a better alternative. The question is whether the Google model can provide that alternative. If so, then it's measurable, it's targeted, it's effective—and we can wave goodbye to the television business model."*[4]

Although the Internet is a vast improvement over traditional advertising avenues, it is still a broken model. Users know how to ignore ads on their big screen monitor, so the pressure to create engaging ads is high. There is a Firefox browser plug-in that replaces ads with artwork. Targeting is minimal in display advertising because the same computer could be in use by multiple people, the user's delete cookies might intercept the ad, profile information might be lacking, and so on.

As an advertising medium, mobile's forte includes targeting, context, and measurements. The mobile device is the most personal of all mediums: Tracking of data is virtually guaranteed, the availability of location adds context, and yes, you can measure the heck out of your campaign: All the pieces are in place to make a viable medium for the advertisers. We will discuss fragmentation and the issues that need to be addressed in Chapter 5. As the industry matures and the structural elements fall into place, phone undoubtedly will become the most preferred advertising medium, especially to target the youth segment. One-on-one tracking allows granular user profile development, which enables great understanding of user behavior both individually as well as in a clustered population, so as to fine tune the marketing message to almost absolute certainty. Thus, effectiveness of campaigns increases tremendously. Advertisers will know the expected return from campaigns as well as exactly which half or what percentage of their budget was wasted.

THE NEW LONG TAIL OF DIGITAL ADVERTISING

Audience reach in this new mediascape is becoming ever more fragmented. But the beauty of all things digital is that it enables a far lower cost in reaching niche audiences and measuring the effects of a campaign. This applies not only to mobile media, but to all digital media. Despite the audience fragmentation taking place, previously inaccessible niche markets can now be reached profitably. Search on the Internet is perhaps the greatest example of this. Combined with more behavioral and contextual data, search will enable precise targeting of user purchasing intent to prevail in the future. The accessibility of more and more niche markets will also apply to mobile media. A new generation of granular messaging aimed at an expanding level of niche audiences will create a long tail of advertising—and mobile will be at the forefront of this development. This long tail of niche advertising is made possible by a new generation of mobile segmentation and targeting. And it is highly measurable with the right mobile analytics framework and metrics.

Reaching the Previously Unreachable

Unilever, the company that markets a range of skin-care products including Dove, Lux, Pond's skin cream, and others, segments their user audience into six high-level categories,[5] as follows:

1. Apathetic Annie—women who spend minimal time caring for their skin.
2. Age-Defying Beauty Queens—older women concerned with wrinkles, sagging, and puffy eyes.
3. Young Beauty Queens—girls with oily skin, mostly concerned with pimples and blackheads.

4. Peaches and Creams—women who want a healthy, clean, natural look; also who want nongreasy and hypoallergenic ingredients.

5. Dazed and Confused—women who view face care as complicated; their goal is radiant, younger-looking skin.

6. Jaded Jane—women who are skeptical of product efficacy.

In the old analog world of TV, radio, and print marketing, Unilever had to look at programs, broadcasts, and print media that might correlate with their targeted audience segments, as illustrated in Figure 3.1, then run their campaigns and see what happens.

Because there is no way to guarantee who is watching a particular program, listening to a certain broadcast, or reading a targeted magazine, a significant part of the advertising campaign may target the wrong audience and hence send campaign dollars into the budget dumpster. Figure 3.1 shows the segmentation of Unilever's six audience categories and the dispersal of advertising dollars. The advertisements and promotional messages hit a portion of the targeted

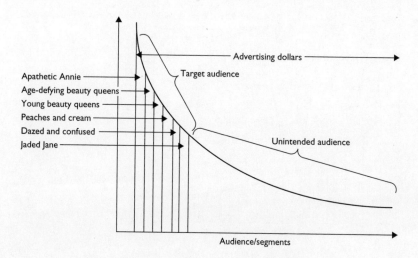

Figure 3.1   Analog world advertising.

audience, while a significant part of the messaging is exposed to an unintended audience, thereby compromising the effectiveness of the advertising dollars.

By contrast in the digital world, especially with enhanced mobile targeting, the brand can focus specifically on the intended audience segment. Although there will be some message leakage to unintended audiences, it will be far less than the analog counterparts and will cost only a small fraction of the overall advertising dollars. Furthermore, the head of the long tail shrinks to beef up the tail and make it meaningful for targeting and segmentation.

To illustrate the benefit of audience segmentation and filtering to achieve tighter segments in the digital world, Unilever's Apathetic Annie segment in Figure 3.2 would be further divided into subsegment categories of women's professional and personal lives, tastes, and dislikes, geography,

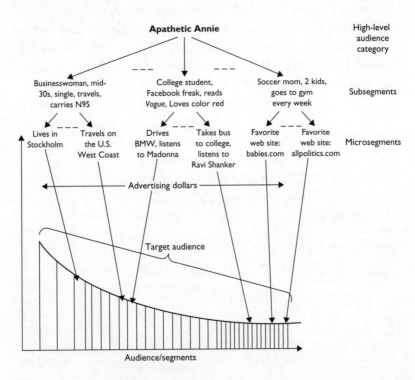

Figure 3.2   Digital world advertising.

motivation, and so on. This helps cluster numerous subsegments and ultimately microsegments, thereby providing a more refined message to each segment. The result is delivery of an advertisement that is a useful and actionable information piece, rather than an in-your-face presentation that invokes resentment.

For each of the lower-level segments shown in Figure 3.2, a digital advertising campaign would need to design a different message and potentially use a different medium. Some segments might respond well to a TXT campaign, whereas others might do better with paper-based coupons.

The targeting of low-level audience segments along with a younger generation of highly connected, mobile consumers use of new daily communication utilities that previous generations had called "technology" will have a tremendous impact on all media. The younger crowd is consuming the new digital media far more than it is using print and TV. To reach the 18-to-28 consumers, digital advertisers need to use mobile media.

The broadband world of this media generation is not flat, but enables a tremendous portion of this new digital sector. It plays an incredibly important part in achieving critical mass in video, community site interaction, and mobile usage. Dial-up consumers are generally not part of this picture and dial-up speeds for mobile media are also nonstarters. More importantly, each localized audience pocket demands localized media. Occasionally, a global phenomenon sneaks through as a hit, but that is the exception, not the rule.

TOMORROW'S ADVERTISING METRICS

For the new media generation, campaigns need to be engaging and interactive. To be engaging, the media and campaigns must be localized for the consumers' interests. A campaign put together from one media and slapped onto another media will most likely fail to engage a critical and oversaturated audience. Consumers of the new media are oversensitized to how broadcasted ads are trying to influence them. These consumers need messages that are specifically tailored to their interests and behavior.

TV, radio, and print will still have a strong position in the future for audiences in the head or shoulder of the long tail graph. Campaigns will typically embrace TV, radio, and print for the majority of consumer reach and ad spends. However, the Internet, driven by contextual and behavioral targeting along with the power of narrowcasting in search, will increasingly take larger portions of campaign budgets. Digital media, including mobile in particular, will play a key role in taking the campaign's messages, and making them more effective by reaching smaller, microtargeted niche audiences. A long tail of smaller and smaller niche campaigns that are highly customized and cost-effective will ultimately emerge with mobile targeting. The far more fragmented audiences in the tail will need more tailored messages to capture their attention.

To accommodate these audiences, new measurements, metrics, and approaches beyond reach and targeting will need to be in place. For the next generation, the combination of tracking engagement, viral responses to campaigns, and transactions in smaller, fragmented, and highly targeted niches, with dynamic campaign modification for maximum effect, should prove to be powerful.

Mobile is unique because of its built-in payment mechanisms. It is not available everywhere yet, but it is being enabled in most high 3G-penetration countries like Japan, Korea, and Finland. Being able to track a campaign down to the purchase is the only thing that matters. Tracking advertising to the purchase of mobile media is in place today. Also, mobile bar codes are coming that can track an ad to the purchase of physical goods. This is the area of greatest promise for mobile in the next four or five years of advertising metrics and transparency.

Mobile is also unique because it has camera phones and can click to read a mobile bar code. This is especially powerful to enhance off-line marketing to take a picture of a bar code in an ad or on a store shelf, thus associating the print advertisement with a transaction that follows. These powerful scenarios can be used to differentiate mobile channels across other media.

These are all somewhat familiar terms and concepts, but they have not been applied to mobile metrics as compared with other media. Mobile offers the potential to leverage them for greater campaign success—or greater failure if they are not understood. Mobile metrics and campaign measurability will be an extension of what is inherent to the Web. The targeting will be with more usage, user, and engagement data in smaller niches and far closer to the point of decision. The measurement power of digital will be taken to a deeper level with mobile.

The following sections discuss the key measurement factors across the five-points framework:

1. Reach
2. Targeting
3. Engagement
4. Viral Effects
5. Transactions

Digital advertisers must understand this framework before they can take advantage of the microniche promise of the mobile advertising world.

Reach

In the past, most advertising has embraced reach. Combined with the frequency of touching the segmented audience, this is the area that all media understand well. Advertising grew up in the world of TV, print, and radio reach, where there are well-understood cost dynamics, measurements in each area, and advertising models.

The old media approaches and gross rating points (GRPs) were based on broadcasting to get the necessary audience reach. Digital media and advertising, especially as driven by search, don't fit some of the old reach assumptions. With digital, reach can now be 24 hours a day and 7 days a week, and on the consumers' terms, as in searching or browsing versus sitting in front of the TV. With digital media, reach is being redefined with time and place. The need to reach a consumer at the right time and the right place with the right campaign has never been more critical.

Well-established metrics like frequency-to-conversion ratios and ad exposure time for richer media types still apply. In fact, mobile does a much better job of frequency management at the user level, so advertisers can keep track of the number of times an ad has been shown to the user and fine-tune the frequency on a per-user basis and thus increase the efficiency of the campaign. But they are the new baselines and not the whole picture with digital media. They are evolving past the basics at a rapid pace and making the analytics gurus the new advertising rock stars. These new metrics are also being applied to mobile advertising right from the onset. Therefore the pace of mobile metrics will accelerate dramatically, since the baseline is far higher than in other media when starting as an advertising platform.

The mobile value enhancers around targeting, engagement, and viral campaigns impulsively aimed at the point of sale are significant extensions of the classically defined reach of the past. The following sections describe how these apply to the five-points framework.

Targeting

In general, advertising buyers in digital media will be increasing their budgets around actual and predictive consumer behaviors. From the advertiser's perspective, mobile is the first mass medium that can uniquely identify every consumer. On TV, Nielsen ratings are the measurement of audience response. On the Web, there are multiple cookies, no cookies, lots of aliases, and false identities. Magazines and newspapers can only sell circulations based on addresses and a few demographics. Meanwhile, every mobile user has a unique phone number, a known address, and an identified sex, which makes it easy to identify them as a segment. This level of detail has never been available in any previous media. To date, there is wide industry consensus that targeting is the key to ad growth in mobile media, as indicated by the M:Metrics survey shown in Figure 3.3.

To build large consumer bases, carriers have invested billions into networks, spectrum, and devices, so it seems natural they would also want to leverage that base by taking control of the access to it. Instead of asking how much they can get from the user by identifying the value of the bits flowing through the pipe, carriers—in their unique position of knowing so much about consumer behavior—need to ask how much value they can add to the mobile data experience or to advertisers. By further emphasis, knowing the answers to the following questions would add tremendous value to a nascent mobile advertising and media ecosystem:

- How can carriers use robust consumer data to help advertisers reach a more engaged audience with fewer ad impressions?

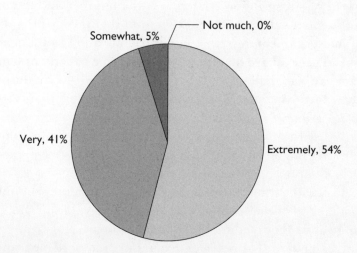

Figure 3.3   Mobile targeting as key to ad growth.
Copyright © 2007, M:Metrics, Inc. All rights reserved.

- How can carriers use the data to help advertisers monetize their long tail inventory and media?
- Most importantly, how can carriers enable this information for mobile ad targeting and not give away any
  personal information?

Even though consumers are often not aware of the process, an ad that is prompted by their actions tends to be
more relevant to their needs and therefore more valuable.
TV ads had time and demographics on their side, whereas
the Internet brought about breakthroughs in context and
determination of user intent from search. Mobile embraces
all these in addition to location and far stronger contextual
and behavioral targeting.

Ultimately, reach and targeting are not enough. The new
genre of consumer-generated content, blogs, and interactive
media will demand a new set of metrics. The future will not
be merely about impressions, but about consumer relationships, conversations, influence, and authority. The industry
is starting to measure how many conversations are influenced by a blog. But the industry also needs to measure not
just the number of impressions, but who is being impressed.
Instead of subscription counts, it is the number and quality
of influences subscribers makes within their groups that really matters; meaning, how many friends and family members did users share that impression or piece of content with,
and what was the impact it had on them (did they ignore it
or was there further transaction?). Mobile media that is *sufficiently contagious* can play a key viral role in these metrics,
starting with engagement metrics and evolving into something that might be called cost per engagement. We explore
this in Chapter 6, the business model overview.

As noted earlier, turning the mobile digital footprint into
consumer's "declared intent" is more achievable in mobile
than in any other medium. Imagine the potential of an advertising campaign that relies on a combination of demographics (zip code, age, calling plans, and phone types), calling
history and patterns, comprehensive mobile data usage and

browsing history, real-time location, and has a simple-to-use voice search interface. Mobile carriers already have all this information and capability, whereas competitive advertising media often do not. This mobile combination could be unrivaled with respect to advertiser value versus any other network or device.

Frequency Management

In the analog world, frequency management of ads is ineffective. The ads are played to a wide demographic at different time slots or printed in newspapers and magazines in different editions. There is no reliable way of tracking who has been underexposed or overexposed. With the Internet, cookies and ad networks like Tacoda track users' behavior and ad exposure across many sites, but even these techniques are inefficient due to lack of coverage as well as overdependence on cookies.

With mobile, frequency management can target or filter the user base. Since tracking may be done at a user ID level, the system can track which users have seen or haven't seen the ads. Depending on the exposures for the given users in the past, the frequency of ad exposure can be fine-tuned for a user on a given mobile channel. Further, the exposure can be controlled across multiple mobile channels (WAP, SMS, Mobile Video, etc.). Thus, if the user is not interested in engaging or has already been shown the impression on a different channel, overexposure might not be prudent.

The system can decide which ads should be shown to which users at what moment using what channel.

Engagement

Historically, advertisers have struggled to define engagement and to assign strong measurement values to various user actions associated with it. This desire has created a strong need for a methodology that can measure engagement and the varying levels of associated attention and interaction. In an unprecedented act of collaboration, virtually all the major advertising associations including the Advertising Research Foundation (ARF), American Association of Advertising Agencies (AAAA), and the Association of National Advertisers (ANA), have come together to provide a standard industry definition: "Engagement is turning on a prospect to a brand idea enhanced by the surrounding context."

This definition is too vague to work with. Beyond that, there is little consensus on what engagement means or how to measure it. Current attempts are shackled by a historical, TV-centric view that is inherently dominated by demographic perspectives. In the field of digital media, engagement definitions must take into account not only the quality of the visitor, but more importantly, the quality of the visit. It should take into account the time spent during the visit as well actions and reactions for example, did they respond, bookmark, save, send to friend, send to computer, created something new and different with the piece of content?

User Experience

Great user experiences are the cornerstone of engagement. If consumers cannot use the mobile media and they have a bad experience, engagement immediately suffers. The small screen exponentially magnifies a bad mobile user experience and will stop even the most passionate consumers. In addition, user experience barriers will instantly limit the ability to effectively measure the success of a brand or campaign. As a result, engagement measurement suffers in a big way.

Online is the only media enabler that can track true interactivity and duration—and these are at the heart of the new metrics for engagement. Moreover, online advertising networks can provide advertisers with a strong platform for both the testing and tracking of interactivity and duration. Ultimately, online and mobile networks will be the keys to optimizing advertising to engaged consumers. Because *every interaction* can be measured in mobile, this media could become the driving force in overall engagement metrics and standardization.

Duration, interaction, and permissions frame the basic value of engagement metrics. Consumers who are having great experiences while immersed in a consumer community are the harbingers of engagement. Whether they podcast, vlog, mblog, generate their own content, upload mphotos, tag, rate, vote, or subscribe to an RSS (really simple syndication), it is all interactivity. If it is repetitive, it involves high duration and this provides a fertile ground for innovative measurement and metrics.

Duration

Duration is the unifying concept behind engagement. As the time that a consumer spends interacting with an advertisement increases, so does the chance that the advertising messages will be consumed and ultimately converted to a sale. Apparently, Nielsen agreed with this because their web measurements began moving away from just measuring impressions and started focusing on time spent. In the near future, the acceptance of engagement and time duration as a key metric will move more quickly through the industry standard committees than it did on the Web. This newer concept of an ad interaction rate based on duration is nearly a standard part of the new digital advertising lexicon.

View-Through Rates

View-through rates or "delayed visits" to an advertiser's site without a direct ad click-through are now fairly common digital metrics to gauge engagement. It is hard to achieve in mobile because of the relative dearth of mobile-specific destination sites, but this is changing.

Interactivity

Interactivity defines the ability to move a consumer to initiate a sequence of actions within an advertisement or the media being consumed. Clicks, mouseovers, voluntary permission-based signups, subscriptions to RSS feeds, video downloads, mobile alerts, blog comments, and blog trackbacks all represent a strong step toward interactivity and engagement. By taking one or more of these actions, the consumer acknowledges the advertising message in some way and thereby expresses enough interest through interaction to indicate that engagement is beginning to occur.

Permissions

In mobile, permissions enable taking engagement tracking to a new level. With permissions, the consumer is asking to get more information and to participate in the campaign. Subsequently, they will allow and enable marketing from various channels, including SMS, MMS, and WAP as the primary channels.

Leveraging Other Mediums

Someday, mobile will rule the advertising world. Until then, successful campaigns will utilize and complement advertising across other media. As discussed throughout this book, mobile makes other channels interactive.

A key aspect of strong engagement is whether the campaign keeps the dialogue going across multiple mediums. Strong engagement can occur if the campaign allows the consumer to continue the conversation on the Web, print, or other media, even though the campaign introduction might have initially been launched on mobile. The level of engagement strengthens by expanding the boundaries and increasing the time spent across channels and mediums, which ultimately makes for a vibrant and successful advertising campaign.

Viral Effects

The essentials of reach and targeting were developed on the historical transitions from broadcast and print. Cost per mille (CPM), which was based on print models, was accepted in the early days of the Internet as the measure of both reach and frequency. Sites were based on brochureware and brand advertising while CPMs were all the rage. This was heavily questioned when the dot-com bubble burst. Now CPMs are back in the world of mobile advertising. But the glow of extraordinarily high mobile CPMs will wear off at some point and they will once again be questioned. On the Internet, the industry shifted advertising dollars to pay per click (PPC), which rewarded effective narrowcast targeting based on user intent and search. This will also happen in mobile search. All this works perfectly well for companies that want to ignore the viral effects of social networks, but the new breed of young consumers are highly connected with mobile, and conversations—often driven by messaging—influence their attention and decisions.

Cutting edge media buyers are already figuring out that it is not only about how widely individual meme makers can spread the seed, but how deeply they can plant it into their immediate network, how deep these folks can plant it into theirs, and so on. Highly engaged customers become the medium for the message. In today's oversaturated media world, brands and products must be sufficiently contagious to succeed. Passionate advocates actively promote brands and products through viral effects such as word of mouth, often without realizing they are doing this. Witness the phenomenon of the iPhone, driven by the master cult members of the Mac computer. Vocal members embrace a common set of values while trumpeting the virtues of the Mac over the PC, which aggressively spill over into the iPhone. Lines camped for a day around the mall have never before been seen for any other mobile phone release. This exemplifies a product sufficiently contagious to bring about a true viral effect with high impact.

The viral effect encourages negative reputations to spread rapidly as well. Negative engagement can hurt. Look no further than Sony BMG's recent spyware problems. It started with a negative, aggressive groundswell in a vocal blogsphere and ignited like a gasoline-fed fire. Never mind the consumer boycotts and an almost immediate class action lawsuit—more telling is that a blog search for "Sony Spyware" returned nearly 50,000 blog posts. That is the equivalent of a giant billboard warning that says, "Arsenic Is in Your Drinking Water," on every road you drive. Consumers were engaged . . . and enraged. It works both ways today.

Transactions

Media no longer represent one-way, top-down communications. Because they are digital, they can lead to transactions. The entire value chain is affected—the media, the advertising, purchases, and delivery. Whether those transactions involve digital media or physical items shipped overnight, interactive media are now channels to market. It is no longer just a communication channel since consumers expect to perform online transactions and will be disappointed if they can't.

The ultimate goal of any advertisement is a sales transaction. Metrics along the way move toward a transaction that may be a sale, a referral, or a walk-in to a store for a promotion.

Mobile allows the advertiser to drive deeper levels of engagement, leading to the performance that marketers want along the way to a clear transaction. Mobile devices ultimately can add payment value directly at the point of sale. Although this scenario is futuristic, except for Asia, it is a long-term and high-value addition to mobile advertising metrics. With respect to the ability to purchase electronically on the Internet today, there is often a murky connection between the sale and the advertising influence that led to the sale. This will also be the case for mobile transactions.

Postclick Conversions

Postclick consumer conversions are increasingly important in search engine marketing (SEM) and search engine optimization (SEO). Well-known best practices to increase postclick conversion rates recommend that marketers create a unified relationship between search keywords, ads, and landing pages. If the advertiser bids on the keyword *Health*

Club, the advertiser should feature Health Club in both the ad and landing page. In practice, few companies have the time or resources to create individual ads and landing pages for every keyword they bid on. Nevertheless, customer abandonment rates have been proven to increase when the expected keyword is not included in the ad or landing page copy. This will have more effect in mobile advertising until a robust mobile search ecosystem and bid-on keywords are connected to actual mobile landing pages.

Offline Sales Lift

Offline sales lift is tricky to obtain and critical to measure. The historical approach includes training sales personnel to record and report lead sources. Web landing pages that encourage prospects to print a discount coupon that they can redeem at a store or landing page, also encourage them to find their local store and register for an enrollment discount. These are basic approaches in refined search-driven campaigns.

More advanced approaches incorporate paid 800-numbers for tracking. Other strategies include implementing periodic, nonconsecutive search ad campaigns when other marketing efforts are at a minimum—this will correlate search spend and leads. In store referrals, a campaign can use call center tracking and sales locator pages to gauge offline sales lift. A campaign can also use surveys, web samples, and focus groups to track the impact to offline sales.

Brand Impact Lift

Brand impact lift is often the goal of advertising and is ubiquitous in mobile advertising today. Measuring the impact in this area involves five core metrics: brand awareness, ad awareness, message association, brand favorability, and purchase intent. In general, digital online campaigns can have positive effects across all five of these core brand metrics. The impact varies depending on the publishing network and environment.

Quality matters in brand perception. Mobile is being deployed as part of major brand awareness campaigns today, partially because the quality of the audience and publishing environments is top notch.

COMPARING MOBILE WITH OTHER MEDIA

The five-points framework can help digital advertisers:

- Understand mobile's strengths and weaknesses in comparison to other advertising mediums
- Ascertain how different channels in mobile fare against each other
- Know which one or which combination might be the best fit for a given campaign

Last and most important, advertisers can use the framework to think through the basics of a mobile media advertising campaign, and then use the framework to design, execute, measure, and post campaign performance. The measurement capability across these pillars forms the core of the framework.

The five-points framework elements of reach, engagement, targeting, viral effect, and transactions also help in evaluating advertising media, including their strengths, weaknesses, and ways they might complement each other for the overall good of a campaign. Advertisers should care about ROI versus the nuances of any specific channel. By leveraging multiple metrics and measurement tools, advertisers will see the increased effectiveness of their mobile campaigns. This leads to cross-media econometrics modeling and a cost per conversion for all media.

Figure 3.4 shows TV, radio, print, outdoor, Internet, and mobile advertising effectiveness with respect to the five-points framework elements, and rates those media on a scale of "high" and "low." Since there is an inherent difference between potential and reality, not to mention between markets,

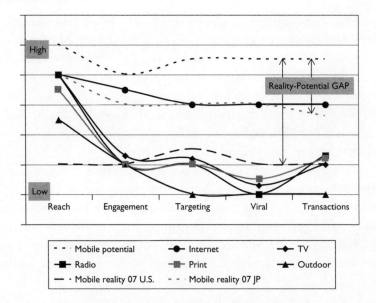

Figure 3.4   Advertising medium comparison in five-points framework context.

Figure 3.4 also illustrates the potential of U.S. mobile to capture the highest ratings for each of the framework elements (applies to all geographic locations). The chart also shows the rating levels for Japan and U.S. mobile realities in 2007.

What Is Possible in Mobile Today?

As a new medium, the reach of a mobile phone is tremendous. By 2007 in the United States, over 80 percent of the population had mobile phones[7] and the majority of the phones can at least do Short Message Service (SMS). This feature now becomes available as a vehicle for mobile advertising. There is the potential that nearly all mobile users can be touched by voice advertising during, before, or after calls such as customer service or directory assistance calls.

It is easy to be engrossed with the glamour and reach, engagement, targeting, viral, and transaction capability of mobile, but what is possible with mobile today? Furthermore, what are the gaps between the realities of today and the potentials of tomorrow?

With over 3 billion mobile subscribers, no other consumer device even comes close to covering the sheer numbers of humanity. With respect to targeting, no other medium can provide the accurate and rich user profile, psychographic, social engagement, and demographic data available from mobile. No other medium has the viral capability that mobile possesses—within seconds following a simple click, a unit of advertisement can spread like wildfire.

The instant and personal nature of mobile makes it an attractive advertising medium. The engagement capability of mobile, where multiple channels engage and interact with users and keep them transfixed for a long duration is beneficial for brands. In addition, mobile allows for tracking sales correlated with advertising and does so better than any other medium. Above all, the critical metrics of the five-points framework are measurable at the most granular level rather than being the result of guessing games and half-cooked surveys with sampling errors.

With time, the industry will fix its flaws and the ecosystem will adjust to a winning formula that provides the best capabilities of the five-points framework. Until this occurs, it would be a mistake to think that mobile is isolated. While moving forward, mobile will serve as a complement to existing media in big and small campaigns.

COMPARISONS WITHIN MOBILE CHANNELS

Mobile has several channels for reaching the consumer. These channels are typically exposed by technology around user interface presentations. The three core advertising methods of interactive campaigns, brands, and search can be applied to any of the channels. This section describes the reach of various mobile channels in addition to comparing other mobile channels with respect to the five-points framework. The reach of various channels in different nations tracked by M:Metrics is illustrated in Figure 3.5.

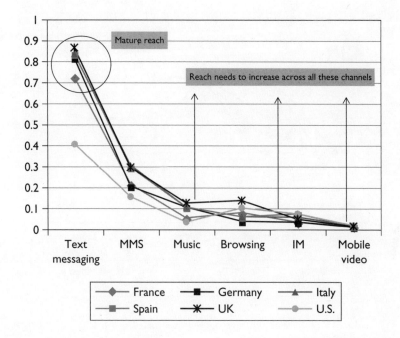

Figure 3.5   The reach of different mobile channels in several major mobile markets.
Source: Evan Neufeld, "M:Metrics May Briefing" (May 2007).

Figure 3.5 shows that TXT messaging is being used by the majority of subscribers, perhaps in part because the barriers to usage across carriers have been largely eliminated. The use of Multimedia Messaging Service (MMS) is on the rise; however, it is still plagued by interoperability and pricing issues. Once you get past TXT and MMS, the industry has major pricing, technology adoption, applications, and general consumer adoption issues. As of late 2007, browsing, which is a big area for brand advertising, is on the rise but it is barely on the map compared with TXT. In Japan and Korea, browsing is into the 90 percent penetration range. New categories of mobile channels, such as mobile video, podcasts, audio, Bluetooth, and mobile search, are just emerging and will take time to reach a critical mass for advertisers.

Figure 3.6 compares the various mobile channels with respect to the five-points framework. We are using the terms

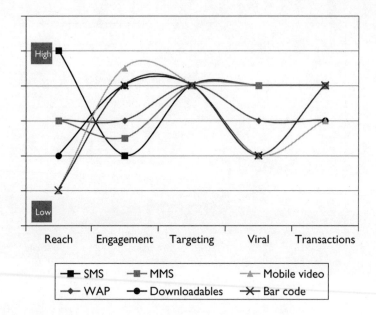

Figure 3.6   Mobile channels and the five-points framework.

TXT, WAP, MMS, mobile video, and downloadables in these charts because they are the channels that brands and carriers use in the implementations of campaigns. With respect to reach, TXT is at the highest level. This is the result of simplicity, cross-carrier ubiquity and low prices. Figure 3.6 shows that the visual media of mobile video, downloadables, MMS barcode based, and browsing (WAP) are more appealing in the context of engagement. The mobile targeting capability is equivalent across all channels, since it is inherent to the medium. Once there is an understanding of a user's profile, advertisers can send a targeted message using any of the mobile channels, depending on the need.

Currently, the viral capability of TXT is the highest due to less friction in the ecosystem, although things get complicated if users are sending more visual content. Typically, this would be done using a TXT-based URL link from the sender, although the user experience will vary widely depending on the recipient's network provider. Interoperability again rears its ugly head once we get beyond simple text messaging and into the other channels. These problems are expected to be resolved by the mobile carriers and technology providers in due time. Last, the transaction capability that turns a campaign into an eventual sale is the strongest for mobile when compared with other advertising media.

THE FIVE-POINTS FRAMEWORK FOR DESIGNING AND MEASURING MOBILE CAMPAIGNS

The main purpose of the five-points framework is to guide the design, execution, measurement, and comparison of mobile campaigns. By using the five elements of reach, engagement, targeting, viral effects, and transactions, mobile campaigns will have a higher chance of success. Some campaigns will excel in one or more areas but will be compromised in others. The key is to maximize the effectiveness of successful areas of the framework to compensate for any deficiencies in the others.

Off-deck campaigns that usually do not have good targeting data, are great for instant reach as they are limited by walled gardens. Therefore, the effectiveness of an off-deck campaign should be maximized to compensate for weaknesses in the area of targeting. Although the ability to do user profile targeting is currently constrained for off-deck providers, this will change as smart phones proliferate, carriers become more open, and the powers of Google, Yahoo, and Microsoft gain enough reach. A carrier that is providing user profile data to a campaign for targeting purposes can do a great job of reaching the customers that matter, but the reach is reduced to the size of the customer base. This might amount to only a fraction of the national or international subscriber base.

Campaign Design

Those who create advertising campaigns can use the pentagon graph of Figure 3.7 to design their campaign model.

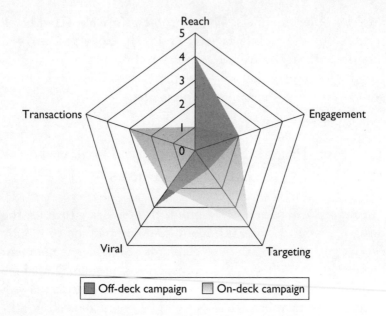

Figure 3.7   Using the five-points framework to design and measure a mobile campaign.

The key to designing a successful mobile advertising campaign is to maximize the areas in the pentagon graph. The goal is to score high points in all five categories of the five-point framework, but that is not always feasible for a given campaign. When building a campaign model, it might be necessary to compensate for the lack of reach by enhancing the viral aspects for overall good results. Similarly, a lack of targeting could be somewhat offset by increasing the reach of the campaign.

No campaign, in any media, will ever get scores of five across all five points. But we hope to have provided a framework to compare and contrast the compromises across media or in mobile channels for a stronger planning perspective.

Increasing Advertising Returns Using the Five-Points Framework

The five-points framework provides a way to measure performance across the five critical elements. Performance measurement can then be documented and compared with other campaigns so that lessons can be learned and applied to future work. Thus, the framework is a useful tool for comparing the mobile medium with other advertising media, evaluating which channel(s) work best in a given geography or network, and providing a way to measure strategy and performance across the five elements. By carefully considering all five elements and measuring the performance of each element, advertisers can increase and track the return on advertising (ROA) of their campaigns. Briefly,

$$ROA = f\Sigma(m_r*Reach + m_e*Engagement + m_t*Targeting + m_v*Viral + m_{tr}*Transactions)$$

Where ROA is a function of sum of the five variables

In this equation, m_r, m_e, m_t, m_v, and m_{tr} are respective coefficients applied to the measurement of the five variables to weight them appropriately. For certain campaigns (e.g., brand advertising campaigns), reach might carry more weight than, say, transactions while in the case of transactional/promotional advertising, the number of transactions could outweigh reach.

Figure 3.7 is an example of measuring campaign performance with respect to the framework elements. It compares two actual campaigns that were run by major consumer brands and shows how well or poorly they performed within the context of the framework. Campaign performance will always be a balance between what the campaign has access to and how it can best leverage the functionality it has. Great user interface (UI) products like the one from Zumobi, discussed in Chapter 7, along with similar active portal startups have tools for engagement, viral effects, transactions, and targeting, but they need work on the reach component.

The key is to measure frequently, modify the campaign as quickly as possible based on real data, and measure again. The most rapid adaptations will win in the marketplace of tomorrow and the best metrics and analytics will be one of the most important keys to creating campaigns that resonate with consumers.

MEASURING ADVERTISING ACCOUNTABILITY

Advertisers have long used the four standard metrics—brand awareness (aided or unaided), message association, brand favorability, and purchase intent. The elephants in the room—purchase and loyalty—are often invisible in the metrics discussion. Measurement and accountability of advertisement and media activity remain on the agenda of agencies and marketing organizations worldwide but without effective measurement capabilities, especially the ones that can tie the advertising dollars to sales and revenue impact. Participants hand-wave and guess the numbers and the impact (see Figure 3.8).

The ultimate goal of advertising is to generate sales and contribute to the bottom line. If that is not happening, the advertising dollars go to waste. The goal of any advertising campaign or program should be to maximize and measure the impact.

Mobile can measure the reach to the right audience, measure activity at each level of the advertising funnel while gathering feedback in almost real time, and optimize the campaigns accordingly. Media attention span for audiences and consumers is now fragmenting across every medium type. That cat got out of the bag in a bad way and tore across town in the mid-1990s. From the perspective of old media, this fragmentation has a lot of perceived downsides. When ads are run on radio, TV, and in print without interactive mobile enhancements, the entire process has to build expensive overhead to cover the poor accuracy around targeting. Compare that with the potential in mobile. Advertisers and the media on which ads ride will eventually be able to tie each message to a specific audience segment. This is the ultimate in advertising, where advertisers benefit from a higher degree of consumer engagement with their advertisement along with the ability to accurately measure that engagement. The combination of mobile's interactivity, targeting, and unique consumer usage patterns is a powerful dynamic. The power of really defining a somewhat vague term like engagement with tangible metrics and data is huge.

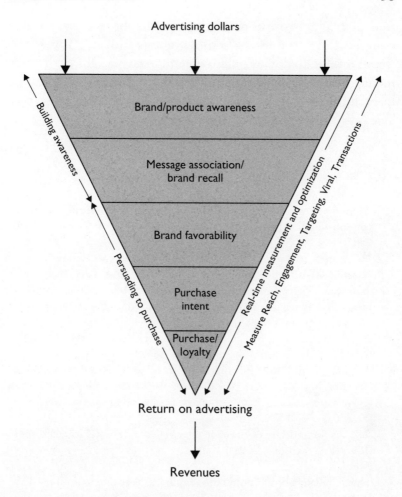

Figure 3.8   Measuring the impact of advertising.

Finally, mobile enables other media, such as print, television, and radio to be interactive. This interactivity enables metrics that are far better than the past generation of measurements. Campaigns that were once not measurable to the degree that mobile interactivity enables are now highly measurable. The interactivity is an engagement breakthrough for the consumer, and metrics are a major step forward for the advertisers and brands involved.

The five-points framework is an effective starting point for framing a mobile campaign and for comparing the five points across other media for the best views across complicated variables. When the mobile industry solves the issues related to device management, massive silos of distinct media, and complex campaign management, it will result in tremendous value in this fragmented consumer universe. The best measurement metrics will win.

NOTES

1. Nicholas Negroponte, *Being Digital* (1996), http://archives.obs-us.com/obs/english/books/nn/bdcont.htm, accessed on November 29, 2007.
2. As quoted in Martin Mayer, *Whatever Happened to Madison Avenue?* (Boston, MA: Little, Brown and Company, 1991), 138. Apparently, this was originally attributed to Viscount Leverhulme (William Hesketh Lever), as quoted in Tony Augarde, *Oxford Dictionary of Modern Quotations* (New York: Oxford University Press, 1991), 136.
3. As quoted in John S. Coulson, "Ads Can Change Attitudes, Hike Sales; Effects Measurable," *Marketing News* (February 16, 1976), 5.
4. As quoted in Linda Formichelli, "Keeping It Real: New Media Are Forcing Marketers to Be More Authentic with Their Target Customers," *Deliver Magazine* (May 2007), accessed on November 29, 2007.
5. Jeff Zabin and Gresh Brebach, *Precision Marketing* (Hoboken, NJ: John Wiley & Sons, 2004), 100.
6. See note 1.
7. The actual subscriber population is slightly less due to double SIMs and subscriptions (e.g., for phone and data card).

4

Introduction to Mobile Advertising

WHAT IS NEW AND DIFFERENT ABOUT MOBILE MEDIA?

Mobile media compose the broad basis for the seventh generation of media and the second big generation of digital media after the Internet. Mobile phones add four significant elements not possible on any previous mass media, making mobile, in some ways, potentially superior. As devices, new mobile phones enable these consumer media capabilities at lower price points than ever seen before. Mobile phones have the following four unique capabilities:

1. They are high volume, personal fashion statements.
2. They are always carried and always on.
3. They have unique user input experiences of cameras and voice.
4. They have built-in payment mechanisms.

These unique device, network, and media capabilities will generate significant new consumer capabilities and advertising models. Mobile will ultimately present massive opportunities to provide *context, immediacy,* and *personalization* that inherently make mobile a strong advertising medium, with significant potential advantages over radio, print, and television. How do we take advantage of those benefits? There are over 3 billion mobile phone consumers—three times as many mobile phones as personal computers. Over a quarter of all Internet access is already from mobile phones. There are nearly twice as many mobile phones as TV sets. Twice as many people use TXT messaging on a phone as use e-mail on the Web.[1] But mobile is, first of all, a communications device.

The mobile phone enables, if only barely, almost all the capabilities enabled by previous media but does not replicate directly from them. At first, mobile media attempted to replicate the earlier media and advertising forms, but those efforts largely failed.

Mobile phones are not just small video screens or dumbed down little web browsers. They are the very heart of a major new mass medium. It is as different from the Internet as the Internet was from TV or as TV was from radio or as radio was from print. Both mobile and the Internet are unique in that they have capabilities from the previous eras of media. And because they are digital, they are disruptive to the advertising world that formed in the TV era.

In this chapter, we examine the present status of mobile media, and look at how some of today's successful models will help mobile advertising become a major force in the bigger world of TV, print, radio, billboards, product placements, and other advertising.

YOU CAN'T MILK A CALF

In all new media, it is critical to develop amazing new user experiences that launch massive consumer adoption. Without this focus, media are limited to islands of geeks and may never see mass consumer adoption. Without a heavy concentration of consumer eyeballs, the media will fail as an advertising platform.

Creating great user experiences is essential in mobile media. The small screen highlights poor experiences that can be masked easily with PC monitor-sized screens. Mobile ads that lack relevance, are poorly implemented, or are generally disruptive to the user experience can easily cripple the nascent mobile media market before it can develop a broad base of consumers. Massive acceptance of mobile media is a strong prerequisite for mobile advertising scale. Mobile advertising can't degrade, invade, or interrupt the user experience or it will halt the adoption of the media.

But this has yet to be proven in scale in the markets of the world. Targeting could easily backfire before it is accepted. Consumer permissions and preferences are critical. Permission starts with understanding the consumer marketing preferences. If you understand, then you can execute permission-based marketing.

If you walked into a store and the clerk asked, "Can I help you," you might say yes and find it a great experience. But, if you walked out of the store without buying and the clerk ran you down, accosted you in the store's parking lot, and stuffed a last-minute offer that did not interest you in the window of your car, you might revolt. Targeting consumers before they get to where they are going can disrupt and delay the user experience. Targeting them in the middle of an experience can easily tip over the edge into interruption. This is especially relevant to the small screens of mobile. If mobile advertising is perceived as TXT spam, irrelevant Bluetooth messages, or WAP sessions that eat into data plans or are generally interrupting a user experience, mobile ads will stall before reaching their potential. Mistakes made on small screens get magnified 10-fold to users. Reactions can be harsh and viral. Bad words can travel like wildfire on TXT before a product can even get off the ground.

How do mobile operators harness the obvious opportunities without alienating their critical loyal subscribers? And how do advertisers harness mobile without negatively affecting their brand values? Operators are moving slowly with highly structured and well-planned processes. The risks associated with an overly aggressive strategy at rollout are massive, potentially killing mobile advertising at birth.

If executed correctly, the benefits of mobile advertising far outweigh the possible downsides. There is a growing awareness of mobile advertising and many consumers expect it to be only a matter of time before advertising on their mobile phones becomes the norm. In addition, some models can ensure greater acceptance, such as free minutes incentives, credits on data portals, and rewards points for signing up friends in exchange for the receipt of the ad. The key to subscriber buy-in, even with incentives, will be in delivering content that is of high value to the consumer. As noted by Harry Kargman, the CEO of Kargo:

> *The state of the market is definitely early. Right now, it is all over the place. There is not clear understanding of what we should be charging, how we should we be charging, and so on. People get $75 based on targeting whereas on an off-deck campaign, it is $5; that is a big spread for the same ad. It is because the market is very immature.*[2]

Most current mobile advertising activity is just getting out of the experimental phases. Publishers are doing the vast majority of tasks, including creative work and delivery of mobile ads. The inventory is limited and fractured by the various mobile application technology types. The mobile advertising business, while ripe with potential and explosive in its growth, is still a relatively young calf. We can try to milk it aggressively with ads, but it is early. We can also never forget that user experience really matters.

Even with these issues, real marketplaces are appearing for mobile media and advertising. And many more will emerge in the next few years. The destination is no longer in doubt. The trajectory will be steep and aggressive, and mobile advertising will be a significant market. The journey promises to be interesting. Here are some starting point examples of successful mobile advertising and a few over-hyped grand failures.

A MOBILE CONSUMER'S PERSPECTIVE

Recently, global mobile content was optimistically measured by Informa to be at $31 billion, which is above the Internet's $25 billion content estimate in the same report.[3] Regardless of the optimism in the report, mobile media is younger than the Web and evolving very fast as a powerful new media channel.

Mobile advertising is at a nascent stage in the United States, as well as most parts of the world except Asia. The 2007 U.S. mobile advertising market was just $150 million, according to the Association of National Advertisers. But this will change rapidly as a younger generation of 11- to 17-year-olds grow up. Advertisers will change their media choices to reflect the fast-moving shifts in consumer behavior. The mobile phone is an extension of everything these new consumers do. They cannot imagine a world without this technology. In fact, our three-year-old daughters will never know a mobile phone that is not a camera phone.

Consumers are starting to see ads in mobile today. Brand-new forms of media and advertising interactivity are taking off on mobile. They primarily fall into three areas:

1. TXT short codes for interactive, response-based advertising on television, print, and on billboards. Advanced use of bar codes and camera phones driving advertising interactivity in print is alive and well in Japan, but has not been seen much outside Asia.
2. Brand advertising is appearing aggressively as banner ads, primarily on WAP. On messages in China and India, SMS interstitials are now appearing as a standard part of a smart brands campaign. Video and mobile TV are primarily brand-based advertising enablers today.
3. The big money kahuna of the Internet—search ad revenues—is a long way out in mobile, except for local search. The grand on-ramp to the internet is showing up as a mini on-ramp for mobile consumers today.

Consumers are embracing mobile media and seeing mobile advertising more often. Advertisers are noticing that younger consumers and previously unreachable niche audiences are reachable by mobile today. Here are some approaches that consumers are seeing in mobile media in the market.

The interactivity of the mobile phone will make legacy media come alive. TV, radio, print and billboards can all be made interactive with mobile, bringing out new forms of advertising even in old media. Mobile will be woven into the center of most campaigns and no longer isolated to tiny mobile-specific islands. Around the world, interactive voting and polling using TXT on TV was a critical tipping point of consumer mobile media usage because it exposed mobile to massive new audiences in an engaging, fresh way. And they are participating in it. It is expanding the demographics to older generations and to new markets at an unprecedented scale. As Jeremy Lockhorn, Director of Emerging Media at Avenue A | Razorfish(now part of Microsoft), says, "Mobile can be the connective tissue between other media."[4]

Mobile Makes Old Media Interactive

The mobile phone has its own unique messaging platform, SMS messaging or TXT. The first of the killer applications for mobile, TXT is compelling. It is simple, cheap, fast, and interactive. TXT is also far bigger, by users and by revenues, than anything on the Internet. There are 1.1 billion people who use the Internet, but out of 2.7 billion mobile phone users, 1.8 billion people use TXT messaging. More than twice as many people are active users of TXT than are active users of Internet e-mail. The reach is phenomenal, and the impact to TV is already massive.

One of the great promises of mobile advertising is that it can make old media, such as TV, print, and radio, highly interactive. Voting on TV, purchasing content out of the Sunday newspaper, and interacting with radio shows are all generating solid consumer usage and revenues globally. An entire TV or radio audience can usually do TXT. They may not TXT, but their phones have the capability. Even though this form of interactivity is catching on, it is complex to provision free TXT campaigns. As Mark Logan, VP and Managing Director of Interactive at Barkley, says, *"It is like getting the Vatican, the Pentagon and Congress to all agree on an agreement for a major series of campaigns. There needs to be a better way to scale the setup of interactive campaigns for this to become a major campaign budget opportunity."*[5]

Even with these short code provisioning issues, this area is a great example of how mobile can make older media interactive and measurable. And it is hugely influential in getting the masses of consumers to understand, use, and embrace mobile as a media type. TV TXT voting and polling leads radio, print, and billboards by a large margin, as seen in the M:Metrics chart in Figure 4.1.[6]

Interactive TV Is Not What TV Executives Planned in 1993
Mobile TXT derailed the best-laid TV executive plans from 1993 around their definitions of "interactive television." TXT and its rapid adoption on TV productions is having a powerful impact on new TV shows. It is also having a positive impact on the overall adoption of mobile data by consumers in almost every country in the world. Although many TV shows allow people to vote on the Web free of charge, the mobile phone is the most effective interactive tool for casting a vote, probably because consumers can participate

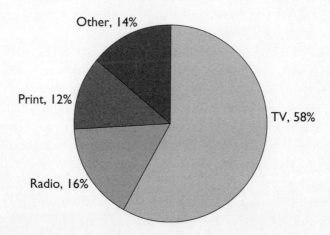

Figure 4.1   SMS responses by medium.
Source: M:Metrics, May 2007. Copyright © 2007 M:Metrics, Inc. All rights reserved.

without getting off their big couches! TV TXT voting is truly a global phenomenon, and no show worldwide has made
this more obvious than the *Pop Idol* franchise and its U.S.
cousin *American Idol*. *Pop Idol* generated over 3 billion viewers in its first six years.[7] And more than any other U.S. TV
show, *American Idol,* achieved breakout status and got U.S.
TXT usage on the map as a true mobile phenomenon.

American Idol's first season in 2002 achieved 110 million
total votes and 2.5 million TXT votes. The only participants
were AT&T mMode's 20 million customers. The first month
barely crossed 50,000 TXT votes. The second *American Idol*
season in 2003 received 240 million total votes and 7.5 million TXT votes. Participants were still limited to AT&T
mMode's 20 million customers.

By the fourth season (2005), TXT and SMS were still
largely unused in the U.S. market. Yet *American Idol* viewers
sent a record 41.5 million TXT votes in out of a total 500 million votes. This was the single biggest TXT event *in the world*.
And the mobile reach was still limited to 50m total Cingular
and AT&T mMode consumers. What is more remarkable is
that 30 percent of those TXT voters *were first-time users*. TXT
innovation was now possible with that type of user adoption.
Mobile trivia, sweepstakes, and TXT chats were all added.[8]
But there was a huge problem. Consumers who were on
other networks could not TXT vote at all.

When all U.S. mobile customers could vote, the numbers
became truly stunning. Mobile vote counts exceeded the
highest vote counts in any U.S. presidential election. The
2006 season had 578 million total votes and 120 million SMS
votes with nationwide, cross-operator TXT capabilities.
There will have to be an equivalent cross-operator effort
to break through to these types of volume for mobile
advertising.

There can be powerful viral aspects to these TXT scenarios. Sanjaya staying on the 2007 *American Idol* show well
past his talent because of rampant TXT voting for him was
a great example of this. Engagement is easily measured.

Responses are almost instant. TXT voting is not exactly what old-school television executives envisioned in 1993 when interactive television was conceived; this is what it has become. But it is generating big TV revenues, massive mobile TXT volumes, and incredible new transparency around performance metrics that were only dreams for TV executives a few years ago.

Mobile Makes Billboards Interactive

While walking in SoHo, you can send a TXT as Lenny Kravitz peers down from a billboard for Absolut vodka. On the billboard, Absolut asks you to TXT to get a free four-minute music track where you are standing. And it works. Ogilvy ran a campaign on a billboard at Times Square for Dove, asking if the model was wrinkled or wonderful. The results were displayed in real time on the digital billboard.

The billboard is alive again as an advertising medium. Mobile users can look at billboards, no matter where they are—on kiosks in malls, on garbage cans, on taxi roofs, on the sides of a bus, and above traffic jams on the side of a road—and download music, get a video clip, or get a coupon. All with a simple TXT message. When mobile bar codes appear en masse, this will explode as it is even simpler to click a camera phone than to triple-tap TXT. It is amazing, considering that billboard ads were considered moribund a decade ago. Mobile is a key driver of this growth moving forward. One of the oldest ad mediums is suddenly one of the industry's most fashionable. Mobile makes it interactive. It is now cool again.

TXT interactivity is powerful. But opt-in should be designed into the campaign. Walking by a billboard that is enabled with Bluetooth sending capabilities and getting scatterblasted with bluespam will backlash with consumers. In Times Square, Walt Disney World advertised a new theme-park ride on a billboard. It asked you to send TXT, and seconds later your phone got a Disney message asking if you wanted more Disney promotions. This is classic user opt-in that is friendly to the consumer. And it is highly valuable for the advertiser to hone in on the right base for higher responses.

Mobile Makes Old Media More Measurable

Surveys are no longer required to measure billboard, television, or radio effectiveness. Direct response has brought engagement to the forefront, and mobile makes it measurable. The results are no longer subject to vague frequency or drive-by audience metrics. The results will also interact with future campaigns in near real time to adjust the campaign based on the engagement metrics. Billboards are becoming a media buyer's new best friend because of this interactive engagement and highly visible metrics. This is a powerful enabler that only mobile interactivity can provide. Because of the ROI and the metrics, we will see more and more of mobile interactivity and resulting measurability in TV, radio, and billboard campaigns moving forward (see Table 4.1).

Messaging-based TXT interactive or response-based advertising has been the lifeblood of mobile advertising to date. In fact, it was the success of TXT campaigns that motivated many analysts to forecast the multibillion-dollar mobile advertising markets that we see today. The primary reason for this success is the acceptance of TXT interoperability agreements among the operators, making nationwide and worldwide campaigns possible.

Some of the pioneers in mobile advertising were companies like ipsh! (later bought by media company Omnicom) and Flytxt (later bought by Italy's Buongiorno) who ran high-profile campaigns for celebrities and media brands. Agencies typically work with the aggregators who have direct links into operators worldwide. Having that point of connection helps remove friction at the operator level.

Although this format is great for interactive campaigns, it is possible to run brand campaigns on other mobile channels, as described in the following sections.

Table 4.1   How Mobile Makes Old Media Interactive

Consumer Engagement Points for Direct Response or Interactive Campaigns	Ad Models and Expected Results	Mobile Operator or Publisher Requirements
Calls to action in print media, radio, and television shows.	TXT short-code based. Very measurable.	Interactivity with polling or voting through high-volume MO-SMS gateways.
Digital billboards supporting TXT short codes.	Immediate response and measurement of calls to action.	TXT short codes required, with advanced lead times.
Consumer pull based with some opt-in push.	Instant win sweepstakes.	
Engagement based, not interruptive.	Great consumer adoption rates for many new TV shows.	Premium message fees for additional message revenues. Strong revenues for high-message volumes.
Excellent reach. All phones can TXT. Most people can TXT.	Popular in major sporting venues.	Revenues typically split 40:30:30—40 percent to the producers, 30 percent to the operator, and 30 percent to broadcasters. Operators then share a tiny percentage with the mobile enablers.
Viral scenarios appearing.	Mobile bar codes tomorrow, especially in print media. With mobile bar codes will evolve into a disruptive, closed loop pay-per-action model.	
Transactions with mobile bar codes.		
Future campaigns ## or ** based, or bar code based, simplifying consumer use.	Measurement around engagement for old media. Higher levels of accountability.	

The Brand in Your Hand

In an ad-saturated world, the mobile phone browser has been an almost pristine canvas. After a few major misfits and false starts in the 2001 to 2003 time frame, and a slow, experimental lift off in 2004 and 2005, banner ads in mobile began to become real in 2006. A number of companies are helping to transform the device that people are loath to leave at home into a personal, pocket-sized banner ad billboard, selling everything from the latest ring tone to tennis shoes. Advertisers are now starting to move aggressively toward the brand in your hand.

Only five years ago, most mobile phones had only monochrome, or black and green screens. WAP was readily available, but only about 33 hard-core users in the world really enjoyed the user experience. Today, midrange phones have bright color screens that are a quarter of a standard PC screen. It is no longer a miserable user experience. It is tolerable, but it is still not great. All mobile phones today have at least TXT capabilities and basic WAP browsers. In three Asian countries; Japan, South Korea, and China, the majority of web access now comes from mobile phones, not PCs. More countries will see this transition point during 2008.

But it is not enough to consider more users. Consider the explosion in recent WAP usage. In November 2006, Telephia and comScore both reported that the first five major U.S. web sites have crossed the threshold with more web users coming from mobile than from PCs. Those first five are Accuweather, ESPN, Weather Channel, Yahoo Weather, and G-Mail. In the United States, 35 million consumers used mobile browsers in 2006 with subscriber access to WAP growing 54 percent year over year in 2007.[9] This is significant in that it is now a big traffic base for mobile banner ads. And mobile advertisers are starting to take advantage of this explosion in usage.

Big brands are noticing this revolution on mobile. The rush of mobile operators supporting banner ads on WAP is on.

Orange UK, with mobile ad partner Screen Tonic, launched one of the first market-scale WAP banner ads in 2006 on its WAP portal, Orange World. Ads from Peugeot, Jaguar, and United International Pictures went live with the launch.[10] At the launch of the service, only four devices could access the advertisements, because of their display characteristics. The problem of too many styles on WAP was highlighted instantly. It was necessary to transcode the ads to the correct formats and sizes for a limited number of devices. This will be a continual problem for ad production moving forward. Too many sizes are required. This set of issues was to be a common theme across all advertisers on WAP.

India's biggest mobile operator, Bharti Airtel, has worked with Microsoft, Canon, and Ford Motor as advertisers since 2005. In October 2006, Sprint/Nextel launched WAP banner ads with Third Screen Media. In November 2006, Yahoo brought banner ads to mobile across their global mobile network. Remember D2C, which started in Japan as the first mobile advertising company back in 2000? D2C says it is running "100 million to 500 million banners on mobile phones a month, with 3 percent to 5 percent of viewers clicking on the ads."[11] This was in late 2005, when the rest of the global operators were just beginning trials in their markets.

This cousin of the Internet banner ad is the grandfather of mobile advertising techniques. And it is surprisingly effective. Advertisers know that mobile users sometimes have too much time to spend. They might be commuting by bus, waiting for a friend, or sitting in their doctor's office looking for things to do. And advertising started having a direct positive impact for consumers as they saw the price of mobile applications fall for the first time.

Also quoted in the *Wall Street Journal* in 2006, "The average price for a four to eight week long banner ad campaign on a content provider's mobile web site is now $75,000 to $150,000, up from $25,000 to $50,000 last year. About 3 percent to 5 percent of phone users click on banner ads on their screens— higher than the 1 percent click rate of computer users, says Jeff Janer, chief operating officer of Third Screen Media."[12]

WAP banner advertising is predominantly branding based today. There are some initial "click to action" or offer-based campaigns, but they require clicks to WAP-friendly sites that, for the most part, are missing today. This is a major hole in the ecosystem. Consumers would have to go to a second, poorly integrated site. Or go nowhere at all.

On-deck mobile banner ad revenues are shared between the ad-serving platform provider, the mobile operator, and the content provider. Today, *on-deck* refers to the "WAP deck" offered and controlled by the operators. They determine the mix of services, content partners, and ultimately the inventory of ad-space. The platform provider typically serves as the clearinghouse in the on-deck mobile advertising scenario. Mobile operators can try to provide a proprietary solution and manage their own ad-servers. In this scenario, advertisers wind up negotiating directly with operators for ad placement and rates. Scaling this process for the advertiser would be complex and difficult.

In the off-deck model, advertisers have to compensate the content publishers to display ads, typically in a CPM revenue model. *Off-deck* refers to services not delivered or accessed via the operator's deck. However, a second revenue share for clicks or actions taken on the advertisements may occur. Pay-per-click (PPC) and cost-per-thousand (CPM) models are still in the early experimental phases with banner ads.

The off-deck platform providers handle the revenue settlement between advertisers and content publishers. They also act as clearinghouses to manage the cash flow. A volume play here results in higher margins for the ad platform company and can be reflected in higher revenue shares offered to the content publishers. AdMob offers up to 75 percent of revenues from advertisers to its content partners. Overall, the industry average for CPM revenue shares comes to around 50 percent.

AdMob was the first company to pursue WAP-based advertisements for the off-deck market. Initially, only smaller advertisers were using its ad network; as AdMob's reach and audience have grown, global brands such as Coca-Cola and Adidas have run campaigns. In a campaign for Adidas, AdMob delivered 180,000 of the total 500,000 unique visits from print, TV, online, and mobile marketing efforts. In 2007, Millennial Media also launched off-deck mobile advertising and gained good traction fairly quickly. Similar companies started to mushroom around the world.

In addition to the exploding usage and massive reach, there is another excellent reason that advertisers will love WAP. The typical click-through rate (CTR) for a regular Internet banner ad is about 0.2 percent, whereas the rate for mobile banner ads is in the range of 2 to 3 percent.[13] With click-through rates (CTRs) of 3 percent, the off-deck Adidas campaign mentioned previously delivered 40 percent of the leads for 4 percent of the budget. That performance will no doubt go down over time as the novelty wears off. But right now, it represents sensational ad performance (see Table 4.2).

Despite some debate in the industry, large global brands looking to generate brand awareness and introduce new products, and not looking for targeted programs, will perform better with off-deck strategies than with on-deck. This is because there is less complexity than delivering the same program on-deck with multiple geographically distributed operators. Assuming the inventory of banner graphics and WAP sites

Table 4.2   Mobile Banner Advertising Overview

Consumer Engagement Point and Campaign Types for Brand-Based Campaigns	Ad Models and Expected Results	Mobile Operator or Publisher Requirements
Consumer pull or opt-in push based.	Text and graphic interstitials as banners.	Primarily WAP and XHTML mobile portals and applications.
Used for awareness and brand reinforcement.	Better reach from emerging ad networks; specifically off deck.	Entertainment applications and entry points to other media applications. Content mostly news, weather, sports, and stock. Search and local search applications also involved.
Mostly interruption based today. Contextual targeting will make this far more engagement based in the future.	Very hard to reach both on- and off-deck with a single buy.	
	Now fairly easy to achieve global reach in a campaign with off-deck mobile networks.	
	Generally CPM based with huge premiums for targeting data.	Banner ad standards starting to be put in place, but still evolving.
		Inventories generally low, contributing to high CPM prices.
		Video, mobile TV, and other forms of mobile media will evolve for brand advertising.

gets solved and the value chain becomes clearer, WAP will begin to begin to take off. This is happening at a fast pace in the off-deck portal world and will apply to operator portals and applications as it gets smoothed out off-deck. Assuming the contextual targeting value for the consumer is spot-on and the banners don't land with a dull thud overwhelming the user experience, they should be a key part of the mobile advertising value chain moving forward.

Mobile Search Is Not Quite a Consumer On-Ramp

The third and perhaps the biggest potential revenue producer is mobile search. In the online world, search dominates the advertising revenues with over 40 percent of the share, followed by display advertising. In mobile, search didn't exist until 2005. Will mobile media search be the most important on-ramp for mobile media usage? Yes, absolutely—but in the future. It is not used as a destination on-ramp today, as it is on the Web.

Will mobile search be the first big battleground for mobile ads? Yes, but it will take more time for the dynamics in mobile to come together around true high bandwidth, sufficient cross operator global media, and content indexes with far simpler user interfaces. Until these are in place, the consumer volumes will not be sufficient to attract significant advertisers. And even then, a strong argument can be made that the on-ramp for a mobile experience is communication, not search. And as such, communications and mobile communities might be more important than search to the nascent mobile advertising ecosystem.

Some mobile ad network upstarts are thinking that this game is all about setting up a new mobile ad marketplace or exchange and matching up buyers and sellers. It is not that simple. The mobile search traffic base is too low overall, as is the advertiser base that is willing to purchase search keywords. Advertisers want good traffic and lots of it, while publishers want monetization. There are web networks out there that have overcome this, but it is very difficult to do.

The core reason advertising is not a dominant force in mobile media is that mobile search does not have the reach or usage to make it so. As yet, there is no parallel with search on the Internet enabling massive reach and usage from one search box. Search is a one of the best ways to find content and the absolute best way for a marketer to determine consumer intent. Mobile search should be about discovery and should be the primary tool to find media and content that has not previously been seen by that consumer. Mobile advertising can be carefully targeted and relevant to what consumers are doing at any given moment and is less likely to be dismissed out of hand.

Mobile search is not the best way to find mobile media today. Typing in any information (e.g., a web address or a search inquiry), using a phone's cramped keypad is a chore many people aren't willing to put up with. And even if the user goes to the trouble of triple-tapping in keywords, the results are often poor. New forms of mobile search technology will enable media, communities, recommendations, and new content discovery. The user intents displayed by mobile consumers will enable specific one-to-one keyword targeted marketing and incredible ROIs. New interfaces with voice search are now on the market. The combination of new interfaces, far better indexing breadth and depth, and recommendations for discovery of new media will make mobile search a powerful paradigm for mobile media and advertising.

About one third of today's interest in mobile search is little more than a manifestation of the poor usability of so much of the mobile web. A large percentage of mobile search usage and volume is for site navigation queries to Google, Yahoo, and free ring tone sites. As the distinctions between mobile content and web content disappear over the next few years, it does not bode well for closed browsing environments with limited content indexes that consumers can search. The days of closed, or walled, gardens and portals are numbered.

Another key reason for relatively slow consumer adoption is the lack of a strong mobile index that is accessible from any phone by any mobile consumer. The new domain registry for mobile, .mobi (also called DotMobi) initiative was supposed to help address the dearth of mobile sites, but it is slow to evolve as well. Mobile search would be able to search an index of .mobi sites. There are not enough eyeballs using .mobi. There are simply too many operator content silos today to build scale in an index for mobile search. Fixing this is a prerequisite for advertisers to get the reach they need for successful large-scale targeting of mobile keywords.

Despite the big missing models around mobile search, the first major battleground between the web giants and operators will occur here. The value of targeting mobile specific ads against clear user intent is simply too important for a strong mobile model not to appear. Things are changing. Yahoo now has a major agreement across multiple major Asian operators for their oneSearch service. The reach is potentially 100 million consumers in more than a dozen countries. This is the scale of reach necessary to attract a real mobile advertising base. Even half of that, 50 million mobile eyeballs, would be great reach for a new group of mobile keyword bidders. In a major statement of support of mobile, WPP invested in JumpTap in late 2006.[14] In theory, WPP will soon offer its existing advertising partners easier access to mobile distribution. WPP's advertising sales channel, mobile search index, and keyword sales programs will enable an abundance of mobile advertisements via mobile search. If JumpTap can gain significant distribution, this might be an important step to move the industry forward. Medio Systems has released combinations of search, with voice interfaces, merchandising with recommendation engines and an advertising network off mobile operators' decks. This combination will help redefine mobile search to a more powerful consumer proposition. Motricity now has a strong position with the late 2007 acquisition of InfoSpace. The combination of a strong portal and media storefront business to leverage with mobile search will have an impact on the market. But time is running out. They are all selling into mobile operators as point solutions that can be operator branded. None of them have reached critical mass for consumer reach yet. Brian Lent, Medio Systems Chief Executive Officer, predicts:

> *Naturally existing players from adjacent spaces want a piece of the growing pie. History has shown that new mediums usually have new winners. How many of the top 10 web sites were media winners of the TV age? Google understands that ad monetization means that other services can be made cheaper. Operators spend billions of dollars a year on building and maintaining infrastructure. Obviously they don't want to pay for infrastructure that someone else gives away for free. The white label solution is to work with the operators and not compete with them.*[15]

Mobile advertisers will flock to the entity that has the best reach to masses of consumers. The most transparent reach is to buy keywords that get to hundreds of millions of consumers at once. The powerhouses of web search, Google, Yahoo, and Microsoft's existing ad services will expand incrementally to mobile. All are testing mobile-specific ad types and paid clicks and calls for mobile search. And they are gunning for premier positions on the handsets through OEM agreements; driving consumer adoption around the operators to gain reach. This reach across operators will inevitably lead to a successful mobile specific keyword auction model (see Table 4.3).

Some believe the pay-per-click rates for mobile search terms could dwarf those paid for keywords online, since someone searching a keyword on a mobile device is likely to be closer to making a purchase, especially for mobile media such as ring tones or games. Although the race is on to extend this model from the Web to mobile or to create mobile operator search models from white label point solutions, those solutions are not enough. One of the biggest opportunities in all of mobile advertising revolves around a potentially high volume, cross operator, off-deck mobile search offering. This would be the prerequisite for a massive mobile search driven advertising model. A compelling

Table 4.3   Mobile Media Search Overview

Consumer Engagement and Campaign Types to Find Media with Mobile Search	Ad Models and Expected Results	Mobile Operator or Publisher Requirements
Consumer pull based on search intent. Highly focused targeting.

Used for awareness and brand reinforcement.

Mostly engagement based, sometimes interruptive. | Text-based ads.

Somewhat variant models today. Pay per click (PPC) will happen in scale in 2008 and later.

PPC is generally very high quality and low volumes of paid keywords today.

Cross operator reach a major impediment for this model.

Local search ad models more evolved and scaleable than media search today.

Media search being combined with advanced recommendation systems to make the consumer purchasing cycles much more appealing. | Highly fragmented from an advertiser's perspective.

Advertisers required to interact with numerous systems at different operators. Almost impossible to span every operator's search box in any one country.

Index sizes for games, graphics, media, and information problematic for mobile ad models in search today.

Complicated, silo-based, integrations required at each operator to create an index. |

consumer experience delivering a new volume of high traffic performance will bring a new mobile advertising network in place.

Location-Based Targeting . . . Whoops, We Missed Again!

Since early 2001, this has been the classic mobile ad scenario. You walk past a Starbucks, your phone beeps, and you get a half-price latte offer. But its delivery cost was around $0.05 and even if the redemptions hit 2 or 3 percent, the costs would have been upward of $1.50. Reaching consumers in enough scale to opt-in would be very expensive, driving the per adoption costs closer to $5.00 to $7.00.

Location is not nearly ubiquitous enough to trigger location-by-location delivery. And even if it were, the operators would probably charge for the location parameter driving the acquisition costs far higher. And consumers would call it spam if their message bucket got charged with a message. From most angles, this approach has been a failure to date. But it will evolve into something meaningful.

The current "hot" implementations (started in Europe around 2003) are based on Bluetooth. Proximity marketing, or bluecasting, is done by bluetoothing offers to consumers in proximity to the advertiser or store. This approach is based on radio technology, which is free to the operator and attractive from a cost perspective. It can't typically be billed.

But it has an interruption-based dark side. Bluespamming is here. Bluecasting is marginally less intrusive than a text message because your mobile phone number is always private. Although this approach requires no opt-in from consumers, the only way to not get a bluecast *is to turn Bluetooth off*. That is insane. Uninvited. Interruptive. A lot like spam.

Bluecasting will be an interim approach at best unless a "one-click" consumer configuration is enabled. This single click would let consumers tell the network if they wanted to opt-in to bluecasts—or not. This does not exist yet, but since consumers are now in control, it will be required for this approach to work. If this one-click configuration is not in place soon, this scenario will be replaced by flat rate data charges made far more usable with preinstalled mobile bar code readers. Click on a mobile bar code and invite the promotion into your life. Consumers will be back in control and bluecasting will be relegated to the tar pits of the past.

Unless these types of models become engagement based and get away from interruption approaches, they are not worth considering. Savvy mobile media grazers will hit the skip button and move on.

Where Am I Going? What Is Nearby?

Mobile media and location devices are great examples of shrinking gaps between content and mobile devices. Location-based search applications and specifically Global Positioning System (GPS) navigation applications make the content versus device separation small indeed. These applications are smart enough to know the location of the user through their phone, and use that information to provide geographically targeted search results. In other words, the device tells the content what to do. This is very different from web content relationships to a PC.

Local search is an enormous web opportunity that has been germinating for more than six years. Mobile search, especially voice-driven mobile search, may be the catalyst for local search business to reach a true high growth tipping point. But to date, the experience has been frustrating on mobile. Triple-tapping keywords is hard for all but elite members of the thumb tribe. Getting bad results is all too common and frustrating. Location capabilities are more than likely not there. Little or no advertising revenues either mean the application is a loss leader for the vendor, or the application is expensive for consumers. But that is all about to explosively change.

Around the globe, TXT access to local business listings is skyrocketing. In Norway, roughly 30 percent of local listing requests are by TXT. Consumers are replacing fee-based operators with self-service mobile search. TXT-based user experiences to get listings are still limited, but this will change radically over the next few years. The pace of innovation in voice search, free directory assistance (DA) for local search, and local search advertising models guarantees this category is a big revenue producer in 2008 and beyond. Go2 Directories had already delivered over 1 billion local search WAP pages and over 50 million ads by early 2007. 4INFO is on track to serve over 100 million TXT local search ad units in 2007. Some of the fastest growing product lines within any operator's inventory are client-based, GPS based local search or navigation applications, typically priced at upward of $9.99 U.S. per month (see Table 4.4).

These market trends, combined with the unique value of morphing this common directory assistance voice call scenario into true, compelling, voice search will be highly leveragable for the next evolutions of mobile and local search advertising. Voice search applications will be integrated with maps and weaved into other forms of rich local data, like calendars of local events, at their core.

Voice mobile search is potentially the largest and most lucrative opportunity but also the hardest to do well. It has taken years for it to arrive in quality, simplified user experiences. Free mobile local search, enabled with cutting edge voice user experiences, driven by powerful indexes that are highly optimized for mobile and powered by pay per click or pay per call advertisements are bad news for fee based directory-service businesses. This disruptive force is covered in Chapter 7, with an overview of the powerful forces behind a major business model shift.

PEEKING AHEAD TO ADVANCED MOBILE MEDIA EXPERIENCES

The advent of powerful media processors; lots of memory; and cool, new, large-screen mobile phones on higher speed networks is a boon for mobile media consumers. This is best demonstrated in the new iPhone, although in the U.S. market, it is shackled on a slow network with a semi-walled garden. Given the high replacement rates of phones, these phones will reach critical mass by 2008 in almost all global markets. These powerful media phones are laying the groundwork for new mobile media applications. But it will take a while to overcome the battery drain issues from the media processing and large screen usage. Consumers are taking advantage of these media devices, with media applications that are often subsidized by new forms of mobile advertising. While these

Table 4.4   Mobile Local Search Advertising Overview

Consumer Engagement and Campaign Types When a Consumer Asks "What Is Nearby"?	Ad Models and Expected Results	Mobile Operator or Publisher Requirements
Consumer pull based. Highly relevant, based on search intent.	Awareness, engagement, and some consideration.	GPS or location APIs required and not as widely available to vendors in late 2007 as predicted.
Some brand reinforcement, awareness, engagement, consideration, and some transactions.	Text-paid clicks. Mostly banner ad interstitials. Some TXT interstitials.	Publishers must have relationships with the sales forces of the yellow pages companies or paid call vendors.
Engagement based, generally not interruptive.	Ad extensions in this area that are derived from directory assistance calls (e.g., a caller may receive a map with directions and ads on it).	Can be TXT, WAP, or client based with or without a voice interface. Might be directory assistance or 411- or 118-call based.
	Text pay-per-click (PPC) and pay-per-call links. Large ad volumes already in mobile local search applications.	Complex connections between the directory assistance capabilities and mobile data applications, and advertiser bases required.
	Local search derived ads typically not campaign based, but come from the world of the Web and local merchants.	Voice search and directory assistance will collide in 2008.
	Audio ads in free directory assistance models in 2008.	
	These ad types will be some of the first to evolve into pay-per-transaction models in mobile.	

applications and consumer views are not the norm, they are coming soon.

Free Media Snacks, with Ad Strings Attached

In 2006, Toyota launched the Yaris on mobisodes in mobile, as well as on conventional radio and TV, and on MySpace. If you were one of the 500,000 lucky people who owned a Sprint video phone at the time and watched the mobisode *Prison Break,* you saw a groundbreaking product launch campaign. Toyota and Fox cut an extensive deal for Toyota to sponsor and more importantly, to be featured in the then new Fox mobisode series, *Prison Break: Proof of Innocence.* The series ran only on Sprint, with some analysts pegging the total campaign in the neighborhood of $10 million. Toyota was placing a giant bet, with the tiny number of video phones on the U.S. market at the time, that the device in the consumer's hand was a viable new target for launching a major new product.

Later in 2006, MasterCard decided to go mobile with product placements and sponsorships in 26 of Fox's mobisodes, *Bones: Skeleton Crew.* Nielsen/NetRatings fueled this effort with statistics saying, "accessing the Internet from a mobile device was the No. 1 online activity among users that make $100,000 or more each year." Those affluent alpha users and early adapters were the core that MasterCard was trying to reach. And they were on mobile.

Mobisodes *24, Prison Break, Bones: Skeleton Crew,* and others are written and filmed specifically for mobile. They are short video snacks full of bright colors and built for small screen images. They are often written by different people from those who create the regular TV version, and they have mobile product placements as part of the video. Product placements in TV, magazine articles, video games, music videos, movies, and now mobile are one of the fastest growing segments in advertising. Consumers are TiVo-ing right past the ads so they can get to the show, which is now full of paid product placements. The same product placement trends will happen in mobile media, starting with mobile video. Toyota was a front-runner in this. The category even has its own measurements from Nielsen and ITVX, who have defined values for the placements. Nielsen has just entered mobile, and so will be bringing its metrics in this category to mobile.

With the introduction of mobile broadcast TV services from MediaFLO (Qualcomm), advertisers are excited about the high quality of mobile video services and the significant measurement capabilities. There are three approaches in this segment: Unicast, Broadcast, and off-deck. Unicast solutions allow for preroll, postroll, and ad insertions between frames. This applies to solutions from companies like MobiTV and services like V-CAST from Verizon Wireless and SeeMeTV from 3 UK.

The measurement capabilities built into the broadcast video solutions, along with the much higher quality of video delivery compared with Unicast approaches, are attractive to mobile advertisers. Using video-stitching technology, caching on the device, and relevant targeting, the ads can be personalized to the consumers' benefit. There is tremendous potential in this area—but it is definitely off in the future of mobile advertising.

It is likely that interactive, consumer-initiated models will resonate best with younger media grazers. Engagement will be the new measure of this type of mobile ad. Interactive advertising, with the option of requesting more information about the product or service, will evolve quickly with mobile media. Click to watch a prerelease of a new music video. Or a new movie trailer. Watch a video of a new Lexus commercial and ask for a test drive. Enter a contest on a video ad.

If the ad is subtle, appropriately integrated, contextually relevant, and viral, we will have a unique media form for advertisers. Engagement will be measurable. Viral forwarding and morphing will be possible with this new ad format in video. Media is becoming social currency. If it is worth anything, it is worth sending on. This will happen to the new generation of mobile media ads. But it is not here yet.

If videos are attached to the beginning of other video applications (apps), will mobile prerolls be the new spam of mobile media? If not done right, they may turn out to be exactly that. There are ways to limit how they are utilized, increasing mobile effectiveness and limiting potential consumer backlashes. Timing could be limited to 5 or 10 seconds. And exposure frequency could be limited; perhaps one preroll for every third or fourth mobile video a user sees. Because of the smallish screens and limited attention cycles, mobile will certainly see 2- or 3-second tags "brought to you by" in advance of videos, and combined with full-length ad units later on (see Table 4.5).

We Interrupt This Idle Screen for an Ad

For years, the most valuable real estate on the mobile handset was media-blind. The idle screen, also known as the home

Table 4.5   Mobile Video and Media Advertising

Consumer Engagement Points and Campaign Types for Mobile Media	Ad Models and Expected Results	Mobile Operator or Publisher Requirements
Some opt-in push, mostly pull based.	Text and graphic interstitials as banners. Some video ads appearing.	Operators reluctant to free content that appears to cannibalize their premium media revenues.
Mostly brand campaign based today.	More aggressive tie-ins to music and video releases and concerts in the future, especially as higher bandwidth becomes prevalent through MediaFlo and other bandwidth solutions.	Ad-sponsored ring tones, wallpaper, games, and other premium media content.
Recommendations from also-bought scenarios, a powerful merchandising approach.		
Awareness, engagement, and some consideration.		Limits possible on promotions of publishers' media if not fully sanctioned in the storefronts.
Brand reinforcement for promotions for the content.	Product placements, especially in mobile video will be strong mobile ad model drivers.	

screen or phone top, is the main screen that consumers see as they journey through various menus and screens to access other media. It is the starting point for calling or texting, buying media, browsing, and configuring settings. Until recently, the idle screen was unexploited screen space. However, over two dozen new approaches have recently been announced or released to utilize the idle screen and bring media closer to a single click by the consumer.

Operators around the globe are quickly moving into "push-based" scenarios to encourage new mobile media discovery. The concept of discovering new mobile media needs a major breakthrough, given the inaccessible messes of the storefronts. In late 2007, the idle screen became the new battleground to access mobile media, find new media via search, and monetize it with advertising.

Once again, the Japanese market is showing the way. DoCoMo and KDDI have chosen Acrodea's Vivid UI as the best solution. Consumers can download their chosen "brand skin" and radically alter the user interface, for example, going from a BMW branded UI to a Barbie® branded UI.[16] The cool part of this solution is that not only the brand changes, but the entire functionality, from keys to applications, can also be changed by the brand. These approaches have turned push-based interruption approaches into engagement models. Consumers will eat these up, right after they hit the delete key on an interruption-based approach.

Promotions of new services or media can be achieved without bombarding consumers with interruptions. It has to be a more subtle presentation. If done correctly to the right audience, it can be effective. One of the first really successful mobile idle screen mobile advertising campaigns was Thailand's Advanced Info Service (AIS) and Honda. The Honda campaign on AIS broadcast motorcycle safety tips and targeted millions of AIS mobile consumers, offering a new Honda moped as a prize in return for registering. Within three weeks, more than three million unique impressions were generated, with more than 100,000 users clicking to participate in the prize drawing.[17]

Advertising on the idle screen does not take priority over the user experience. Since a well-designed idle screen is as much about accessing mobile communication as it is about media, it would be a mistake to infiltrate screens like the address book or the IM session with ads. Casual reminders of offers could easily stray into intrusions and insults to the user because the idle screen is so close to every action required to do anything on the phone. Please see Chapter 7 for a case study on Idle Screen.

While You Wait, We Bring You an Interstitial

Far less intrusive than interrupting idle screens are interstitials presented during load time or in the bottom of TXT messages. Interstitials can be based on SMS, WAP, or downloadable applications. Interstitials are ads that play during the dead time of WAP page loads or application downloads. Or they can be in the footers of every SMS message, as is the case in India and China today (see Table 4.6).

From a consumer perspective, watching an ad inserted during a WAP page load or a mobile application start-up is almost unobtrusive. It is certainly no worse than watching

Table 4.6   Idle Screen and Interstitials Overview

Consumer Engagement Points and Campaign Types for Idle Screens	Ad Models and Expected Results	Mobile Operator or Publisher Requirements
Mostly consumer push today.	Text and graphic interstitials as banners.	Entertainment: video and music.
Used for brand awareness, brand reinforcement, and tie-ins to other campaigns.	Click to video is appearing.	Information: news, sports, stock, and weather.
Interruption based today. Perhaps with contextual targeting, idle screen campaigns can be turned into engagement models. If not, they will fail.		Sponsored news, sports, etc. evolving. Infomercials inserted. Promotions and tie-ins to other media campaigns being tested.

a progress bar move ever so slowly. When implemented effectively, ads actually provide useful and actionable information. There is no argument about who owns the dead space between downloads. It is the operator's turf. Like the overview provided in Table 4.6, interstitial implementations will be greatly simplified. Once that happens, far more global operators will be implementing interstitial advertising between applications and start-up screens.

If taken too far, interruption-based, idle screen advertising represents old-school media control thinking. It does not take advantage of finding new media through personalization or from community discovery of hot media. Nor does it take into account the incredible media control consumers are exerting on the Internet and the move toward engagement in advertising. This avenue for advertising can be incredibly successful for the long term—if it is not overrun by push-based interruptions in the short term.

Mobile consumers are open to mobile advertising. But there are major caveats. The messages have to be relevant. The benefits need to be tangible. And they have to be presented with an opt-out at every stage. These are significant prerequisites as mobile consumers try to protect themselves from spam and an invasion of their privacy via their always-on mobile phones. Finally, the core value chains need to be defined and simplified. This is one of the major missing ingredients in mobile advertising today—the value chains are fractured, complex, and confusing for the stakeholders with the budgets. The brands and agencies get dizzy and weak knees wobble trying to figure out a new cube of 3D-like complexity.

Basic Mobile Advertising Value Chains

Even though the mobile advertising opportunity is a significant potential market, the mobile value chain is incredibly complex. Different from the Internet or any traditional media, there is significant fragmentation at multiple levels. While partnerships, consolidation, and technologies are facilitating growth and simplifying distribution, it is going to take time before a true friction-free ecosystem emerges where advertisers can reach consumers in relevant, scalable, and revenue-generating ways.

In its most basic view, the mobile value chain comprises advertisers, agencies, solution providers and enablers, content publishers, operators, and consumers. Phone manufacturers or original equipment manufacturers (OEMs) are enablers in this value chain rather than active participants, although Nokia is trying to change the pattern by acquiring advertising companies, like Enpocket and mapping companies, like Navteq. At each link of the value chain, we can find a number of participants. The irony is that even though mobile operators are limited in number, the number of vendors in the value chain is exceedingly high and the problems they solve are massively complex.

The preceding scenarios were brought to you primarily by the vendors shown on the chart in Figure 4.2. They have worked incredibly hard for a long time to build point solutions that are for the most part exiting the experimental phases. They are moving into the formation and early stages of building new value chains that will morph and change as solutions are defined, integrated, and merged.

Most of the value chain points discussed in this chapter are applicable to North America and Europe. Over time, as the industry matures, these value chains will converge and collapse just as we have seen in other media. In Japan and Korea, this has, for the most part, already occurred.

Comparing Industry Value Chains

Compared with advertising mediums before it, mobile is closer to the Internet than TV/cable, radio, and print. Mobile uses similar technologies and distribution techniques as the Internet. And, like the early days of the Internet, mobile audiences are tied to specific networks. This all sounds a lot like 10 or 15 years ago, when we had AOL and Compuserve doing the same thing. A major difference is that in mobile, we have the operators, who play the role of both portals and ISPs.

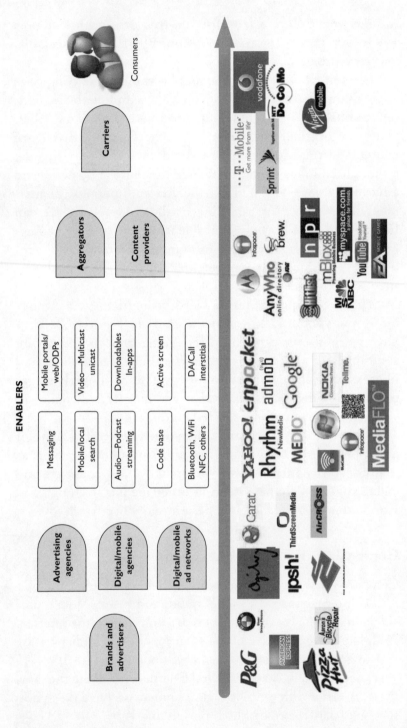

Figure 4.2 A mobile advertising value chain.

Today's big problem in the mobile advertising space is that there is no single value chain. Instead, there are many, and they are confusing and fractured along technical lines. But a clear distinction is evolving between off-deck volume plays and on-deck quality plays.

SIZING THE MARKET

There is a wide array of options for mobile advertising—from tried and true TXT to upcoming broadcast mobile video services of MediaFLO and DVB-H, QR Code, NFC (Near Field Communication), and others that we haven't thought of yet. So, the question arises, how big is the market? The next few sections add perspective to the mobile advertising opportunity.

How Big Is the Market?

Market forecasts are valuable, but we definitely need to use them with caution and common sense. This can be hard to do with the level of hype that usually occurs in the early stages of an interesting, emerging market.

Mobile advertising opportunity is a mash-up of two gigantic multibillion-dollar industries that have been on the path of convergence for some time: telecom and advertising. According to the Telecommunications Industry Association, the global telecommunications market is going to be worth $4.3 trillion in revenue. In 2006, Europe was the largest market with $1 trillion, the United States was second with $923 billion, and Asia-Pacific third at $715 billion.[18]

Advertising on the other hand is almost a $500 billion industry globally, with the United States accounting for 42 percent, Europe 23 percent, and Asia-Pacific 20 percent. Figures 4.3 and 4.4 show the global advertising spend by medium and the distribution by regions.

Despite Internet advertising being around for over 12 good years, in 2006, it only accounted for 6 percent of the

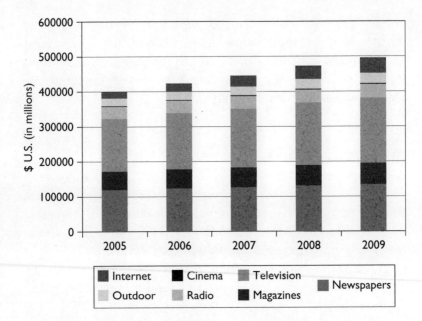

Figure 4.3   Global advertising expenditure by medium.
Source: ZenithOptiMedia, February 2007.
Note: Similar numbers are available from the PricewaterhouseCoopers study
"Global Entertainment and Media Outlook: 2007–2010." The global media and
entertainment industry is approximately $1.5 trillion in size with the United States
accounting for 41 percent; Europe, Middle East, and Africa (EMEA) 33 percent;
and Asia-Pacific 19 percent according to the study.

overall media spend and is forecasted to cross 10 percent
only after 2010. The traditional heavyweights—newspapers
and TV—accounted for a whopping 67 percent share in
2006, and that share will only decline slightly to 65 percent
by 2009. So, the shifts in advertising dollars and market
share happen over a very long time, especially in terms of
Internet age.

Given all this, how does mobile figure into the picture?
We will get to the mobile forecasts in a minute, but should
probably discuss the importance of mobile in developing
nations where majority of growth is going to come in the
near future. Figure 4.5 plots out Internet penetration versus
mobile penetration for some of the major economies. Asia
had over 400 million users but only 10.7 percent penetration

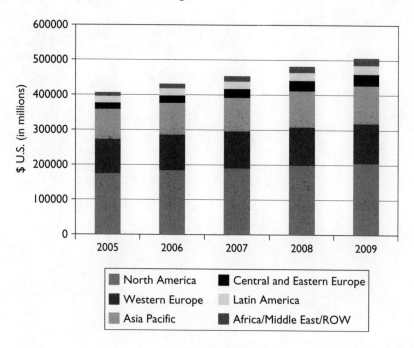

Figure 4.4   Advertising expenditure by region.
Source: ZenithOptiMedia, February 2007.

while North America had approximately 233 million users and 70 percent penetration.

While the penetration ratio stays between 1 and 2 for developed nations, it is a totally different picture for developing nations—between 3 and 8 times as many phones are available than there are traditional Internet connections. Based on the advent of mobile data services, 75 to 90 percent of the population in such areas will experience digital advertising on their mobile. Although Internet penetration is bound to increase with time, it might never get close to mobile penetration in these countries in our lifetime. This creates an incredible mobile reach proposition for advertisers as far as digital advertising is concerned.

Getting back to the mobile forecasts, it is worthwhile to start with something that we can easily audit, that is forecasts made about 2005 in 2001. Figure 4.6 shows the analysis of mobile advertising forecasts for the U.S. market

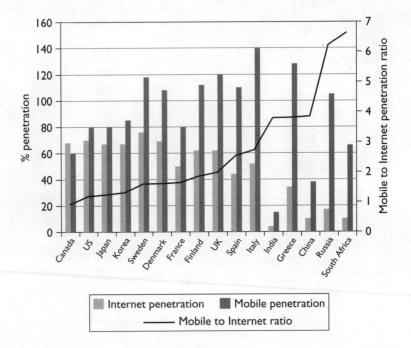

Figure 4.5   Mobile to Internet (PC) ratio in select economies as of March 2007.

Comparative estimates: U.S. mAdvertising spending, 2000, 2002, 2003, and 2005 (in millions)

	2000	2002	2003	2005
Forrester research (2000)	$0	$27	$159	$890
Jupiter (2001)	-	-	-	$2,100
Myers Reports (2001)	-	-	-	$2,600
Ovum (2000)	$4	$363	$1,212	$4,218
The Kelsey group	-	-	-	$6,800
The Yankee group (2001)	$7	$409	$1,271	$6,100

Figure 4.6   Mobile advertising estimates for the U.S. market in 2001. *Source: eMarketer;* various, as noted, 2001.

back in 2001. Within four years, the market was projected to become a $4.8 billion industry. The real numbers ended up being less than $200 million by most estimates.[19]

The point of this discussion is to show the perils of forecasting a young industry; you just don't know how things might grow. In general, all forecasts are too optimistic and don't take

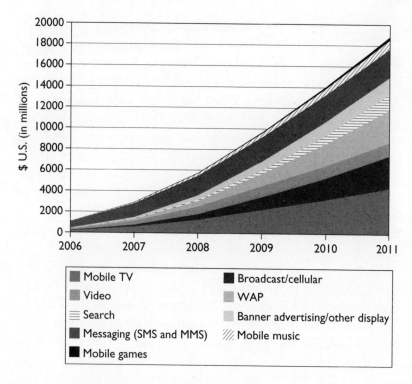

Figure 4.7   Global mobile advertising revenues.
Source: Informa, ABI Research, Mobile Advertising Estimates, 2007.

into consideration the complexities of the ecosystem of an emerging segment that needs to mature. Figure 4.7 presents the average industry consensus on global mobile advertising revenues. Are we about to repeat history? As you will notice, these forecasts don't even take into account certain categories of mobile advertising such as NFC, WiFi, Bluetooth, Application, Voice, Directory Assistance, Active Screen, and others. There seems to be no common understanding and definition of mobile advertising on which to build reliable forecasts. Needless to say, you must be cautious in banking the farm on forecasts of nascent markets.

Japanese Mobile Advertising Market

To get a grip on the potential market in the United States or Western Europe, a look at Japan[20] is the harbinger of what's to come. Japanese subscribers are very active mobile Internet users with all operators providing unlimited data service plans. The number of people accessing Internet through mobile exceeds the number accessing via a PC. As a result, mobile advertising has been an active industry in Japan for some time. According to Dentsu Inc., mobile advertising revenues for 2006 was approximately 39 billion yen or approximately $321 million (for 2007, this figure jumped to $556 million) or close to $3.4 per subscriber (for the year). By 2009, this number is likely to scale to over $6/sub/year (Figure 4.8).[21] According to InfoPlant, almost 60 percent of the Japanese consumers use mobile coupons and discounts more than once a month.[22]

The U.S. market is just starting to get organized and move from TXT marketing to mobile/local search marketing, interstitials, in-content ads, banner ads, and so on. In 2006, the United States did less than $1/sub (for the year) in mobile advertising revenues, the bulk of which will be

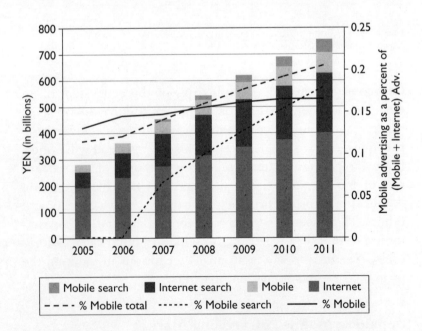

Figure 4.8   Japanese advertising market—Mobile and Internet.
Note: Calculations based on numbers reported by Dentsu, Financial Report, 2007.

TXT marketing. Europe is also slowly waking up to the possibilities around mobile ads and has been experimenting with some clever business models such as operator 3 subsidizing usage and phones in lieu of advertising on the phone. These models are also being offered in the microenvironments of downloadables, subscriptions, video streams, and so on. Even in Japan, some form of advertising is just starting. Mobile search as a revenue stream started becoming meaningful in 2007 with almost no activity prior to that. Japan has the most experience with mobile advertising, but it might not be the most sophisticated or advanced. Most of the developed nations are at the same level of maturity. While Japan's mobile advertising revenues in 2006 were around $321 million, it was only 10.7 percent of the digital advertising revenues and an almost negligible 0.65 percent of the almost $50 billion Japanese advertising expenditures in 2006.[23]

Though relatively small, mobile advertising expenditures have been growing at a healthy pace of 30 to 40 percent each year and are expected to touch 128 billion yen by 2011 (roughly 3.3 times the 2006 figures). We are pretty sure that doesn't account for numerous categories that are still being envisioned or accounted for (mobile search didn't even fit into the equation until 2007). The third generation of developments in wireless communications (3G) played a big part in the growth of the Japanese mobile market over the course of this decade. By 2008, over 90 percent of the subscribers will have 3G devices in Japan. Also, the packet flat rate that was started in 2004 helped in expanding the early adopters and heavy users to the mass market. Various studies showed that the time spent on and access frequency of mobile web sites by packet flat-rate subscribers are around five times those of nonsubscribers. As a ratio of packet flat-rate subscribers increase in the future, viewing opportunities of mobile ads will also increase. Introduction of mobile search helped in discovery and usage. From almost 6.5 percent share of search advertising expenditure, mobile search will grow to over 18 percent by 2011 according to Dentsu.

The largest growth is expected in the mobile advertising market with the spread of mobile search and flat-rate data plans expected to reach over $1.1 billion by 2011—almost 3.5 times the size of market in 2006. On the mobile search front, KDDI partnered with Google, and NTT DoCoMo chose Mobile Content Network (MCN) as their mobile search partner. However, Yahoo! Japan remained the most popular mobile search service (by a factor of two compared to Google) as of 2007. Also, the consolidation of mobile marketing packaging to the user is going to rise due to mobile wallet, broadcast services, helping the industry maintain a healthy growth rate in Japan.

The future of mobile data services and wireless industry remains bright. The opportunity of mobile marketing is potentially a big one but we must be cautious of the estimates if past history is any indication. We should also remember that it took over a decade for the Internet advertising market to take hold. Focusing on standards, usability, and economics made it happen. Though the opportunity for mobile advertising is enormous, the mobile ecosystem is much more complex.

In summary, brands are running many experimental campaigns. The campaigns are beginning to scale. The inventories are improving. And the models and metrics are coming together. Old media that has not been interactive to date is coming alive with mobile. TV, radio, billboards, and print are all embracing mobile as an extension. For some TV genres, mobile TXT is at the very core of a new value proposition. For others, like mobile interactivity in radio, it is evolving. And for printed media, mobile bar codes will blow open massive new advertising possibilities. Local search is working from an early adopter perspective. The ads are relevant to the consumers and the ads are low lift for the merchants to create and track as they are really just extensions of web versions.

Although there are profound positive differences with mobile media and advertising, it is largely unmet potential today. Mobile advertising is fraught with fragmentation and, for the most part, is stuck in advertising experimentation. At the same time, mobile has tremendous potential as an advertising platform. On the supply-side, over 20 start-ups are attempting to be the value-adds between the operators and advertisers. This fragmentation means it is far too expensive for most brands and advertisers to use mobile as a single channel. Channels of application complexity also require advertisers to modify, sometimes radically, a campaign from one mobile channel to another. This is all prohibitively complex and expensive, and severely retards advertiser reach. As a result, mobile ad inventories are small. Standards for ad inventory are just being put in place. These smallish inventories are artificially propping up advertising rates, especially for banner-based brand campaigns.

Operators need to adopt advertising as a core part of their business and not as a peripheral or fringe effort, as is sometimes the case today. There are significant issues around the various business models —or worse, no business models—that need to be created and standardized.

NOTES

1. Tomi T. Ahonen, "Putting 2.7 Billion in Context" (Communities Dominate Brands blog, January 2007).
2. Interview with Harry Kargman, CEO of Kargo, June 2007.
3. Nick Lane, "Global Mobile Media" (Informa Telecoms & Media report, May 2007).
4. Interview with Jeremy Lockhorn, Director of Emerging Media and Video Innovation, Avenue A | Razorfish, August 2007.
5. Interview with Mark Logan, Vice President and Managing Director, Interactive at Barkley, August 2007.
6. M:Metrics, U.S. Market, May 2007.
7. Alan Moore, "Pop Idol: The Fake Plastic Trees of Reality TV or Participatory Democracy in Close-Up?" (whitepaper, October 2006).
8. All *American Idol* stats from 2002 to 2005 are from AT&T Wireless or from Sue Marek, "American Idol, Still a Hit for Cingular,"*Wireless Week* (July 1, 2005).
9. M:Metrics, June 2007.
10. Orange UK (press release, August 2006).

11. Li Yuan and Cassell Bryan-Low, "Coming Soon to Cellphone Screens: More Ads Than Ever,"*Wall Street Journal,* August 16, 2006, http://online.wsj.com.

12. See note 11.

13. ABI Research, November 2006.

14. JumpTap, "WPP Makes Strategic Investment in JumpTap, Leaders in Mobile Search and Advertising" (press release, January 30, 2007).

15. Interview with Brian Lent, Chief Executive Officer, Medio Systems, July 2007.

16. Informa Telecoms & Media, "Activating the Idle Screen: Uncharted Territory" (May 2007).

17. Celltick, "Honda Campaign Reached Millions of AIS Subscribers Using Celltick's LiveScreen Media" (press release, February 12, 2007).

18. TIA, "Broadband Demand Drives Highest Telecom Industry Growth Since 2000" (January 2007).

19. Based on average industry consensus.

20. Japan is the second largest advertising market in the world behind the United States. Japan is also the first country to exceed 50 percent 3G penetration earlier this year.

21. Dentsu Financial Report, 2007, Chetan Sharma Consulting.

22. www.wirelesswatch.jp//modules.php?name=News&file=article&sid =2021/, accessed December 1, 2007.

23. D2C, Mobile Advertising Estimates, 2007.

5

Challenges and Accelerators
for Mobile Advertising

The elements of *context, immediacy,* and *personalization* that inherently characterize mobile give it significant advantages over other advertising media, including radio, print, and television. The potential for these advantages is evident, but it will take some time to reach critical mass and broad advertiser acceptance. The question is: How many years will it take before the industry exceeds $1 billion, or even $10 billion in revenues? As a matter of reference, it took two, four, and five years respectively, for U.S. broadcast, Internet, and cable advertising to cross the $1 billion revenue mark. Also, it took five years for Internet and broadcast advertising to cross the $5 billion mark, while none of them crossed the $10 billion mark in their first 10 years of existence. Figure 5.1 shows how this revenue growth occurred.

Is it likely that mobile will deviate from this growth pattern? Instead of being a blip in the advertising revenue stream, when will the mobile segment start rivaling the revenues generated by advertising on the Internet, radio, newspaper, and TV? Is this growth possible—and what will it take to get to that scale? What technical, business, and legal issues must the industry address before advertising agencies respond by allocating dedicated staff and real dollars to tackle mobile advertising, instead of using experimental market development budgets? Also, who will be the

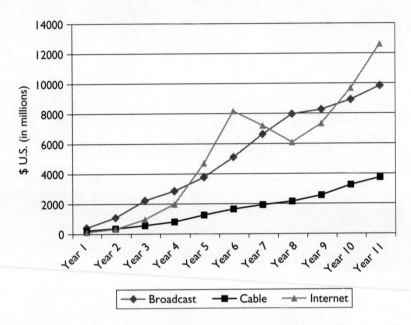

Figure 5.1   Annual ad revenue growth in broadcast, cable, and Internet in the first 11 years of growth.
Source: IAB Internet Advertising Revenue Report, 2005 Full Year Results, PricewaterhouseCoopers.

dominant players controlling the mobile advertising ecosystem five years from now?

What needs to happen for mobile marketing to go from the levels of high buzz to that of a really big business? The industry can feel good about the success of Internet advertising, but everyone should remember that it didn't happen overnight. It is also useful to avoid the assumption that mobile advertising and marketing will replicate the Internet experience. This time around, it will be helpful to consider business strategies in the context of these questions: What do advertisers want and how can they achieve it? What unique capabilities can the mobile industry offer advertisers? What major accelerators are required and what obstacles must be overcome to achieve billions in revenue for this new industry and advertising medium? This chapter answers some of these important questions.

GROWING CAMPAIGNS FROM $50,000
TO $1 MILLION OR MORE

After a dozen years of web advertising history, it is only now that web-based advertising agencies are finally starting to harness the massive power of the Web to create highly innovative Internet advertising campaigns. For example, here is the Coors Lite 4:53 campaign:

> *At 4:53 PM local time on weekdays, the Coors Light brand symbol, an old-fashioned train called the Silver Bullet, will race across entertainment, news and sports web sites that are frequently visited by the brand's core audience of men ages 21 to 34. In the online environment, you can really target consumers in a precise way. Surveys show that 71 percent of the Internet use of men 21 to 34 takes place at work and 61 percent of that is done at the end of the day, 3 to 6 PM.*[1]

The power of the Web as an interface that ties previously unreachable segments together and makes sites reachable in a fairly ubiquitous manner is a powerful dynamic that is difficult, if not impossible, to achieve in today's mobile media world. The Coors Lite 4:53 campaign could only have been successful with robust advertising networks that stretch across many hundreds, if not thousands of web sites. In mobile advertising, these capabilities do not yet exist.

In the course of writing this book, the authors interviewed many people who are knowledgeable about mobile campaign budgets. The consensus among those interviewed is that $1 million campaigns are beginning to be seen; however, they are the exception rather than the rule. Historically, budgets for most campaigns have come out of market development funds or emerging technology funds. For the most part, they were not coming out of mainstream campaign budgets as a percentage of the overall campaign.

Almost everyone recognizes the potential in mobile advertising. The conceptual value is now far more understood than even a year ago, but it still has a long way to go before attaining true revenue scale. Essential to mobile advertising success is the power to reach upward of 20 million consumers as well as smaller but highly targeted segments. But a single, critical question looms large—how can advertisers overcome the overwhelming complexity in the new mobile media world?

Complexity Is Everywhere

In mobile, a campaign similar to the Coors Lite 4:53 campaign might consist of the following:

- Build out half a dozen campaign variations across half a dozen mobile operators.
- Build out a separate off-deck campaign.
- Make the campaign work in MMS and on WAP v1.1, v1.2, v2.0, and XHTML mobile profile; then map it across 500 plus handsets in seven classes of graphics and screen size capabilities. Use a variety of tags to handle retrofitted mobile ad graphics.
- Provision a variety of TXT-based short codes across at least half a dozen approval processes.
- Or maybe implement a WAP push variation for those operators who will not enable specific WAP or MMS access. Or maybe not as WAP push, as it is not available across all operators.

The campaign should also get operator-by-operator-by-operator and maybe even publisher-by-publisher-by-publisher campaign approvals, and the various integrations should be done at least three months ahead of time. Campaign managers should be prepared to work with at least four ad servers, and it should be no surprise if three or four cycles of user acceptance testing are required. Also, it is inevitable that new devices will be shipped while testing is in progress. Since these will be unavailable ahead of time, it will be necessary to test them at the last minute. In no earlier than three months, campaign managers can aggregate the data to determine the effectiveness.

Such a process seems incredibly complex for advertisers to scale right now, particularly when they are used to the relative simplicity and standardization of ad types on the Web. This complexity severely hinders rapid mobile advertising growth. An advertiser's dream of doing text, graphics, video, or audio across multiple application types, devices, and networks all at once seems impossibly complex in the emerging mobile advertising ecosystem.

For mobile ads to reach their full-scale potential as a standard medium for campaigns and to enable interactivity in print and other media, the industry needs to make this fractured mosaic of technology more transparent. This presents a large opportunity for a new breed of mobile advertising delivery companies and advertising networks.

My Silo Is Bigger than Yours!

The mobile advertising industry needs to learn how to deliver value and scale in such a way that it hits a high volume stride and makes money for all involved. In general, there are too many mobile silos, splinters, and segmented applications approaches for an advertiser to muddle through. It might be helpful to look at examples set by other industries, such as cable companies, that have built their businesses on the cheap and efficient delivery of advertising to mass markets. With the collective maturity and mass audience reaches of TV or the Internet today, it is far easier to run a campaign or buy media for a semitargeted reach.

For mobile advertising to be capable of competing for overall advertising dollars at the level of TV or the Internet, the industry must fix the massive media storefront and discovery problems it has created. Both mobile media and advertising are stuck in the quagmires of these old silo-driven approaches. Today, it is not cost-effective for brands and advertisers to try to make these individual silos work in high volume, mass markets of targeted consumer reach.

Sending multiple messages to somewhat segmented audiences in other digital media costs virtually nothing compared with the current approach to mobile distribution.

A major hindrance for mobile operators is their business infrastructure; they are large organizations and understandably must be organized into logical business units. But the implications and difficulties those organizational silos pose to broad-reach mobile media and advertising might not be so obvious. No two operator data groups are organized the same way. They are typically organized into technology or revenue groups, such as MMS, TXT, location, and media groups. Mobile operator organization can also be fractured by unique application and UI types, application on-boarding processes, storefronts, user profile systems, location APIs, and messaging silos.

Many Point Solutions in Many Silos

As shown in Figure 5.2, no one player offers a complete range of mobile advertising solutions. In this embryonic stage of the industry, as you would expect, start-ups are focused on niche areas, while the bigger players are playing catch-up. What you see here today will change tomorrow.

As the industry evolves and grows, we can expect consolidation of scalable businesses within each segment. Almost every segment represented in Figure 5.2 is highly likely to consolidate. In the end, there are likely to be three or four large vendors and some smaller ones focusing on niche areas. The biggest question in this entire area is whether mobile operators can control the ecosystem and determine how mobile advertising revenues flow or must they allow the big web brands of Google, Yahoo, and Microsoft determine how advertising revenues will flow throughout the ecosystem.

In Asia, mobile operators will continue to play a stronger role working directly with the advertisers while in the United States and Europe, operators are likely to be dependent on the enablers and advertising networks to bring innovation to them. As consolidation continues, traditional infrastructure

	Messaging		Browsing			Search		Applications				Streaming			Others/Device		
	SMS	MMS	On-deck	Off-deck	Mobile/Media	Local/411	DA	Games	Downloads	Communities	Applications	Unicasting	Multicasting	Audio	Codes	Bluetooth	Active screen
AdInfuse	•	•	•	•								•					
Admob	•	•		•													
Air2Web	•	•	•														
AirG	•	•	•	•													
Amobee	•	•	•	•				•	•	•		•					
Bluecasting																•	
Enpocket (Nokia)	•	•	•	•													
Facebook										•		•					
FAST	•	•	•	•	•	•				•							
Google	•		•	•	•	•	•			•		•					
Greystripe								•	•								
Morricity					•	•											
ipsh! (Omnicom)	•	•															
JumpTap					•	•											
MediaFLO																	
Media			•	•	•	•	•			•							
Microsoft (w/TellMe)	•			•	•	•	•	•	•	•			•				•
Millennial Media				•	•	•		•	•		•						
Mobile Posse										•							
MobiTV												•	•	•			•
Myspace										•							
NeoMedia															•		
Quattro Wireless			•	•													
Rhythm New Media												•					
Smaato											•						
Third Screen Media (AOL)			•	•	•	•											
Verisign (mQube)	•	•		•													
Yahoo	•	•	•	•	•	•	•			•							
Zumobi	•			•		•											

Figure 5.2   Mobile advertising vendor map as of November 2007.

players are likely to emerge as solution providers for the mobile advertising value chain as well.

In any event, if you are a brand or an advertising agency, figuring this out for the first time is complex and difficult. That has to change and simplify for the industry to scale dramatically. There is a lot of work to do if mobile is to become the third screen of media—or perhaps even the first screen.

MOBILE WAS ONCE A FLEA MARKET

Today, the mobile industry is coming out of what might be considered the equivalent of a flea market. It was a massive market and a busy and somewhat frazzled one as well. At this mobile flea market, consumers found a somewhat confusing physical bazaar as they wandered around. The atmosphere was generally one of curiosity, discovery, and sometimes heritage. In the words of Paul Reddick, formerly a Vice President of Sprint/Nextel:

> *Those models are fairly outdated. The revenue required does not support adding in additional value for the consumer, who have to support the whole model. The mobile world needs advertising to add overall value to the model. With ring tones and other content, the operators let a number of products just sit out there in the stores, and if they sold, they sold. If they didn't sell, well they didn't sell. It was basically a flea market.*[2]

In this scenario, the burden of discovery and the search for good media are squarely placed on the consumer. The content is sometimes not all that compelling, and the churn is higher than it should be. Incredibly poor mobile storefronts cause massive confusion and complaints from consumers.

Digital Distribution Stuck in an Old Physical World

Mobile storefront management and media distribution are stuck in the old dictates of the physical world where shelf space is all there is. Within that problematic model, merchandising revolves around the inherent physical limitations. When mobile consumers buy mobile media in this scenario, their experience is severely hindered by the directory tree navigation structures that the mobile industry imposes on itself in the name of customer service.

Over time, the power of the top-down directory tree arrangements of mobile storefronts and decks will erode and become less relevant. The market dynamics that are causing this change are deep, and many digital industries are being impacted at a very rapid pace. Mobile will not be immune from these changes, but today the storefront approach is stuck in ancient roots of the physical world, which has led to the notion that shelf space is scarce and information must be arranged, controlled, and tightly managed. David Weinberger says it best:

> *We have entire industries and institutions built on the fact that the paper order severely limits how things can be organized. Museums, educational curricula, newspapers, the travel industry, and television schedules are all based on the assumption that in the second order (physical) world, we need experts to go through the information, ideas and knowledge and put them away neatly.*
>
> *But now we—the customers, the employees, anyone— can route around the second order. The miscellaneous order is not only transforming business. It is changing how we think the world is organized and—perhaps more importantly—who we think has the authority to tell us so.*[3]

Weinberger's insights apply to mobile storefront management as much as to digital inventory management in any other industry. By contrast to mobile storefronts, other digital media, such as on the Web, is breaking free of these physical constraints. The old way of managing the storefronts is as much about the hierarchy of decision making and political authority as it is about making things easier for mobile consumers. Mobile will not be a giant, isolated exception to these inevitable digital distribution macrotrends. The dynamics are too powerful outside mobile for it to be an isolated island and the last harbinger of physically limited structures while the rest of the world is driven by the new rules of digital distribution.

There are many examples of these new rules on the Internet, with Amazon storefronts perhaps being the most profound. Amazon's classification systems do not follow the old library-based filing rules. Rather, they drive buying patterns into massive collaborative filters that consumers can customize and use to find what they are looking for. They also have system-generated recommendation scenarios that are consumer friendly; and a massive search system is the glue that holds it all together. The Amazon consumer does not encounter any silos, and the system often presents new products that consumers might never find on their own.

Opening Up the Gardens, While Keeping the Weeds Out

Physical classification systems are generally derived from top-heavy power struggles and are based on limits in the physical world. The analogy of the physical retail storefront is a perfect parallel. There are winners that wind up on a shelf in a storefront, and there are losers. This zero-sum game is almost always physically driven and the motivations are fierce because shelf space is rare and valuable. But those physical limits and rules do not apply to digital distribution, where inventory is unlimited and the discovery process can be consumer friendly. Mobile operators seem to focus their merchandising efforts on the media storefront, as if they are displaying physical items with physical space limitations that require the application of tight controls and management.

Physical classification methods applied to mobile storefronts are related to organizational boundaries, subcategories, links, and references in the storefront. Operators will typically spend months analyzing whether a creative new mapping product goes into a "Maps and Directions" category, the "Maps" category, or into a brand-new "Navigation" category. They might further deliberate whether it should land in the backwaters of the old "Search and Directory" category.

If they make the mistake of putting the product into all the categories, deck clutter follows. So does endless discussion about matters such as whether it should go on the top deck as a promotional highlight and what is the storefront end cap fee? After all, the space is severely limited. Wait . . . this calls for a meeting and a decision! All should come prepared and plan on being superpatient as this meeting may well adjourn sometime next year.

Freeing up the storefronts and getting to true consumer-driven merchandising capabilities are major prerequisites for massive mobile media usage. Storefronts derived from the old physical world rules can't be fixed—they must be replaced with a new digitally driven, consumer friendly paradigm. Replacing the current media shelf space with an innovative media discovery paradigm is a future consumer-friendly tipping point to get to a scalable mobile advertising ecosystem. Not replacing it forces the shelf space by default into the hands of the big Internet advertisers, who can either afford to buy the shelf space outright or already have the traffic justification in place to monopolize the space with their brands. This could easily result in tilting the nascent mobile advertising ecosystem power curves in the same direction as the big Internet brands.

In the new world of digital media, consumers will organize, classify, rank, and share the importance of new media. Mobile directory trees will become obsolete because the leaf, as defined by consumers, can be tagged to hang from any branch or many branches on any tree. The old binary decision process in the big meeting rooms for a one-line change on the top deck is obsolete.

Mobile operators provide tremendous value in the consumer ecosystem for mobile media. One of the big keys to the next generation of consumer value is in opening up media discovery, access, and viral sharing for youth markets. To make this possible, there needs to be more mobile media to discover. To create this next generation of media, third-party developers must unleash their creativity into a mobile media ecosystem that is not bound by the limited physical shelf space rules that exist today. Operators can play a valuable role here by providing the massive collaborative filtering, search, discovery, and advertising ecosystems to make this happen.

Combined with open, unfettered access to the Internet, digital rights free media, and flat-rate all-you-can-eat pricing, these model dynamics will have a powerful and liberating effect on the availability of new and creative mobile media—and subsequently on consumer demand. This will enable massive new scale in mobile advertising reach, thus helping to create an industry.

A HUNDRED THOUSAND SHORT CODES? NOT YET!

Provisioning interactive mobile campaigns for direct response is simply too slow and complex. For interactive or direct response campaigns, which are making television, print, and radio more interactive and measurable, the provisioning of volumes of TXT-based short codes is an onerous, brutal process. Sometimes they go smoothly. But if you use the word *free* in any campaign definition, the process breaks down rather quickly. Mobile operators do not like that word, and their approval processes will stall out if it is used. Not only is it sometimes difficult, it is a lengthy process, because each one has to validate and approve the campaign. The chances of missing tight deadlines are high. Mobile advertising is the most interesting for making media interactive and creating direct response. Creating an interface between the physical world and the consumer through their mobile device, which is always on and always in their pocket is powerful. The market simply needs to make it far simpler for the big brands to participate and set up campaigns. Tim Jemison, CEO of Zoove, explained the power scaling this mobile interactivity succinctly:

> *Whether it is using a TXT short code, texting in **or taking a picture of mobile barcode, these are a few steps away from making print, billboards, and other media*

interactive. Mobile is the perfect link between us and the world around us. Yet, there are under 2500 active short codes in the U.S. market. There should be a million. So clearly, short codes aren't taking off. What we think the market needs is a fundamentally better consumer experience with something simple like hitting **and getting information. And a fundamental overhaul in how these campaigns are provisioned to get to millions of them.[4]

Gaining constant ISP or cable company approvals across the board every time a campaign is run is never seen. In any media other than mobile, it is not even considered. For mobile to attract large-scale, cross-operator campaigns, this issue needs to be addressed.

We are confident that we will see innovative new approaches to bypass these lengthy deployment and approval issues. Zoove is implementing an innovative ** system where a consumer hits ** and then a number for the interactive portion of the campaign. More importantly, once they have ** configured, the brands can implement campaigns far faster.

PUSH VERSUS PULL

Push- and pull-based advertising models are driven by distinctly different approaches to consumer advertising presentation. Back in the old days of mass markets, products, and media, companies could just throw massive amounts of money at a marketing problem and buy gross rating points. They could sell anything by buying more GRPs and pushing ads into the faces of consumers. Push advertising worked, especially for the advertising agencies, since their returns were based on a 15 percent commission for the purchase of TV, radio, and print space where they pushed out the ads. It was inconsequential whether the ads were boring, annoying, or clever since they didn't have to be engaging in an interruption-based advertising economy.

Push-Based Advertising

As a result of this history, almost all traditional advertising uses a push-based approach to deliver their messages to potential customers:

- A TV program is interrupted for an important advertising message from the program sponsor.
- Direct mail flyers fill the mailbox for a few seconds and then visit the recycle bin.
- Telemarketers call over dinner.
- Pop-up ads appear on computer screens.

All these methods are pushy and consumers are exposed to them whether they want to be or not. Another characteristic of traditional advertising is one-way communication. The advertiser talks while the consumer listens, making interaction nearly impossible.

Mobile advertising certainly has the technical possibilities to push advertising to consumers. After all, alerts and mobile e-mail are often based on push technology.

Pull-Based Advertising

The Internet is different, and most marketers will fail if they don't take these new consumer-driven differences into account. Remember, the consumer is in far more control in this new digital world. Generally, the Internet facilitates a pull-based approach to advertising. Web users are drawn to a particular home page and they come in massive volume if there is sufficient interest. Rather than a strict one-way conversation, the communication can be two ways and interactive. The brand and the consumer both talk and listen. In general, pull-based advertising has been extremely effective at acquiring profitable traffic, especially for search with its focus on the power of user intent and bidded keywords that show up right at the point of consumer intention. Other examples of pull advertising are search engine optimization (SEO), directory merchant ads, and shopping portals. For example, SEO is now often matched with a corresponding positive experience on the landing web site. The same text and words used in the SEO efforts make a consistent transition for consumers and give them a pleasurable experience— to pull them back again in the future.

Push and Mobile Advertising

Back in the late 1990s, right before the dot-com blowout, along came push, the next big Internet thing. Pointcast was the poster child of this complete consumer miss. Consumers scratched their heads a little and had a really hard time understanding what was the big deal. Push has arguably evolved into today's Internet Real Simple Syndication (RSS) feeds, and many people do in fact find them useful. RSS is a seismic shift in the industry, but it is under the consumers' control. They find it useful and time efficient.

Mobile can also be a powerful push-based system. The ferocity of Blackberry's push-based vibration e-mail mode, which is a discrete form of notification, is a major example of a successful implementation of push scenario in the mobile industry. Also becoming very popular are mobile alerts to get the latest sports score. At this juncture, it is important to ask some relevant questions:

- Just because mobile can be a push-based system, does it mean that the industry should use it to push advertising to consumers?
- Is push the next big thing as an underlying fabric for mobile advertising?

The answer to both these questions is absolutely not. The industry should ban push-based advertising or banish it to the smoke-filled backrooms of fringe bit players.

Push-based location scenarios fly straight into the face of this consumer, pull-based market dynamic. Moreover, push-based advertising is no longer viable in general because the power has shifted from the marketer and brand to the consumer. Thanks to the Internet, video-on-demand, TiVo, digital radio, and now mobile media, consumers decide what media they want and when they want it. The new rule is to get consumers to engage in the media and advertising messages by pulling them in with engaging scenarios. Pushing the messages out to consumers in broadcasted, head-thumping, interruption-based scenarios is no longer the way.

Successful campaigns of the future, especially those targeting younger consumers through mobile media, will turn the old advertising buy process and push approach on its head. Successful campaigns will start by first analyzing how consumers live and use media in their daily lives. The agency creating the campaigns will then work backward to create messages most appropriate for those channels and build up the campaign into an engaging experience for the consumer. With Nike, this meant coming up with an approach to use TXT to custom-design shoes on an interactive billboard in front of the consumer's eyes in Times Square. The dynamics at work here are so powerful that they may eventually force the agencies to revamp the old 15 percent fee structures into new ones based on a brand's objectives or growth. These new arrangements may well turn agencies from outside contractors into business partners.

Mobile can help redefine the concepts of engagement and targeting in advertising. But it could also take major missteps into consumer quicksand with push-based approaches that do not provide proper consumer opt-in or context—just because the technology can enable it. It is important to avoid these mistakes before perceptions about mobile advertising values are cemented into the world of advertising in general. If consumers opt-in and the proper consumer context is discoverable, push might be an important technical enabler for a campaign. But the industry should use this device with caution and forethought.

BUILT-IN, NOT BOLTED-ON METRICS

On the Web, campaigns can employ targeted advertising and the results are quickly quantifiable. In addition, advertisers have the option to pay only when a prospective customer clicks on their ad. Results are almost immediate and provide instant traffic to the advertiser's web site. The formats, options, and ad models are all relatively quick to deploy, and are tested and proven ways of promoting online products and services. Advertisers can very quickly experiment with different keywords, titles, descriptions, and targets and can easily measure advertising effectiveness.

On the Web, however, two major market dynamics collide, which can make the old methods of campaign management and measurement fade away, even before they appear in mobile media. The clutter of advertising is making simple exposure to an advertising message irrelevant. At the same time, interactive digital media that can demonstrate consumer engagement is emerging as a strong new approach. This engagement metric is valuable to media buyers who need to target through the ad clutter to obtain effective returns. Engagement will definitely supplement the vaunted concept of frequency in media plans. In this environment, mobile could be a key media driver and measurement metric of engagement in digital advertising campaigns; however, mobile is too fraught with unresolved issues for this to happen soon.

The basics of mobile campaign management are not much different from those on the Internet. The selection of a country, mobile sites, and ad locations within those sites is similar to Internet campaign management, except that the ISP or cable company rarely enters the picture. In mobile, campaign managers must figure out which mobile operators they will work with. From this point forward, complexity spirals exponentially.

The campaign that targets specific users or the variances within the channels quickly gets complicated. Mobile ad reach is either created or crippled in the ensuing steps of campaign management. Targeting the details of handset models or user interface (UI) types, UI modalities, and user profile selections is hard, but getting campaigns targeted to the next level of application, channel, or silo can be difficult. TXT targeting is easy and serves as the lowest common denominator. Multimedia messaging (MMS) and Wireless Application Protocol (WAP) are not that easy. Idle screens and applications, such as Global Positioning System (GPS) navigation or games, are orders of magnitude harder and their reach in campaigns is limited.

Although some advertising and content standardization is in place, much more is needed. The complexities of these silos are simply too visible for advertisers. As a result, campaign complexity is too difficult to quickly scale, and reaching across innumerable silos is too hard and time consuming. Standards will help this situation by simplifying and accelerating negotiations between content providers, publishers, and mobile operators, resulting in a dramatic increase of mobile advertiser inventory. In turn, this will accelerate mobile cross-media promotions directly to the consumer.

A Unified Front for Mobile Metrics

As discussed in Chapter 3, the use of metrics to plan, manage, measure, and modify digital campaigns will be a powerful and profound change. The influence that mobile targeting will have on the next generation advertising metrics is potentially massive. The keys to this happening in mobile revolve around industry-wide agreements on standards and interoperability issues about supporting data. In the past, mobile has done this on a massive scale with voice-roaming agreements and with fraud management agreements. So the mobile industry has proven that it can be done on a large scale and in a timely manner. When the revenue incentives are truly visible, it will happen.

Do advertisers really know how well their mobile campaign performed and how much it actually cost? If there are visitors but no transactions, the problem might not be the campaign but the mobile site. Whoops, they might not even have a mobile site to click to yet. Is a mobile site needed? Is that the most effective way to get user traffic from the campaign? These open questions form another big area of confusion in today's mobile advertising value chain and a key reason many mobile advertisers are mobile media providers.

An entire mobile cottage industry is evolving around solutions to the problems of campaign management. As a result, campaign management is just now becoming possible for mobile advertising. The Mobile Marketing Association (MMA) designed its Global Measurement Committee (GMC) to solve some of the problems in campaign management, audience metrics, and general standardization. Under the guidance of this new committee, the industry will create a framework for the measurement of mobile marketing campaigns across all mobile channels.

Mobile operators are savvy enough to cooperate fully on device or campaign management. But they need some help to get the necessary mobile audience measurement data to metrics companies such as Nielsen, comScore, M:Metrics, and others. This will happen because the stakes are high with respect to mobile advertising campaign returns. Additionally, mobile operators will have to justify audience sizes and silos for competitive ad spending because high mobile ad rates will not stick unless audience metrics justify them long term. The limited reach of mobile today versus other media, especially with the large Internet ad networks in place, will have to be addressed to maintain the relatively high ad rates in place today. The combination of audience engagement-based metrics measurements, validated by third parties, will be critical to get true scale in the mobile industry.

If the industry can truly capture targeting accuracy and combine it with effective metrics, mobile could be at the forefront of targeting and engagement measurement. To the detriment of other media that cannot measure specific targeting, this can put mobile at the forefront of media buys instead of the tiny microslice of the pie it commands today. This is both a powerful enabler and a large cooperation effort. As a successful cottage industry, targeted measurement will have the tremendous effect of attracting the scale of advertising budgets necessary to achieve the billions in revenue forecasted by various industry analysts.

WHERE ARE THE MOBILE AD MODELS?

In a semiconfused attempt to be all things to all people, mobile ad models are all over the place. The models are almost always mixed up and confusing. Compared with other media, extraordinarily high CPMs (cost per milles) surprise even the most savvy media buyer. But the high variety of pricing models will settle and diminish as leading models emerge. More accountability and transparency to advertisers will drive this emergence, and simplicity will scale those ad models that work really well.

Media people who are not deeply involved in mobile nuances sometimes find the following basic questions hard to answer: What do I buy? Whom do I buy it from? How much should I expect to pay? What is the cost per unit? Why are CPMs so high in some cases and so low in others? This model topic is important enough that the entirety of Chapter 6 is devoted to it.

As mentioned in the Internet historical overview in Chapter 2, display advertising on the Web began to really take off when companies like DoubleClick began to establish virtual marketplaces where advertisers could easily purchase placement inventory. These ad exchange concepts have matured considerably since those early days of 1997 and 1998. Today, we have established ad networks like DoubleClick, 24/7 Real Media, and ValueClick. Google, Yahoo, IAC/Ask, and Microsoft also are capitalizing on the public's enormous appetite for search-based marketing. They have created their own marketplaces, complete with keyword auctions, to efficiently sell the right to target prospective consumers. An entire advertising ecosystem has evolved around the Web, with companies providing everything from campaign management to keyword optimization services.

Without a more transparent mobile ad marketplace, mobile advertising models will remain mixed up and confusing to buyers. As a result, big media buyers may just rely on tried and true, well-established advertising mediums. For mobile to be a standard component of major campaign media planning and buying exercises, campaign, ad, and device management, along with campaign measurement tools, will have to evolve as standard tools. One-offs will not work.

This represents a tremendous new opportunity. An "out-of-the-box" solution that makes the various handset and interface variables, application silos, and network types invisible to a campaign is a significant mobile market opportunity.

MOBILE AD ACCELERATING FORCES

Despite the plethora of issues previously discussed, mobile advertising has transformational potential. But potential is not enough; it must be made real, tangible, and easy to buy and to use. The most important question to answer in the entire value of mobile advertising is "What is in it for the consumer?" If the industry rises to the occasion and answers this question in a positive and aggressive manner, the mobile media and mobile advertising business will accelerate to massive proportions compared with where it is today. Mobile media consumers will be the single biggest variable causing this young industry to flourish—or to flounder.

Perhaps the most significant consumer benefit from mobile advertising will come through dramatically cheaper mobile media that is far easier to access. Mobile media is expensive to create and distribute to mobile consumers. Advertising subsidies will eventually enable richer and more interactive mobile media that is available on far higher bandwidth networks and better media handsets. Given the dramatic increases in costs to produce great mobile media, mobile operators are forced into developing new approaches to subsidize these costs.

Mobile advertising will also provide mobile media consumers with access to media of which they were previously unaware. This will be especially true if the power of social networks is opened up to mobile consumers so they can discover, share, and virally spread new mobile media.

Last, there is huge potential for targeting specific microgroups of consumers in mobile. This potential can separate mobile from all other forms of advertising, but it has yet to be truly unleashed. No other device or network knows so much about an individual phone number or consumer.If conducted in a consumer-friendly manner, this targeting can be one of the single biggest value-adds for all of advertising, especially in consumer control and audience fragmentation.

THE PRESSURE IS ON

The market pressure is on the operators to compensate for slow voice revenue growth. Mobile data and media revenues will also drive part of the revenue solutions, which will then drive mobile advertising at accelerated rates.

As cellular migrated from analog to digital, and with the advent of TXT in the late 1990s, consumers started getting exposed to something different than voice—data services. Starting from Scandinavia and then spreading to Western Europe, Japan, Korea, and North America, texting gradually became a popular application. To this day, a good portion (40 to 50 percent) of the data revenues come from messaging.[5]

It is a consistent trend in all major markets, from the developed markets such as Japan and Korea to developing markets like India and China, that with increased subscriber penetration, there is pressure on voice average revenue per user (ARPU). Voice has become commoditized over the past few years, with rates dropping to U.S.$0.01/min in India. This market dynamic is forcing a major operator push into mobile media and data to make up for the declining voice revenues.

Mobile media and data ARPU is now contributing in excess of double digit percentages in all major operators worldwide. This will have a profound accelerating impact to the implementation of mobile advertising globally.

REACHING GENERATION C, THE NEW MEDIA GRAZERS

There are 3 billion people under 25 years of age on this planet and 60 percent of them live in Asia. They are Generation C,[6] the mobile connected and new media generation. It is only natural that content and connection should come together in mobile media. To understand this dynamic, look to Asia. Very connected consumers use TXT, music, camera blogs, and other mobile media to send information to all their friends over wireless networks. These activities will radically impact media and mobile advertising.

From a survey of 1,500 U.K. youth, aged 11 to 20, Q Research reported that 32 percent of mobile consumers were willing to accept ads. When they were asked whether they would be willing to accept ads that were related to their areas of interest, the response jumped to an amazing 71 percent. When asked if they would accept ads that offered discounts and coupons, the response was 76 percent. Last, when they were asked if they would accept ads that gave credits for their prepaid phone accounts, 84 percent said yes.[7] Response rates such as these indicate an amazing potential; if the advertisements are relevant and nonintrusive, they will be accepted; if they drive special offers and discounts, they will be sought after. This market segment is also centered in the sweet spot of a marketers' demographics, as illustrated in the M:Metrics data in Figure 5.3.[8]

Tomi T. Ahonen and Alan Moore summarize this incredibly important connected generation and the underlying connections to the new and rapidly evolving use of mobile phones to tap into communities: *"Generation C is defined by their use of mobile phones to connect to digital communities. Only communities on mobile phones are always connected and always on."*[9]

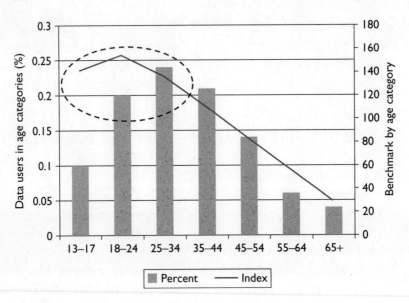

Figure 5.3   Generation C data users index.

Generation C is highly connected, multichannel, and mobile. Going forward, they will be incredibly influential in mobile media and the adoption of new mobile advertising forms. They are the new Borg!

FILTERING, THE MOBILE WAY

Next generation advertising targeting must center on delivering excellent consumer value. Achieving this creates sales. For today's consumers, it may be important to shift our mind-sets from "targeting," which implies *pushing* a message to consumers, to "filtering," which has a *pull* orientation. Filtering enables the focus to be more on what a specific segment or consumer group is likely to consume, giving the messages a draw or pull. By contrast, if an advertising message is pushed out of context, consumers will want to ignore or block it. The world is moving from interruption to engagement. With that significant shift, we have to earn customers' attention instead of buying it.

Higher advertising rates will result from increased effectiveness and measurable responses from consumers. This applies to all media. A significant value proposition for mobile is the potential of an advertising campaign to precisely target filtered and select groups of consumers, along with the ability to track campaign effectiveness. Mobile handsets and networks could be true superfilters of context and behavioral data, enabling far better one-to-one targeting.

New Mobile Operator Value Creation

Mobile operators have access to many sources of consumer data they can use for filtering and segmentation, but they have a hard time focusing the internal resources to harness that power for mobile advertising. The inherent potential here is generally an underutilized crown jewel or "superfilter." For the most part, proactive management and the systems that tie it all together are weak or nonexistent. Web services can be the software glue for third parties to integrate campaigns against this targeting or filtering data. But there is a tremendous industry opportunity to weave this into mobile advertising platforms that are unique to advertising effectiveness.

This could all result in more relevant offers and advertisements for consumers, who dislike being hammered with too many ads from a multitude of advertisers. Over time, it would mean presenting less clutter to the mobile consumer, which would make ads more effective. Finally, mobile operators could deliver unique offers more frequently by understanding the values of the segmented consumer base. Special rewards, offers, and membership programs would be more effective with strong filtering functions.

Mobile Targeting and Audience Fragmentation

As consumers increasingly gain greater control of their media and as they accelerate into highly fragmented slices of audience groups, the value of mobile targeting rises exponentially. The practice of splattercasted, interruption-based messaging, repeated over and over across a broadcast channel to bludgeon audiences into brand awareness, is rapidly dying. It is being replaced with engagement, interactivity, and the messages needed to penetrate increasingly smaller audience fragments. As consumers form more and more niches in this digital landscape, the relevant usage, demographic, and context data that a mobile device and network can provide could achieve a fundamental breakthrough in filtering out the wrong audiences to get to the right targets. The following sections look at some of the powerful tools that mobile can enable to reach these fragmented audiences.

Mobile Geo-Targeting

Targeting based on location will allow mobile to take advantage of the first mass market of consumer GPS devices, which should prove to be powerful. Approximately 25 percent of all mobile searches have a local component. This potential of search has to be balanced with the historical view that local search has also been one of the most overhyped scenarios in mobile data. Mobile location and GPS enable a whole new consumer value proposition for location-based search and eventually for geo-targeted advertising.

The mobile nomination for stupid geo question of the year: "What is your zip code?" as you step off a plane in a strange city and fire up a mobile search application. Finally, 2008 will be the year when this question fades into consumer irrelevance.

Contextual Targeting

Contextual targeting is a relatively new on the Web and could be powerful in mobile advertising. Contextual targeting is refocusing advertising to deliver the right message to the right person at the right time. It takes advantage of what consumers are looking for and places ads nearby. If they are looking for a ring tone, contextual recommendations could show a new music release targeted for that person.

Contextual targeting can vary based on time of day, season of the year, or the day of the week. The value of location and placement context, against the editorial environment of a mobile media deck, has tremendous value to advertisers in reaching closely targeted mobile consumers. In the near future, the most popular mobile sites that have the ability to facilitate contextual targeting will most likely also have the most limited inventories—demand outpaces supply. If this occurs, contextually targeted mobile ads may wind up with the highest prices of any mobile advertising.

Behavioral Targeting

Behavioral targeting is the fastest growing advertising targeting approach on the Internet. In this area, spending growth has shot up from $220 million in 2005 to a forecasted $1 billion in 2008.[10] The market power of this kind of spending will increasingly impact mobile requirements. Mobile has a chance to lead this area—not follow. The idea behind behavioral targeting is to show an advertisement of interest in an unexpected place. The targeting can be refined based on a combination of current mobile data usage, mobile media purchase history, friends and connections, and similar data. Online click stream data is valuable because it can help determine that some consumers like cars since they go to Autoblog.com daily; some love new gadgets because they go to Engadget.com daily; and others have a Mac because they go to the Mac Rumors blog every week. Consumers such as these are far more valuable to an advertiser because they are well defined past their basic demographics. The Web's first advertising implementation, the ubiquitous banner ad, will soon be changed. The banner ads of tomorrow will hone in on users' real needs and wants. This intelligence will be based largely on personalized knowledge of your browsing habits and history. Ads that appear on web pages may well become a true resource.

Mobile behavioral targeting is catching up to the Web fast. The combination of personal sources of implicit data—such as mobile applications that are purchased, viewed, or used—plus explicit data, such as user profile information, can open up a powerful, new, and creative world of recommendations and mobile ad targeting. Making this invisible to the end user with an opt-in approach enables behavioral targeting to be combined with other unique aspects of the mobile data network, such as location or mobile payment mechanisms.

Respecting Consumer Privacy

Maintaining consumer anonymity is supercritical to a campaign. Privacy violations will destroy industry value before mobile advertising even gets going. Advertising campaigns must implement mobile advertising cautiously around filtering or targeting. The last thing advertisers or operators want is a big consumer backlash, and this means no spamming. Sending obnoxious TXTs to consumers, either due to frequency or because they are poorly targeted, will backfire. To that end, the Mobile Marketing Association has developed codes of conduct, and the major and reputable mobile advertising firms and brands are signing on.

In general, consumers do not want to divulge more and more of their personal information, especially to marketers. Consumers only provide details when they see the value of doing so; they provide personal information when they get value in return. Over time, mobile operators, publishers, and advertisers who do a great job filtering valuable commercial offers for consumers, and who *never* misuse consumer data, will build exponential consumer trust. This trust is one of the most critical parts of the entire mobile marketing equation.

Back to the Basics for Mobile

Conceptually, mobile advertising enables myriad targeting options that no other industry enables, with the possible exception of interactive television. This will eventually lead to major breakthroughs for both consumer value and advertising returns. However, the advertising industry, especially parts of the industry not steeped in digital already, does not yet know how to take advantage of these new digital targeting capabilities.

It is sometimes easy to forget that mobile can offer basic segmentation and targeting data that no other consumer media business can provide or even begin to enable. In the short term, mobile can enable basic data such as age, sex, addresses, and perhaps location at time of use. If these basic data points can be standardized among a group of mobile operators, they could easily surpass even the most sophisticated metrics and data enabled on the Internet, while blowing away television and radio enablers. The advertising industry is just starting to get a basic handle on how to use this rudimentary data effectively. After all, it has never been supplied to them by any other industry—so how could they already be set up to use it?

Complications that look sophisticated on paper do not add any value if the brand or agency can't manage them in the planning of a campaign, or if the definitions are different from every operator that the agency works with. Simple, consistent, and reliable data could make the mobile industry greatly appealing to a new group of cutting-edge marketers and advertisers who want to reach far better segmentations of a fragmented audience.

This simplified data in a cross-industry format could be one of the single biggest accelerators in mobile advertising. No other industry, with the possible exception of interactive television, could compete with it if it were presented as a unified front. The industry that pulled off something as complicated as call roaming could accomplish this feat if it set out to do it. It would provide tremendous value and help make mobile a key advertising platform.

Mobile is evolving fast and along the way, mistakes and issues will pop up. Push-based location bluespamming will occur. Nascent user experiences around idle screens, which have media transformational power, will be interrupted by push ads. These errors and false starts will be short lived if consumers with their powerful vote have anything to say about it. But even now, there are positive examples that should be recognized. Old media that has not been interactive to date is coming alive with mobile. TV, radio, billboards, and print are all embracing mobile as an extension. For some TV genres, it is at the core of a new value proposition. For others, like radio, it is evolving. For printed media, mobile bar codes will blow open massive new advertising possibilities. Local search is working from an early adopter perspective. The ads are relevant to the consumers and low lift for the merchants to create and track, as they are really just extensions of the web versions. They may also be disruptive around free directory assistance and voice search. The brands are here, but mobile campaign budgets are often filled from the experimental buckets and are on the small side. Campaign budgets need to exceed $1 million or more across a multitude of campaigns before the industry can claim any scale. Campaigns also need to reach this critical mass in the U.S. market—after all, the United States consumes 50 percent or more of the world's advertising budgets. The U.S. market is the place to watch for the crossing of the $1 million mobile advertising campaign threshold.

If the issues don't become overwhelming and the consumer experience is great, the accelerators will kick in at some point in the next few years. Generation C, as the new media grazers, will have a profound impact on mobile media and advertising. Their influence is analogous to throwing a can of gasoline on a bonfire. Cheap mobile media, supported by ads and made viral by the discoveries of the community, will have positive and explosive impacts on revenues.

NOTES

1. Stuart Elliott, "Cue the 4:53 Silver Bullet to Happy Hour," *New York Times* (March 20, 2007), www.nytimes.com.

2. Interview with Paul Reddick, ex-Vice President, Sprint, August 2007.

3. David Weinberger, *Everything Is Miscellaneous: The Power of the New Digital Disorder* (New York: Times Books, 2007), 22.

4. Interview with Tim Jemison, CEO, Zoove, August 2007.

5. MMS or multimedia messaging is also part of this equation. However, the percentage of revenues coming from messaging has been decreasing steadily over the past two to three years. By the end of 2006, most of the major carriers (DoCoMo, KTF, Verizon, Cingular, Sprint, SK Telecom, and KDDI) reported 60 to 70 percent of their data revenues coming from non-TXT applications.

6. Tomi T. Ahonen and Alan Moore, "Generation C," in *Communities Dominate Brands* (London: Futuretext Limited, 2005), 135–153.

7. "Q Research," *New Media Age* (April 19, 2007).

8. M:Metrics, May 2007.

9. See note 6, p. 136.

10. David Hallerman, Senior Analyst, "Behavioral Advertising on Target…to Explode Online," *eMarketer* (June 11, 2007), www.emarketer .com.

6

Mobile Advertising Models

To scale consumer usage of mobile media, some fundamental, market level changes need to be made. Mobile media usage, while interesting compared with even a year ago, is not at the level needed to attract major advertising budgets. The eyeballs around mobile media usage simply aren't there for major advertising budget allocations. The audiences and eyeballs will appear over time, but model structural changes that make it easier for consumers to figure out the total cost of ownership and make mobile media more cost effective and far more discoverable—will dramatically accelerate the market for advertising.

Assuming mobile can generate the eyeballs, traffic, and infrastructure to enable large brands to easily identify, reach, and measure a campaign's effect on their brand, we will examine how mobile advertising models work today. We will also look at how mobile ad pricing models, costs, and click performances compare against other media.

SAY'S LAW: SUPPLY DRIVES DEMAND

Have you ever owned a personal computer that was too fast? What about a network that was too fast? Hmmm . . . not for long, if at all. All that speed was consumed by new, memory-intensive, creative applications and great multimedia on the Internet. These are both examples of the famous economics law of Jean Baptiste Say (1767–1832), stating that there can be no demand without prerequisite abundant supply.

In other words, supply causes demand. This could be likened to the chicken and the egg dilemma.

Demand for bandwidth is highly elastic. New opportunities for media development on higher bandwidth networks, including the new mobile video and mobile TV networks, will flourish. Creative individuals, low cost, open source development tools, and low-cost servers will all create a rush of fast-moving sparks that can create raging wildfires if the model dynamics are right. Or quash them before they get going if the models are wrong.

Simplistically, total advertising dollars spent on the Internet is a function of the ability to monetize a page (or a link or interaction) and the number of pages (or links or interactions) available. If the dollars spent online increase dramatically, either ad rates will rise or the number of pages will increase, or both. The amount of content that has to be created to support these advertising dollars has to continue to rise dramatically. This will happen, but today it lags behind the Web. As the audiences grow, these online conversations also become more fragmented. But these smaller and smaller segments can be reached with evermore precision as demonstrated by search, or by the highly targeted capabilities of behavioral-enabled ad networks. More and more, advertisers can reach precisely the consumers they want at whatever time they need to. This is happening on the Internet with the new wave of consumer-generated content. However, a similar wave is not occurring in mobile without a rush of user-generated site traffic.

There are really only three key reasons consumers adopt new media or technologies: dramatically lower prices, significantly greater convenience, or visibly extended functionality. Paid content on the Web is a niche business and free content on the Web is for the mass markets. How many web sites require subscriptions? The answer is only a few. Content on the Web demands to be free. It is too easy for consumers to move to web site number two or three if they are asked to pay.

Removing the physical barriers to mobile media and off-deck media while stripping away the behavioral constraints imposed by today's pricing will drive the demand. High mobile media pricing reduces the addressable market for the mobile media, making it difficult to scale a sustainable mobile advertising business. A critical key to this market dynamic is to open up media creation to radically increase the supply. New supply will then drive demand to unprecedented levels of mobile advertising revenues. This will make flat rate, all-you-can-eat pricing, linking, sharing, and forwarding the discovery of new media a possibility for mobile media consumers. This will enable new viral adoptions of mobile media that will help create an industry for mobile advertising. So, as predicted way back in 1800, new supply may well create new demands for mobile advertising.

FLAT-RATE DATA PLANS: THE PRICE IS RIGHT, BUT . . .

Today, the total cost of mobile media is too high for mass-market penetration in most parts of the world. Cost is the single biggest challenge to mobile media as an industry. It is too expensive, especially for young consumers where high costs hit the hardest in the emerging mobile media categories of video, music, and social networking. Most mobile media consumers are cost-sensitive. Even though the industry will hit critical levels (not mobile advertising tipping point levels) of mobile data plans in 2008, most of them will just be subscribers who have some sort of data plan. A true tipping point level will not occur until a critical mass of all-you-can-eat and flat-rate data plans is reached. Until critical mass is hit for all-you-can-eat plans, consumers will avoid services that require hefty deposits and unknown, variable use monthly costs on their bills.

In Europe, there is a movement toward flat-rate data plans, and there is an almost 50/50 split between prepaid and postpaid subscribers. Prepaid data plans are not conducive to variable cost data access prices. Operator 3 in the United Kingdom announced their X-Series flat-rate pricing in 2007 and made the eye-popping promise of unlimited Skype calling and unlimited mobile instant message (IM) usage.

The price of the service is right. For 5 pounds, or $10 a month, you get over 80 hours of Skype, 10,000 MSN Messenger IMs, and a gigabyte of Web or e-mail. It is basically unlimited for most consumers. Video will smack that usage up for heavy users, but that is covered in an upgraded plan. For 10 pounds, or $20 a month, you get 80 hours of SlingBox and Orb. This allows your mobile device to play TV shows, MP3s, and other multimedia files on your PC. The Skype, and MSN support in particular, is frightening to most operators. They are often perceived as competing directly with voice and SMS, the two services that provide the biggest revenues for operators today. Orange, Vodafone, and many others are following this lead.

But a flat-rate data fee is not enough by itself to make mobile media really take off. If it were, mobile media would have taken off in the U.S. market by now. In the United States, the top four mobile operators have offered flat-rate data pricing for years, ranging in price from $15 to $50 per month. Most of them let you use your mobile phone as a modem, something that most European flat-rate models prohibit. What is the result? Some happy smart phone users, but nothing like the mass migration toward mobile data predicted when the X-Series flat-rate pricing plan was announced. Although most of the flat rates have caps and caveats beyond 50 mb of usage, they are not all-you-can-eat plans. Prepay, service metering, and data caps are not exactly conducive to great consumer volumes and tipping point media usage.

If this massive mobile media ecosystem were enabled, driven by flat rates, and had all-you-can-eat mobile media pricing supported by a new search model with recommendations for finding new mobile media, advertisers would have something unique to build on. Flat-rate pricing by itself is not enough to scale mobile media usage. Mobile advertising is one of the key missing ingredients to help the industry get more flat-rate pricing with all-you-can-eat plans.

FREE MY PHONE

In late 2006, Google's CEO Eric Schmidt said, "Your mobile phone should be free. It just makes sense that subsidies should increase as advertising rises on mobile phones." Generation C consumers were raised in the Internet era, where content is perceived to be free. They are bringing this perception to mobile media. No matter what people in focus groups say about ads, Generation C consumers are reluctant to pay for content in any media. So the old-fashioned model of advertisers funding access to content is going to transfer to mobile. This will only work if brands produce creative, relevant mobile advertising that consumers find useful, valuable, or entertaining—just as in any other media or channel. But "free" can also be taken to extremes, as in a new breed of ad-supported Mobile Virtual Network Operators (MVNOs) offering free voice services.

The new MVNO, Blyk is pursuing free voice services as an MVNO in the United Kingdom. Blyk launched its service in September 2007 targeting 16-to-24-year olds in the United Kingdom, offering 217 TXT and 43 minutes of voice calls every month for free in return for users agreeing to receive advertising on their mobile phones. If the ad-based mobile service manages to work with customers in the United Kingdom, the company will have helped pioneer a new form of ad-supported business model.

Blyk also proposed a convoluted user experience whereby customers must complete forms with user preferences to receive relevant ads. Even if those preferences are refined automatically based on usage, this is an incredibly annoying consumer intrusion. Mobile phones are very personal devices and visibly imposing a registration process between consumers and their communications is not good. Compare this with the experience of Google users, where it is incredibly simple: Users type in a search term; receive a complete list of relevant web links; look for the relevant advertisements; click the ad; and they are done. In this simple system, there are no intrusions. This powerful user experience is in the underlying system that makes this almost invisible to the consumer.

Mobile advertising can be used successfully to subsidize content, services, and applications, and this will be one of the next big phases in mobile. Ad subsidies are very different from ad funding—doing the math reveals that advertising models that are entirely funded by content or advertising alone often do not add up. The underlying economics of the MVNO back office and network are high and the costs are too great to support an advertising-only revenue model. Internet-based models are incredibly efficient in distributing content in low-cost models, but throw the overhead of an MVNO into the equation and it quickly goes upside down.

To highlight this point, the content-centric U.S. MVNO Amp'd declared bankruptcy in 2007. Supposedly, what made them different was targeting younger consumers and subjecting them to high prices for all sorts of multimedia content. About $360 million in venture funding later, the content-centric model did not sustain MVNO costs. When it comes to advertising models, it is an untenable sin to forget that in mobile, communications are what drive consumers.

There is no doubt that mobile ads will heavily subsidize more and more media and services. But unless a magical combination of great user experiences, low network and distribution costs, and incredible ad network reach can be attained, it is unlikely that network, device, and voice calls will truly be free in the short term. Going forward, there is assurance that advertising will subsidize mobile media, but subsidizing the entire network and voice calls is beyond the reach of a niche-based MVNO model. However, a full-scale ad network could enable a heavily subsidized phone service.

MOBILE MEDIA MODELS ARE "OMNIA OMNIBUS UBIQUE"

There is little doubt that mobile advertising will play a key role in mobile media. Advertising is a fundamental value proposition for every other media and will evolve with cohesive mobile models as well. But today, it is all *omnia omnibus ubique*, which is to say, "all things for all people everywhere."[1] This will eventually change, but for now, a true mobile ad-driven media model simply does not reflect reality in mobile space. The entire mobile advertising ecosystem has to evolve, from creation to display, targeting, inventory, and myriad models, to a marketplace for ad transactions.

Dramatically increased mobile media usage and consumer eyeballs are prerequisites to arrive at a solid set of mobile advertising models. Operator structural model issues underlie the inability to get the dramatically increased usage and users that the industry needs for wide-scale mobile advertising. Today, mobile advertising models in the industry are complex, if they exist at all. There are too many start-ups dealing with too many operator channels and silos of mobile data, resulting in confusion among advertisers and brands alike. This leads a few of them to bravely take the risks associated with advertising experimentation. There is a lot of replication of models that are working on the Internet. Ultimately, a few yet-to-emerge mobile advertising models will fully leverage the mobile ecosystem, rather than simply translate other advertising models to mobile. But if there is no system, there can be no scale in the models. In the words of William Edwards Deming, *"What we need to do is learn to work in the system, by which I mean that everybody, every team, every platform, every division, every component is there not for individual competitive profit or recognition, but for contribution to the system as a whole on a win-win basis."*[2]

Most Web advertising models are extensions of traditional media broadcast models. The broadcaster (in this case a web site) provides mostly free content and services like e-mail and IM, all mixed with advertising that is usually in the form of banner ads and at times with syndicated search. The advertising works best when the volume of traffic is huge or highly specialized. Ad revenue may be the sole source of revenue or it may be complemented by subscription fees if premium content or an ISP portal is involved. This approach, in its entirety, has been carried over to mobile in its most basic incarnation.

Business models are perhaps the most discussed yet least understood aspect of mobile advertising. Mobile media and advertising will give rise to new kinds of business models—this much is certain. But the industry is also likely to reinvent tried-and-true models. Auctions are one of the oldest forms of brokering and have been in use throughout history to set prices for a wide variety of goods. Interestingly, auctions were reinvented on the Web, not once but twice. The second time had a profound effect on all advertising. Something of similar impact could evolve in mobile advertising, but this is not where things are today.

There are three basic types of advertising in mobile, combined with multiple supporting pricing and tactical approaches:

1. Broad-based brand advertising.
2. Interactive, direct response campaigns.
3. Highly targeted search advertising.

This chapter provides an overview of these basic mobile media models and the ways that advertising models fit in today.

Brand Advertising

A lot of the experimental campaign budgets are from cutting-edge brands trying to influence tough-to-reach Generation C consumers. These campaigns take advantage of user filtering and targeting, but for the most part are broad based. This media model can contain the following components:

Subsidized premium mobile media: For video, ring tones, graphics, music, and so on. Various ad models will evolve to maintain ad-supported subsidization in mobile media.

Sponsorships: A simple "Sponsored by a Big Brand" tagline across the bottom of mobile media, seen frequently in mobile video and with mobile podcasts.

Larger advertising units might not work for a small window, but they will undoubtedly appear at least experimentally.

Video prerolls or intromercials: Full-screen ads placed at the entry of a site or video before a user reaches the intended content. These are seen today in mobile videos, mobile TV, and mobile games.

Postroll videos: Presented at the end of a mobile video, mobile TV, or mobile game session. In games, they may be presented in between the game levels.

On-demand mobile media: A metered usage model based on a pay-as-you-go usage approach. Unlike subscriber services, metered services are based on actual usage. This is different from the classic mobile data "packet charge" models that were content agnostic. Mobile TV and mobile video pay-as-you-go models will appear when advertising is at a point that complements the revenue streams.

Contextual or behavioral advertising: The sale of targeted advertising based on an individual user's mobile media activity. This area could be the most powerful area in mobile advertising models. Mobile could take CPM rates and turn them into models around cost per target because of the underlying potential in mobile context and behavioral data.

Interactive Advertising

These models are basic extensions of where mobile is today. Moving forward, there is no doubt that they will work, but the registration value to the consumer will have to keep rising for them to return to the service.

These models apply when consumers tell advertisers that they want to receive certain types of advertising on an opt-in and ongoing basis. In exchange, the consumers usually provide personal information to the advertiser for targeting purposes:

Mobile portal subscriptions: Consumers are usually charged a monthly fee or sometimes a "day pass" or discounted annual fee, to subscribe to mobile data services.

The sad fact is that subscriptions do not work for most mobile media. It is common for mobile sites to combine free content with premium, fee-based content. Subscription fees are incurred irrespective of actual usage rates. In 2007, subscription and advertising models were more frequently combined. These portal models should have been subsidized by mobile search advertising by now, but they are not. Personalization of these portals would enable even more targeted advertising based on subscribed or customized consumer content.

User registrations: Premium content sites that are free to access but require users to register and provide demographic data. Registration allows better user tracking and higher value in targeted advertising rates and results. This is common on the Web as a marketing tool. In mobile, a registration usually implies a full subscription. This is often done via TXT as an opt-in approach and is often tied to legacy media such as radio, billboards, or print.

TXT short codes: Campaigns that require the brand to provision an MO-SMS or TXT short code for presentation in print, television, or radio. TXT short codes will be complemented by mobile bar codes and ** numbers in the future. The goal of all these is to get a direct response from the segmented, targeted audience.

Targeted Search Advertising

Eventually, the group of capabilities described in this model category will evolve into smaller and smaller audiences with focused niche interests. Hypertargeted audiences in the long

tail of niches will be enabled in mobile because of its unique
targeting capabilities. But initially, the value of basic age,
sex, and address information provided by mobile should not
be overlooked. Today, this value is far better than with any
other advertising-enabling network or device:

> *Paid placement or paid inclusion search*: Favorable link
> positioning as sold for specific search results. Also
> known as sponsored links or advertising keyed to
> particular search terms in a user query. This is already
> occurring in mobile search, but the search ecosystem
> is not yet robust enough to truly scale. This could
> hammer user experiences before they even get going,
> if not implemented cautiously.
>
> *Content targeted search advertising:* Pioneered by Applied
> Semantics and acquired by Google. AdSense extends
> the precision of search advertising to the rest of the
> Web by identifying the meaning of a web page and
> then automatically delivering relevant ads when a
> user visits that page. Mobile may see variations of this
> approach once the off-deck sites reach critical mass.

That Magical Second Act

The big theory in venture-driven conversations around the
world in the web space is that advertising is a great starting point. But does the company have the potential for that
magical second act of generating revenue? Typically, this
means a subscription model as well as advertising. A side
note is that there is usually only a single advertising fund-
able service in any one category. But this is tangential. The
reason the second act is often referred to as magical is that
it is so uncommon. If it happens, it is almost always a subscription model that complements the advertising revenue,
or vice versa.

For examples of the magical second act, look to cable
or to XM/Sirius. XM/Sirius features commercial-free music

stations but has some commercials on talk and news shows. Broadcasting coast to coast, satellite radio offers brands a national presence for advertising, an opportunity not available with other radio. So they have a value proposition for brands that may generate between 6 percent and 10 percent of revenues from advertising. They may also offer the ability for subscribers to purchase songs and media they hear on the radio as they listen, offering a third revenue stream.

For an example of how this magical second act might work in mobile, look to the first mobile mass market community launched in 2003 by SK Telecom called *Cyworld*. In only four short years, Cyworld has taken South Korea by storm. Cyworld, in a country that is only one-sixth the size of the United States, has more video uploads than YouTube does worldwide! Right from the start, Cyworld had a solid business model to generate mobile revenues while tapping into the power of the youth markets with their penchant for creating and discovering new media. That business model was a solid key to their success. Cyworld users can buy and sell mobile media using a payment mechanism called the *dotori*, or "acorn." Acorns can be easily purchased from a mobile phone.[3] Cyworld has achieved the "magical second act," with mobile being a key part of that second revenue stream. Over 30,000 businesses advertise or have a presence on Cyworld. Over half a million items of virtual properties are already for sale, with their own currency. The revenue share is 40 percent to Cyworld and 60 percent to outside content owners. This translates to $7.78 per user per year.[4] It is a nice money machine, and it shows how communities might evolve in mobile and of how two revenue streams, or more, might be achievable.

Since mobile media has its roots in subscription-based mobile models, it is not too much of a stretch to imagine a magical second act of revenues. The key to achieving this is to provide extremely high consumer value and a lower total cost of media. If the total costs are too high—as they are today—the market will never take off to the levels required for massive consumer adoptions. Looking toward the demographics of the young, who are growing up with a very different perspective of media ownership—where they just want to pay $5 for a monthly stream of music or video—this is a ripe area for advertising to capture a second revenue stream.

Measurement: A Problem for the Millennium

Since media time immemorial, advertisers have been grappling two basic questions:

1. How many people were exposed to the advertisement?
2. How effective is my advertising?

Irrespective of the medium, the basics haven't changed. In this section, we review the audience measurement strategies prevalent in different mediums and contrast them with mobile.

Television

TV audiences are measured two ways—diaries or meters. The survey unit is generally the household or might be based on number of TVs in a given household. A diary generally runs one to two weeks in quarter-hour units. The focus is generally about someone watching a program rather than who in the household is watching. Diary surveys might be complemented by phone or personal interviews. Meter surveys are generally based on many months or even years. The participating households are fitted with a meter that is hooked to each TV set and a phone line. The meter automatically records the TV channel on a per minute basis (so recording the channel number and start and stop times for the channel). The research company then dials the meter each day and downloads the viewing data from previous day. The household members are also asked to indicate their presence while watching TV which gives an idea about the demographics (age group and gender). The main measures of TV audiences are:

- *Ratings (households/people):* The percentage of people watching programs; could be reported based on demographic groups.
- *Households using TV:* A rating for all channels combined, or the number of households watching TV.
- *Target audience rating points:* Ratings for a target audience, something that advertisers are quite interested in.
- *Reach:* The number or percentage of people who see a particular program or channel or a commercial in a given time period.
- *Frequency:* The frequency of advertisements presented to an audience.
- *Program ranking:* The ranking of the programs by time duration.
- *Audience share:* Generally expressed in person-hours.

TV time is generally bought in GRP (Gross Rating Points = Reach × Frequency), CPP (Cost per spot/Rating), and CPM (Cost per Thousand = Cost/Thousand people). TV time is bought in upfront markets, scatter markets, or opportunistic markets. For syndicated shows, it could be based on first-run syndication, off-network syndication, and the ancient barter system. The most prominent TV measurement organization is Nielsen.

Radio

In most countries, radio audience is still measured by diaries at an individual level. Some companies have introduced digital and automated ways of collecting the data like IMMI's mobile phone technology; it collects samples randomly—10 seconds of room audio every 30 seconds.[5] Arbitiron's special purpose portable Peoplemeter is an approach that uses inaudible identifying codes or watermarks inserted into broadcast programming or a wristwatch like measurement device. However, the most common measurement format is a radio listening diary that runs for one week and is filled in by one person with quarter-hour units. (Though for most countries the unit is quarter-hour, in some developing countries, this could vary widely.) The main measures of radio audiences are:

- *Average audience:* The average number of people listening to a particular station in a particular time period (quarter-hour, day, week, etc.).
- *Reach (or cumulative audience):* The number of t people who listen to a station in a time period.
- *Frequency (average and distributed):* Determines how often the listeners heard the advertisement.
- *Audience share:* Expressed as a percentage of person-hours (not percentage of people) for a given station.
- *Duration:* The average time spent listening.
- *Impression:* The sum of the audiences at specified times, for example, ad broadcast.
- *Loyalty:* Time spent with the station as a percentage of the total time spent listening to radio.

Radio time is generally bought in AQH (Average Quarter Hour = [AQH Persons × 100]/Population), GRP (AQH Rating × Number of Spots), and Cume Estimates (Reach Potential × 100/Population). Radio time is bought for network, local, or spot radio. The most prominent radio measurement organization is Arbitiron.

Print

Print media audiences are generally measured in two ways—circulation and readership. Circulation refers to the number of copies circulated in public and is measured from sales figures. Readership is the number of readers for a specific issue or a publication over a given time period and is measured by surveys. Circulation is typically broken down into paid distribution, free distribution, and nondistribution. Readership is generally measured in average issue readership (how many people read the issue).

Print advertisements are generally bought in CPMs on the basis of ad size, ad frequency, color, bleed, and gatefolds. The most prominent print measurement organization is Audit Bureau of Circulation or ABC (others are Business Publications Audit and Standard Rate and Data Services).

Traditional Media Measurement Issues

The measurement issues in TV, radio, and print are obvious. It is guesswork in the worst cases and only an approximation in the best ones. First, most measurements are done to measure audiences of the media the ad resides in, meaning they don't track advertisement audiences. In the best-case scenario with TV peoplemeters, the meter records the duration of the program being watched and hence the likelihood of the advertisement being watched in that time period, but whether that person is in the room is not known. Second, audiences are not always represented accurately (e.g., in the case of radio, children under a certain age are not included). And in the case of both radio and TV, wealthier and educated households are underrepresented. With either radio or TV, it is not known whether they are just playing in the background or the audience is actually paying attention to them. The bottom line from the advertisers' point of view is that they don't have a clear grasp whether a given person or household watched the advertisement. Print (especially magazines) is plagued with miscounts of subscriptions that only get corrected in long monthly cycles; there also is no correlation between subscribing to a magazine and seeing the advertisement. In most cases, the purpose of surveys is to determine if the audiences were exposed to the ad. After a few days, the audience can't, with certainty, recall whether they saw the ad.

Even if the person saw the ad, there is no way of understanding the true impact of that ad as it relates to persuasion and purchasing behavior. Some of these problems are alleviated on the Internet, but they are also highlighted by the caches, cookies, and Web 2.0 applications that make even the online measurements suspect.

Can Mobile Measurement Solve Some Legacy Issues?

The value of mobile measurement starts by answering the most basic and fundamental question—did the person watch the ad or not? In mobile data, almost everything gets logged and measured. Although mobile will, no doubt, have its own set of major issues with measurements, it offers the potential of accurate measurements starting from exposure to persuasion to transactions. When mobile phones become payment devices, as they already are in South Korea, Japan, and Scandinavia, the impact or the effectiveness question will be answered to the finest transaction detail possible. Operators play a significant role in enabling the measurement ecosystem for mobile advertising, although Internet brands are extending their online measurement capabilities to mobile. But they also face significant challenges in pulling things together to be effective, which is discussed in Chapter 5.

Companies like Telephia and M:Metrics are also using both mobile metering applications on the phone and surveys to accurately measure the exposure and impact. In terms of variables tracked, it will evolve and be based on the channel and the goal of the campaigns. The five-points framework described in Chapter 3 can help define the parameters that are important in mobile advertising:

- *Reach and frequency:* For unique user and the number of impressions for those unique users.
- *Rich media:* Measurements for video and audio that enable completion rates, time viewed, interaction rates, replay counts, and viral measures for counting how many people it was sent to.

- *Direct response:* Click-through rates (CTR), cost per click (CPC), cost per lead, and cost per sale, transaction, or customer acquisition.
- *Branding measurement:* Aided or unaided brand awareness, ad recall, message association, purchase intent, and purchases or transactions.

INTERNET MODELS MOVE TO MOBILE

Today's mobile advertising models, for the most part, are derived from their Web cousins. They will evolve into the unique value propositions that the mobile phone, network, and media can bring to the world of advertising. But for now at least, they are rooted in the previous generations of media.

CPM (Cost per Mille)

This old standby is still alive and kicking in mobile advertising, albeit on semiwobbly legs. Why there are better models and why the high CPM rates in today's mobile ad market may not be sustainable are discussed in detail later in the chapter.

Pay per Click (PPC)

Sometimes called cost per click (CPC), this model will be brought to mobile search. It is here today in large volumes in mobile local search applications in the United States. As more businesses become aware of the value of mobile search and as the search vendors get more cross-operator traction, this model will apply to more content.

Cost per Call

This is really a variation of a PPC model. We are seeing strong growth in mobile around pay per call in local search applications. This is transparent for merchants and easy for them to buy. And it is easy to implement in mobile data applications. It is the first major step toward a scalable mobile ad model as the production costs for merchants on mobile are zero versus on the Web.

CPA (Cost per Action)

Mobile has the unique position of being the closest to the point of transaction as it has built-in payment mechanisms and mobile bar codes. Mobile is also unique as it is highly interactive. Therefore, it should be the place where CPA thrives. But it is not. The dynamics behind a CPA model are a long way off in mobile advertising. On the Web, CPM and CPA buys are complementary approaches that fill different needs. Typically, CPM drives brand advertising, and CPA primarily drives response-based approaches to advertising. But direct response doesn't work for every product or every campaign. The major difference between CPM and CPA approaches depends on who bears the risks for converting an impression into customer interactivity. When publishers sell media space on a CPM basis, they generally know how many page views are required to fulfill that obligation. When ad space is sold on a CPA basis, it is generally not known in advance how many page views are needed. Many factors that affect yield, like landing pages and conversion processes, are beyond control or influence of the budget holders. Therefore, CPA-based placement sellers generally charge a big premium to accept the risk of an ad yield.

Some domain hosters have begun to game the cost per click model, which might tilt some inventory to CPA in the near future. With CPC ads, domainers create semibogus web sites where confused consumers click on ads in an effort to escape. This is about turning the Web into a giant pile of junk clicks. But with CPA ads, clicking is not enough. You have to get consumers to take action. Google's new pay per action may prove to be a scalable model in the smaller niches and crannies of blogs and social media sites. Both of these dynamics may bode well for future CPA approaches.

In mobile, CPA has not really appeared yet. When it does appear, CPA-only deals will limit placement options, as very few mobile publishers, if any, will accept them for the foreseeable future. In the future, choices will still be limited primarily to sites with lots of unsold inventory and low demand. The basic view on selling ad space on a true CPA basis in mobile is that it is a long way out, or not going to happen at all, based on the unknowns involved. If CPA does appear in mobile, there may be a parallel to the Web where the blue-chip advertisers almost always buy on a CPM basis, while lower-tier companies in the same categories generally rely on CPA models.

Syndication

Although it is rare, if your mobile application or widget distributes content widely, the content owners might want to pay you to get their content in your application or widget. This model will most likely be seen around widgets and on the Web in high-volume sites. Think MySpace or YouTube distribution levels.

Revenue Sharing

Last, and certainly not least, is revenue sharing with your host. This is a given in mobile. The operators take part of the revenues generated. But what if this were reversed? What if the world of mobile development were turned upside down around revenue shares? If operators were supersmart, they would build an ecosystem for mobile widgets, attract the coolest of the cool widgets, and share some advertising revenues with them as an incentive. Naaah, cancel the daydream and get back to reality.

In this model discussion, the brands have to do the heavy lifting of figuring out the best reach, relevancy, and targeting. And even then, going across operators for an on-deck media buy is almost impossible. Going across a massive web site base is possible, transparent, and effective. And until there are cohesive mobile ad models in place, mobile cannot compete with other media for large advertising budgets and campaigns.

Getting to a return on investment (ROI) mechanism is, in the final analysis, all that really matters. On the one hand, some marketers may not consider that lower prices can easily translate into less-productive media and lower ROIs. Or on the other hand, fewer impressions, on the right media and with the right segmentation and targeting, could lead to better ROIs and acquire better performing customers. To get to this ROI, it is essential to get to fully loaded costs. A customer's true lifetime value is based on its revenue streams minus the cost to acquire and maintain it. This varies wildly in mobile media. No matter how you purchase mobile media placements (PPC, CPM, or CPA), you must manage customer acquisition on a CPA basis that includes all marketing costs to understand your true ROIs. We cover this fully later in this chapter.

IS YOUR ISP AN ADVERTISING SALES FIRM?

Imagine, for a moment, if your ISP sold advertising space. Really. Try again! Pretty hard to fathom, right? Well, AT&T plans to push a new advertising model, using it as the cornerstone of new wireless services initiatives. They plan on selling advertising on AT&T Wireless mobile phones, AT&T television and broadband Internet services. They are supposedly expecting upward of a billion dollars in advertising revenue per year. They have already pulled together an ad sales team that has begun briefing Madison Avenue. They plan on developing new advertising services based on its U-verse package, which is a combination of wireless, Internet, and TV aimed at its base of 58 plus million wireless and 67 plus million land-line phone customers. This is one approach, but it is a massive mind shift to think that a network operational centric mind-set can effectively enter the creative world of selling advertising and succeed on Madison Avenue.

Mobile advertising and models to support it are still in formative stages and evolving fast. Some of the older ISP precepts do not apply here. Part of the perception is that mobile is different. But is it—really? There are three major structural approaches and models mobile operators could embrace for mobile advertising:

1. They could form joint ventures with key advertising agencies and get out of the way. This is happening primarily in Japan and South Korea today. DoCoMo's D2C partnership with Dentsu is an example.
2. They could become content producers, destinations, and advertising sales channels and try to stay ahead of Internet brands. China Mobile in China, Reliance in India, and AT&T in the United States are examples.
3. They could abstract core functionality out of the networks and open them up for third parties to embrace and extend. This primarily applies to Europe and North America. Vodaphone in Europe, BT's Twenty-First Century Network initiative in the United Kingdom, and the Sprint/Google WiMax partnerships are examples of this open approach.

For a mobile operator to execute well on the first model, they have a tremendous investment to make to become a destination or become a functional agency within an operator. Companies like Reliance in India and China Mobile in China are dedicating major resources to creating content and becoming an advertising channel. Reliance is part of a larger conglomerate of Reliance Industries, which owns TV, print, radio, and an ISP along with Mobile. Even with that market clout, Reliance is not trying to become an agency. China Mobile is a gigantic government-backed machine with more subscribers than the U.S. market in total and is trying to become a do-it-all company, hence the move to acquire a mobile advertising agency. Sprint has come close to this model, but has outsourced the inner workings to Enpocket. AT&T now has the three-screen vision of being a television, wireless, and ISP enabler and has announced the advertising sales channel, but has not invested much in the overall mobile creative capabilities yet.

A Joint Venture Approach

When it comes to mobile advertising, Japan and South Korea are not necessarily more advanced, compared with their Western counterparts, though they have had more experience with it, especially Japan. As mentioned in Chapter 2, in mid-2000, NTT DoCoMo, the biggest Japanese operator and Dentsu, the biggest advertising agency, created a joint venture named D2 Communications (D2C) and formed the world's first advertising agency exclusively devoted to mobile advertising.[6] This joint venture was to form a new model that focused expertise on mobile advertising. Looking to Japan where each of the big three operators have created a partnership with an advertising agency for mobile is an excellent validation of this approach. The joint venture agency can work on the creative aspects to make sure the brands can attain the right mix of reach and media. These joint venture agencies also have the in-house expertise around the variances and myriad details to make sure the networks and devices can handle the campaign effectively.

Other Japanese operators followed and struck their own alliances: KDDI, the second largest operator in Japan, partnered with Hakuhodo to form Mediba, and then Vodafone (now Softbank) partnered with Cyber Communications to form JMobile. There are also some independent players such as C.A. Mobile and DeNA. Similarly, in South Korea, SK Telecom, the country's largest operator, partnered with AiCROSS in late 2000 while KTF created a joint venture with Dentsu called mHows. The main difference between Japanese and South Korean business models, compared with model structures in North America and Europe, is that operators take an active role as part of their joint investments into advertising agencies.

Table 6.1 shows the joint venture structure in Japan.

Table 6.2 shows the investment structure in South Korea.

The joint venture and investment model has worked well for South Korea and Japan. Operators realized that

Table 6.1   Joint Venture Structure of Mobile Advertising Agencies in Japan

	D2 Communications	Mediba, Inc.	Japan Mobile Communications, Inc. or JMobile
Operator	NTT DoCoMo	KDDI	Softbank
Founded	June 1, 2000	Dec. 6, 2000	July 6, 2001
Capital	980M Yen	490M Yen	490M Yen
Shareholders	NTT DoCoMo (51 percent)	KDDI (51 percent)	Softbank Mobile (45 percent)
	Dentsu, Inc. (46 percent)	Hakuhodo DY media partners (35 percent)	Cyber Communications (46 percent)
	NTT Ad, Inc. (3 percent)	Asatsu DK, Inc. (8 percent)	
		D.A. Consortium (4 percent)	
		Delphys (2 percent)	

Table 6.2   Joint Venture Structure of Mobile Advertising in South Korea

	AirCROSS	MHows
Operator	SK Telecom	MHows
Founded	June 1, 2000	December. 6, 2000
Capital	980M Yen	490M Yen
Major shareholders	SK Telecom/AirCross	KTF/Dentsu

advertising is not their core competency and agencies knew they needed help understanding the intricacies of the mobile world. Operators are typically more conservative, and agencies like to think out of the box and show boundless creativity. By bringing in the expertise from the two groups, operators could hit the ground running and position the new companies as "got to" organizations for handling mobile advertising. Since these agencies are already handling other forms of advertising, they can proactively integrate mobile into the full branding and advertising exercise of any campaign.

In this joint venture model approach, there is still plenty of room for an advertising network broker to reach across operators or around the world in global campaigns. The ad networks could run campaigns for reach or with targeting and interactivity in mind. Or they could reach into the high value-add enablers of mobile transactions or bar code infrastructures. This is a large shift away from the perspective that an operator should actually sell mobile advertisements. It is an excellent option for staying engaged in mobile advertising as a company, while creating a powerful ecosystem and expertise base that is outside the operational cultures of a typical operator's mind-set.

Create the Whole Thing

China and India, along with some of the other developing nations, have relatively low overall ARPUs. They also have a high consumer propensity to use data services due to lower PC penetrations, making these markets ideal for mobile advertising.[7] Companies like 21 Communications in China and Quasar in India are enabling advertisers to launch mobile campaigns.

Mobile operators in China and India are often seen taking an active, aggressive, role in creating mobile media and advertising. With some 495 million subscribers and growing, China is a booming market for mobile media and advertising, but it is also rife with speculation. China Mobile has been aggressively purchasing value-add enablers in mobile recently. They have set up several service divisions recently, including a mobile media shop in Shanghai, a mobile music shop in Chengdu and a location services division in Tianjin. It also recently received a government license to create and execute its own mobile advertising and marketing services.

This is one approach for a few countries and cultures. Mobile operators will attempt to be all things media to all consumers in some regions; it is a viable model and approach. But is it the most effective, long-term scalable approach? We are not so sure about that, even in India and China. Being a strong network operator and a strong media player involves two very different cultures and value propositions.

Ultimately, content wants to be network and device agnostic as well, making this a shaky long-term model proposition.

Abstract the Value and Get Out of the Way

In the past, the ISPs and cable companies built and competed on bandwidth, security, basic systems services, and reliability. They offered e-mail, Web, and blog hosting, and some applications. But they do not offer ad networks or sell ad inventory. Said another way, they generally compete on the access, control, and transport layers of the network game; not so much at the applications level; and hardly ever at the device level of the equation. In this world, access, control, and transport layers are all advertiser and media enablers. Access, control, and transport revenues are not used to fund the applications and media services. The barriers to entry are high for ISPs as well as for mobile operators, perhaps higher for mobile operators, because the 3G spectrum, a necessity for mobile data, was generally bid into the auction stratospheres. The billing, user management, network location, and presence management assets deployed at these layers are also substantial assets for mobile media and advertising. If only they could be exposed for the content, media, and advertisers to maximize against. However, core competencies around media and advertising may not be an operator's strongest suit. It is a totally different mind-set from running a voice or data network. Mobile operators have to make sure their networks don't go down, and backward compatibility is a massive requirement. Operating a voice network is a conservative engineering mind-set. Advertisers are on the other side, coming up with out-of-the-box creative ideas all the time. These two cultures don't mix and match very well.

Operators often know that media or, more specifically, advertising is not at the center of their core competencies. The best way may well be to do it as DoCoMo did with D2C. Partner with an agency who knows the digital space inside out. Set up an independent company that has a sole, maniacal focus on mobile advertising.

Higher up on the network stack ride the applications and devices for accessing it all. The ISPs may offer hosting and applications, but generally never offer devices. The closer to the application layers or to the device layers, the fiercer the competition. The ISPs and network operators are not application builders, and they are even further from being advertising experts. Mobile operators build applications and are building developer networks and mobile advertising ecosystems. It is just a tiny step away to build a full advertising sales support system. So some operators will take that major step toward selling advertising. That will prove to be a strategic mistake. The opposite direction offers the best long-term value. Abstract the core value out of the network—open it up to select third parties—and step out of the way to make a valuable ecosystem flourish. There are signs that some of the large operators have gotten the message, and they starting to formulate strategies around opening their mobile platform. For example, Sprint-Nextel with its broadband wireless initiative and Verizon Wireless with its "Any Apps, Any Device" option[8] for consumers are moving in this direction.

When advertising disrupts the incumbent business models, it will impact how the money flows in the ecosystem. From an operator's point of view, they can leverage their billing relationships and consumer data assets into advertising assets. Adding intelligence about the consumers to the world of advertising is a massive value proposition. If operators can figure out the right way to share that to improve the relevance of not only the advertisements, but the overall mobile user experiences, then it becomes a valuable asset for both publishers and advertisers.

Success in ad-enabling mobile operator infrastructures will be supercritical for operators as markets become more open and competitive for mobile services and applications. Opening up this targeting data, anonymously and with great respect for consumer rights, will be key for mobile operators to create a value for advertisers that is unrivaled by print, radio, or television.

COMPARING AD RATES ACROSS INDUSTRIES

Let's briefly review what CPA and CPM stand for. CPA is an advertising payment model by which the advertiser pays the publisher when a specific, visitor-initiated action occurs, such as the completion of a registration. In this case, you only pay for the customers or action you get. CPA typically focuses on delivering conversions (actions). CPM typically focuses on brand awareness campaigns. Brand advertising is where the big money is. A CPM from a brand advertiser generally pays many times more than a CPA performance ad.

When the dot-com shakedown occurred in 2000 and 2001, most advertisers either left the Internet altogether or demanded a cost-per-action model in place of the CPM approach. With the return of the volumes of brand advertisers to the Internet, the balance of power has reverted to the web site publishers, who favor the old standby CPM models.

Mobile CPMs

CPM is probably the best cross-industry metric. It is generally understood across media types, including mobile media, and implemented on all of them as a purchasing type. Today, brand advertisers pay an average CPM cost of about $3 to $5 on the Internet. They pay upward of $50 or $60 on mobile today, which may not be sustainable long term. We have some campaign evidence of mobile CPMs as high as $120. This compares with an average $30 CPM for traditional broadcast prime time. As more and more brand advertisers enter the arena, competition will increase for premium ad placements on the leading sites, causing overall CPM rates to rise in all media.

Figure 6.1 shows CPM rates across industries. We used price ranges from various industry sources to frame a perspective on CPM rates across various media.

It is critical to look at costs up front and compare them with other media buys, but it is even more important to look

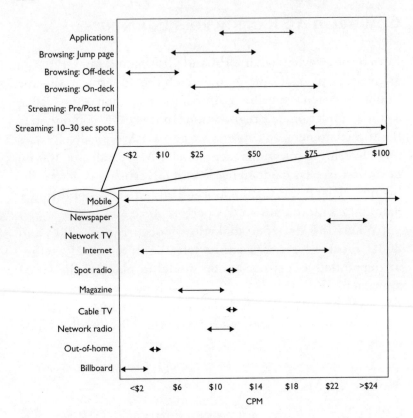

Figure 6.1   Comparison of CPM across advertising media.
Note: Mobile CPMs are author estimates based on our research. The mobile rates
are just a snapshot in time (2007) to give a relative framework versus actual figures
since these will change as the industry matures.
Source: For CPMs other than mobile — Media Dynamics.

at the performance in front of consumers to get calls to action
and sales.

Click-Through Rates (CTRs)

A mobile ad that takes the consumer to a page for more
information or to take advantage of an offer can be tracked
with click-through rates. This enables consumers to get more
information on the product and creates an opportunity for the
brand to interact with the consumer. The typical CTR for an
Internet banner ad is around 0.2 percent; for mobile banner

ads, it's in the range of 3 to 6 percent, or higher in some cases.[9] Off-deck CTRs are generally lower than 1 percent on average though some of the campaigns might yield on-deck CTRs that are in the range of 2 percent to 10 percent depending on the level of targeting. The active screen CTRs are typically the highest as shown in the Mobile Posse case study in Chapter 7. Rates can go as high as 20 percent depending on the promotion.

Typically, brand advertisers in mobile measure their campaigns by CTR. Engagement can also be measured through downloads of content, viewing of video clips and sending links virally. With an average CTR range of 3 to 6 percent, mobile response rates are higher than they are online, or in any other advertising approach in almost any other media. As Mike Baker, CEO of Enpocket notes:

> *It is no secret that mobile has been delivering CTRs that are orders of magnitude higher than the Web, averaging around 4 percent. But we are seeing some campaigns that yield much higher results—as high as 7, 10, and 12 percent. There are a number of ways to optimize CTRs in mobile advertising, including demographic targeting, behavioral targeting, predictive analytics, creative optimization, and creating an overall compelling ad experience.[10]*

Why are there such great response rates? Because the mobile user experience can be very engaging! The calls to action can be compelling new media, like ring tones from a new concert tour, brought to a slick-looking mobile site that features viral send-to-friend capabilities. Or they can be along the lines of the Hookt campaign from Boost, which is highly targeted to the right audience and was a very engaging approach. Although these end-to-end integrated mobile experiences are the exception, they are appearing more often; and where they appear and engage the consumer, they are generating higher CTRs for brands, compared with any other media. But are these high-mobile CPMs and CTRs supportable over time?

While WAP or banner ads follow the traditional CPM/ CTR model, some of the other channels within mobile follow a CPC model (e.g., mobile and local search rely on a cost per search or cost per call model respectively). In mobile search, for the majority of the white-label implementations, enablers are paid on a per active user basis rather on a per search basis. However, they participate in the revenue stream that results from the search results of ring tones and applications that are in the operator catalog. Local search is typically based on the cost-per-call model, which is in the range of $5 to $10 per call and going as high as $30 to $40 per call for high-value leads such as real estate and insurance. Some search models are also based on cost per click in the range of $0.20 to $0.25.

These CPM/CPC models are obviously going to adjust and trend downward as the market matures.

$60 MOBILE CPMs; TOMORROW'S REALITY?

At least half a dozen press releases popped up during the writing of this book claiming a $50 or $60 and higher CPM rate for mobile ads. A brief look back at Internet advertising from 1998 to 2002 shows that a $50 CPM, or anything near it, is not defensible for very long. For the CPM model to work at any price point, even in the short term, these networks need a critical mass of advertisers willing to spend branding (versus direct marketing) dollars on a new, untested medium that will appear in a wide range of content. That is going to be difficult, if not impossible, to find. Since the agency ecosystem is rooted in print and TV, it is also anchored in CPMs and GRPs (gross rating points). For the near-term future, CPMs probably will determine the ratio of dollars spent in mobile. But the ecosystem is being yanked into the digital world with more transparent ROIs that gauge new levels of consumer interaction and impact. Outcomes need to be tied to more than just the theory of eyeballs in the living room.

Assuming for a moment that the mobile ad networks can find enough advertisers, it will increase the attraction for publishers to run ads on their networks, adding more inventory and depressing prices. In addition, web-based interactive agencies were already burned once by ad networks with prices above a $30 CPM. It is likely that the entire mobile CPM model will shrink, as it did on the Web. In both the PPC (pay per click) and CPA (cost per acquisition) models, more responsibility is put on the content providers, insulating advertisers from some risk until the consumer clicks toward a transaction or sale. However, the implementation and success of CPC and CPA models rely on huge impression volumes, an ad sales system more scalable than is required for CPM models, and a mobile infrastructure capable of monetizing consumer clicks or actions. All these are a long way off for mobile advertising. As noted by Larry Shapiro, VP of Disney: *"We might have 10 percent to 20 percent of click-through rates (CTRs), but 90 percent of unsold inventory and CPMs are high indicating the early stages of the market and all of this will trend down like the way you had on Internet when we had $30 CPMs, 10 percent CTRs, and 95 percent unsold and all those numbers changed in the mature market."*[11]

Two major groups are using mobile for advertising today. First are the companies that want to advertise on mobile to get consumers to click to their point of sale to buy a game, mobile music, ring tones, or video. For these advertisers, mobile advertising is about accelerating the process of acquiring a new customer. Their ad spending will be measured and driven by the lifetime value of that new customer. Mobile CPM rates above that are not sustainable for this group. For lifetime economics in these scenarios to make sense, CPM rates must drop to between $5 and $10. As mobile search-based keyword auctions appear, these advertisers may well move their budgets over. But is this type of advertiser really going to scale mobile advertising revenues? No. It will basically be capped by the marketing budgets of these smaller companies. Beyond the CPM and economic issues, aren't all mobile application providers essentially competing with each other for the same time and service spends from the same consumers? How do mobile portal managers feel about semicompetitive mobile media advertising on their prime real estate with the goal of stealing a customer's attention? Will every ad have to be preapproved? Will this really be the market force that drops CPM rates? No, it will not.

The second group of mobile advertisers consists of companies outside the mobile industry looking to increase the awareness of their products and services in a high value, personal scenario. These companies are just beginning to understand the unique value of mobile advertising for relevant, targeted, effective presentations to their audience. Selling these companies on the concept of mobile advertising and getting them to spend more than just their trial budgets is a long, arduous cycle. And the high CPM rates are often confusing to this group. Compared with $10 for a run on an untargeted network to $20 for a targeted web site group, there is still a question of cost and value of the $50 CPMs in mobile. Part of this high mobile CPM rate is driven by lack of mobile inventory today. Once the inventory arrives, that pressure will force the CPMs down in mobile.

Similar to the Web, the mobile CPMs will bifurcate into a lower cost, less targeted run-of-network (off deck) with CPMs between $2 and $9. The higher tier will be targeted mobile sites with specific audiences, where CPM rates will be around $12 up to $20 on the high side. The CPM rates simply follow the degree of targeting value. Better targeting equals higher CPM rates. In mobile, these will be mostly on-deck with high degrees of targeting based on proprietary mobile data being exposed anonymously for the ad campaign. Today's mobile press releases touting costly, untargeted inventory is absurd and won't last. Off-deck mobile ad networks, with less well-defined targeting approaches, will turn into the equivalent of the Web's run-of-network buys, where inventory should always be inexpensive. CPMs will be tied to a certain size of advertising buy, but it won't be an unreasonable premium for smaller buys.

But with the potentially higher value of mobile targeting into niche audiences in a fractured mediascape, is there another level of ad targeting rates, metrics, and value beyond the tried-and-true CPM of yesteryear? Yes, there is!

Is There a New Cost-per-Engagement Model?

A lot of thought is going into Web CPM ad rates for niche, highly focused sites, especially to find 18- to 24-year-old crowds. CPM was originally designed around large horizontal media, primarily print. Is it really the right model for anything but large horizontal traffic bases and consumer eyeballs? Sure, it makes sense for the largest web sites on the planet, as CPM models were primarily designed for large, wide, broad demographic sites like MSN or CNN or even ESPN. The demographic is widespread and the advertiser knows that their actual target is only 5 percent of the total reach. CPM was designed around the broadcast based scatterblasted approaches where the advertisers waste 95 percent of their ad impressions to get to that 5 percent that they really want to reach. So is CPM the best model for rapidly evolving mobile media sites with niche audiences that could be laser-like targeted with the mobile data discussed in Chapters 3 and 4? Engagement-driven campaigns can be effective and measurable, as noted by Scott Ferris, Senior Vice President and General Manager of Atlas Solutions (now part of Microsoft):

> *When programming content and advertising can be separated out, like in mobile and interactive television, you can measure exposure durations. You can also measure consumer interactions with that message at a fundamentally better level. Consumer engagement is far more measurable than even a few years ago and this is going to impact the targeting efficiencies for brands. It is also going to have a significant impact, over time, with how advertising is priced and sold.*[12]

Next-generation engagement modeling and filtering to get to the right segments will enable a new long tail of advertising and that may demand newer models versus the older, broadcast-based CPM centric models. The old approach of CPM simply doesn't fit this new world of niche sites in the long tail of consumer markets. If CPM approaches were foisted on niche sites or niche audiences that were previously unobtainable targets, they would be grossly undervaluing their value to advertisers. Effective niche targeting can be taken to another level in mobile compared with any other media. While TV and print-driven advertisers have made strides toward improving CPM as the right metric with demographics and geographic targeting, digital targeting goes so much further that it makes CPM seem a tad clunky. The right measure for advertising buys with digital media may not be CPMs at all.

The real question on ad rates in a digital world with targeting is: How much will it cost me to reach the exact person I want to reach and ignore the rest? Is this just a highly focused, highly refined CPM model? Or is it a newer cost per engagement approach enabling a comparison across sites and audience variables that would equalize a broad audience with high numbers of generic eyeballs and a small audience on a highly focused niche site? It may well evolve into a newer digital centric metric over time. Cost per engagement would get closer to the actual goal of targeting the right consumer at the right time with the right message. As the metrics around the five-points framework defined in Chapter 3 become real, it will be apparent that the capability to measure cost per target could be a strong mobile differentiator versus other media.

THERE ARE TOO MANY PIGS AT THE TROUGH

The value chains and revenue splits are fairly clear in online advertising. In general, the splits are outlined in this value chain (see Figure 6.2). Although the time frame can be argued, it

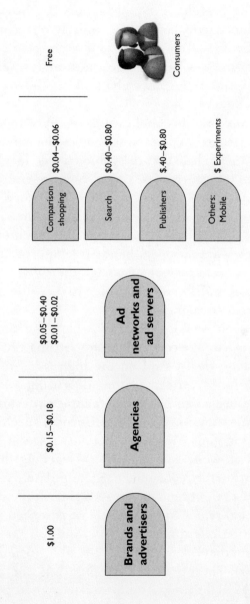

Figure 6.2   Revenue split in the value chain for online advertising.

has also taken the better part of a full decade for these splits to settle into consistent terms and definitions.

The multibillion-dollar questions of the year for mobile advertising are twofold. First, what are the base mobile adverting value chains and their underlying economics? Second, what role will the mobile operators play and how many bread crumbs will be left to the brands? Will there be enough revenue in the value chain for mobile media and advertising to flourish?

While researching this book, we have talked to the most engaged, experienced experts in mobile media from around the globe. And it is clear that the value chains, for the most part, are still in their formative stages. Some operators want to sell the advertising and manage the inventory. Others want to partner with—under their control, of course—a select third-party vendor to sell and manage the inventory. And some operators want an open, hands-free approach, where they let each content provider manage their own inventor. And very, very few ISPs want anything to do with managing advertisements or revenue share.

We have seen mobile scenarios where the publishers actually get close to 0 percent of the advertising revenues in nonrevenue share deals. And on the high side, publishers are getting up to 40 percent of the advertising revenue in revenue share deals. The larger percentage revenue share models are appearing in Asia and in Europe, specifically in the United Kingdom. Mobile ad networks are in the formative stages as well, especially those reaching deep into operators for valuable consumer targeting data. And those that can get this targeting data across a single operator base in any one global region are extremely rare, indeed.

Add in the various application silos, and you have a complex value chain that is hard, if not impossible, to understand (see Figure 6.3). There are too many pigs eating at too many feeding troughs right now. And even if we could get down to a single trough, there could easily be too many pigs trying to get at that trough. There are going to be some hungry little runts running around with young ribs poking out.

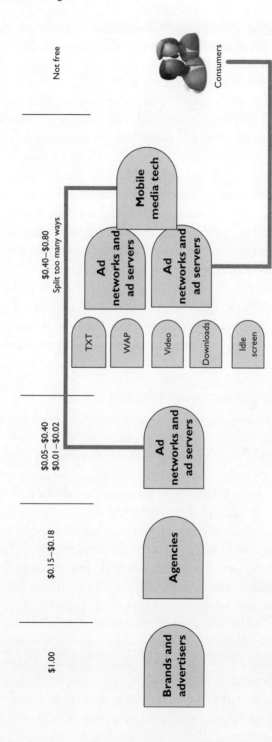

Figure 6.3   Revenue split in the value chain for mobile advertising.

Because over 50 percent of the global advertising spends are in the United States, it is almost surprising that Asian and European operators are sometimes more aggressive in revenue sharing with publishers and advertisers. Perhaps it is just good risk reduction for an operator to shift the risks externally. If it is wildly successful, they will renegotiate it all anyway. Too much of the revenue may wind up going to the big operators. The money will flow, but the majority of it will go to the operators in most parts of the world. Significant structural changes need to be in place before there is enough money flowing to publishers and advertisers for this to scale. What if this mobile media ecosystem and advertising revenue share were turned upside down around revenue shares? If operators were supersmart, they would build an ecosystem for mobile widgets, media, and applications to attract the coolest of the cool apps. And then they would turn around and share some advertising revenues with them as an incentive. Oh wait, we were dreaming just then . . . back to reality.

WHAT AN APPROACHING AVALANCHE SOUNDS LIKE

In views of mobile advertising, most of the models are mixed up, the timing of a major industry revenue impact is far out, and the path to get to clear value propositions and major revenue scale is not yet determined. As noted, there is massive potential in mobile advertising. When the right combination of consumer user experiences, consumer pricing that is close to free, technology enabling a more cost-effective end-to-end solution and market dynamics are all in play—the results can be the equivalent of an avalanche headed your way. If you are the entrenched incumbent, you are about to get caught in a massive scramble because of the impact of mobile advertising. That is the case with today's directory assistance businesses.

The impact in that portion of the industry is here right now and it is potentially heavy. That crack you just heard in the $1.75 average consumer price might just be a major avalanche coming down the hill to get to free. Although there is more to this market dynamic than just mobile usage, it plays a significant role in the equation.

Mobile phones are first and primarily communications devices. At their core, they are all about voice communications. The biggest voice revenue driver outside of person-to-person voice communications revenue at any global operator is a call to directory assistance. According to the Pierz Group, in a study they did on the global directory assistance market, revenues will reach $26.2 billion in 2010, a 60 percent increase over 2005 revenues. The U.S. share of this market will reach $11.4 billion in 2010, an increase of 42 percent over 2005 revenues.[13] At its essence, a directory assistance call will quickly evolve into a voice search call. Some of the biggest pent-up demand in all of mobile is for consumers to find out "What is nearby?" and "Where am I going?" This category used to be called "maps and directions," but with the advent of location or GPS, unique to mobile, it is changing. There is early evidence that mobile search is predominantly local search. This pent-up demand is reflected by one of the largest markets in mobile search. The old model of calling 118 or 411 to ask an operator for a merchant listing is a big white elephant in today's fast-moving voice search market. Combined with scalable local search advertising that is mobile friendly, it is only a matter of time before it is cannibalized at its core.

Voice search is the biggest area of mobile search innovation. By early 2008, mobile voice search will be here and now. It will no longer be "the next big thing" in mobile data. Voice-based directory assistance (DA or 411 in the U.S. or 118 in Europe) and TXT are where the volumes of mobile data and mobile search usage are today.[14] The best single revenue-generating short code in the United States is 411. Both 411 and 118 have huge consumer usage bases, and new mobile data opportunities are part of what is driving innovation in the global directory assistance market.

In just this past year, we have seen tremendous change. The 2007 Microsoft acquisition of Tellme gives the combined companies a tremendous strategic opportunity. In 2007, Microsoft/Tellme handled more local directory searches than Yahoo and Google combined. However, Google's entry into automated voice-based mobile search (800-GOOG411) establishes a competitive landscape that will likely mean a further decline in call volumes and revenues for traditional directory assistance.

Players in this creative burst and new product area include Jingle Networks with 800-FREE411; Tellme, now owned by Microsoft; 800-Yellowpages, now owned by AT&T; Google with its 800-Goog411; and regional players such as 800-SanDiego. These toll-free voice search services are all mobile device agnostic, a huge mobile distribution advantage. They can all send TXT listings and most will be able to send WAP push-based maps and directions. And a few, such as Microsoft/Tellme will integrate into client-based voice search applications.

The combination of pay per click and pay per call derived Internet local search ad models; voice recognition systems, and evolution toward pay per transaction advertising models will have a big impact on directory assistance in 2008 and 2009. Operator-assisted 411 calls are very expensive at around $0.19 wholesale.[15] If voice search costs can drop that cost per call to the $0.04 range and a derivation of pay per action type advertising can scale revenues behind the solution—the game will change. Radically. A free mobile data-driven directory assistance business is a logical adjacent market for an audio ad serving business. Audio ads could be served in front of directory assistance calls or as podcast derivatives.

Local coupons will also come out of this space. Paper coupons have been around for decades, but they are never there when you need them at the store. Mobile coupons are a simple concept, but even if the need to have a client on the handset that reads the coupon is eliminated, there is still a major redemption issue.

These new mobile local merchant ads will come from a different ecosystem, derived from the powerhouses on the Web and their local search ad systems. They will not come, for the most part, from Madison Avenue. If the advertiser models can enable local merchants to participate from the Web and get involved in mobile with little or no lift, this mobile market will be a huge advertiser base. If toll-free type numbers are used to create pay per transaction, closed loop, performance tracking systems, it will be cost-effective for merchants to further fine-tune and hone ROIs and advertisement spends. The scale and power of this advertising-driven model shift will come from Microsoft/Tellme, Google, Yahoo, and other big Web local search players.

When the perfect storm of technical innovations, consumer user experiences and value propositions, advertising reach, and merchant or brand value are all achieved, the results can be extraordinary.

But this is only one example. For an industry to be created and mobile advertising to scale to huge proportions, the use of mobile media needs to scale to new levels. This is especially true for the younger crowds, who can make or break new media almost overnight with viral adoption. Right now, mobile media is simply too expensive overall for them. The industry needs flat-rate pricing and all-you-can-eat models to free up major consumer volumes. The encouragement of a viral component to mobile media is critical for the growth of mobile advertising and also for the measurement of engagement.

Models are forming around the three basic advertising types—interactive campaigns, brand campaigns, and mobile search. But they are formative and early in their evolution. Five years out, we will see more clarity, more transparency on pricing, and more measurability. All these elements are necessary for mobile advertising to attract the major budgets it needs to scale to the levels of other media.

NOTES

1. *Omnia Omnibus Ubique* is the motto of Harrods department store; it means "All Things for All People, Everywhere." David Rittenhouse at Ogilvy pointed this out to us.
2. William Edwards Deming.

3. Tomi T. Ahonen, http://communities-dominate.blogs.com/brands/ 2005/12/cyworld_when_ha.html, accessed on November 30, 2007.

4. Erick Schonfeld, "Cyworld Attacks," *Business 2.0* (October, 2006): 84.

5. The mobile phone also receives a signal from IMMI Bluetooth beacon when the panel member is at home, so the servers can interpret media exposure as "in" or "out-of-home."

6. NTT DoCoMo Press Release, "NTT DoCoMo, Dentsu, NTT AD to Jointly Launch" (June 1, 2000).

7. The Philippines have been active in mobile messaging. Messaging alone helps uplift the data ARPU to approximately 50 percent of the total ARPU. Consumers send over 120 million text messages a day, a higher rate than in the United States.

8. Announced November 11, 2007, http://news.vzw.com/news/2007/11/ pr2007-11-27.html, accessed December 3, 2007.

9. ABI Research, December 2006.

10. Interview with Mike Baker, CEO, Enpocket (now Nokia), June 2007.

11. Interview with Larry Shapiro, Vice President, Disney, May 2007.

12. Interview with Scott Ferris, Senior Vice President and General Manager, Atlas, a division of aQuantive (now Microsoft), August 2007.

13. Pierz Group, "The Directory Assistance/Enquiry Market: A Global Forecast 2005–2010" (April 2005).

14. Greg Sterling, "Text Messaging: Where the Volumes and Dollars Are Today," *Sterling Market Intelligence* (February 2007).

15. Pierz Group, 2006 data.

7

Case Studies from around the World

We have covered a lot of ground in the preceding six chapters. From the basics of defining mobile advertising to taking a deeper look into the market, business models, companies, and value chains, we have provided a breadth of perspective. We have tried to include examples and case studies of innovative business models, companies, and campaigns from around the world. In this chapter, we delve deeper into some of the case studies to show what works, what's coming, and what's unique in the emerging world of mobile advertising.

In addition to discussing mobile campaigns, we look at unique value propositions, business models, and geographic intricacies. We discuss the following case studies:

- User experience: Zumobi
- On-premise solutions: Enpocket and Feeva
- Off-deck advertising: AdMob
- Voice: Bevocal and Vodacom
- Measuring the impact: Lenovo
- Complementing other mediums: HipCricket
- Mobile advertising in the fast-growing markets: China and India
- Local search using location: NearbyNow
- Code-based advertising: Northwest Airlines
- Mobile video: Rhythm New Media
- Bluetooth-based advertising: Bluecasting
- Advertising based on near field communications (NFC): NTT DoCoMo

- Grocery store advertising: Modiv Media
- The new currency: *FREE*
- Idle screen advertising: Mobile Posse
- B2B mobile advertising: Vodafone
- Other noteworthy campaigns

USER EXPERIENCE: *ZUMOBI*

As discussed throughout the book, the user experience matters a great deal on mobile, especially when it comes to advertising. Start-ups such as Zumobi are taking a fresh perspective on the user experience as it relates to mobile advertisements. TV programs are bookends to commercials, they need to entertain to attract an audience and hence have a shot at becoming useful to the advertisers. This is why shows like *American Idol* can cost on average about $340,000 for a 30-second spot,[1] whereas shows like *Big Day*[2] on ABC barely register anything. Shows need to become destinations with a buzz factor to keep the viewers engaged for the long haul. Similarly, on mobile (or for that matter online), sites need to adhere to some basic principles—be wickedly entertaining, be engaging and easy to use, as viral as 1-2-, and continuously bring fresh content while maintaining a high degree of discipline for quality.

Addressing a group of industry executives, Kathy Riordan, VP of Kraft Foods, said "On mobile, it is more important as to what are you going to *DO* for that mobile consumer; not what you are going to *SAY* to them."[3] Zumobi has this principle at the core of its DNA.[4] Born out of Microsoft Research, the user interface of the technology is compelling and makes the navigation from one piece of content to another fairly easy and fun to use. The industry pays lip service to user experience, but like Apple, Zumobi gets it. From its point of view, content is arranged into tiles that are personal miniportals of content, sites, and information that people want quick access to all the time. The design is around making things simple for the user. Around 90 percent of the content is cached and the user goes to the server only 10 percent of the time, making the transition from one screen to another snappy. The underlying technology and design was developed from the very beginning to embrace the way people really want to use their mobile devices, not simply to port the PC experience to them.

The application is FREE; each tile has some advertisements interlaced with the content, based on the user's profile and tile history (Figure 7.1). These ads are downloaded in advance, and since users get value out of the experience, they don't mind ads. Another key design decision was to mark the content space and advertisement space, so that user is unconsciously aware of the differences. All the ads appear at the bottom. Many brands have been fearful of jumping into mobile because of the risk of bad user experience. Mobile can be a magnifying glass if something goes wrong, and top brands don't want to be associated with bad user experience. They like what they see in Zumobi: a simple, but great mobile user experience. Many big digital and Internet brands have jumped at the opportunity to create a user experience that combines content, information, and advertisements. Companies like ABC News, Amazon, Nike, and others are looking to launch tiles and campaigns around Zumobi technology.

From a business model perspective, the company is simultaneously pursuing the operator, the developer, and brands and agencies routes. The company has made their software development kit (SDK) available to help developers build

Figure 7.1   Zumobi tiles.
Source: Zumobi.

tiles. It offers partners monetization frameworks crafted to provide a positive brand and product experience for all in the value chain. The advertising revenue is shared with the developers. For commerce and retailer tiles, Zumobi gets a cut of the transaction. Each tile has a send, personalize, and feedback (virtual) button—and that feature makes it powerful. It allows even a student working in a dorm to create something compelling and reap the benefits from the application's viral nature.

Zumobi or companies like them are approaching mobile and advertising from a different angle, bringing a fresh perspective to the challenge and opportunity of mobile advertising. In the short term, however, they face the challenge of reach and getting deployed on handsets. Over the long term, when devices and networks are more open, we won't even be considering such issues.

ON-PREMISE SOLUTIONS: *ENPOCKET* AND *FEEVA*

In contrast to off-deck solutions like AdMob (case study later in the chapter) or hosted solutions from companies like Third Screen Media (now part of AOL), on-premise solutions are tightly integrated with the operator infrastructure. The solutions can take advantage of the user profile and segmentation gold mine that the operator has and be able to deliver highly targeted ads. While CPMs off-deck are worth a few cents, targeted ads can yield from $60 to $80 CPMs (though this is not sustainable long-term as discussed in Chapter 6). The CTRs are high and the relevancy of ads is better than off-deck placements that are completely random in the first round. In this section, we discuss Enpocket (acquired by Nuance) and Feeva—both of them unique but tightly integrated with operators to extract value from the network and use it for advertising.

Enpocket, probably the first firm in the United States that implemented banner ads with an operator, launched the initiative with Sprint Nextel, the third largest provider in the country. The company has embraced the on-premise services model.

Sprint wanted to increase purchases of mobile media, including ring tones, wallpaper, and music downloads among their actively downloading base, while taking advantage of the reach, power, and profiling capabilities of mobile marketing. The objectives of the campaign were twofold: Increase the conversion rates, and increase downloads of premium media.

Sprint launched the Sprint Predictive Analytics trial in July 2006, using the Enpocket Predictive Engine to accurately provide users with the most relevant content recommendations. Approximately 2 million users received a TXT message with targeted recommendations, while the control group, of approximately 1 million, received a TXT message with random recommendations. Users that had previously purchased mobile content would receive a free TXT recommending an item that, based on their purchase history, would be received favorably.

Sprint routinely achieved a 400 percent increase in conversion rates over the course of the trial, resulting in approximately 345,000 purchases over the course of the campaign. The metrics of the Sprint Predictive Analytics campaign dwarfed the control group during the trial. Those users who received messages from the Enpocket Predictive Engine generated a far superior response: Their click-through rate was nearly 2 percent higher, the conversion rate was more than four times higher, the opt-out rate was 1 percent lower, and there were more than three times as many purchases (see Table 7.1).

Feeva has a different angle in the advertising space. They are neither an ad network nor an advertising technology provider but their technology helps the whole value chain—the operators, the technology providers, and the ad networks. Their value

Table 7.1   Results from Sprint's Advertising Campaign Test

	Sprint Predictive Group	Control
CTR	7.44 percent	5.64 percent
Conversion rate	1.22 percent	0.289 percent
Number of purchases	345,150	98,339
Opt-out rate	2.24 percent	3.26 percent

Source: Enpocket.

is on-premise *real-time segmentation* of user population per session and the information that is delivered at runtime.

They first focus on the broadband network operators though their model and technology are access-agnostic. It relies on the user profile and segmentation information that the operator has and turns it into an abstracted useful signal for the ad network, which in turn can take the input to serve a targeted advertisement instead of a generic impression on a given web site.

Feeva's technology extracts information that is normally dormant in an Internet access network and converts it into real-time data to improve the reach and effectiveness of online advertising. This turns any IP telecom network (mobile, broadband, IPTV, WiFi/WiMAX) into a valuable advertising channel. Instead of becoming the "dumb pipe," it uses the goldmine it has to abstract value elements from operator network assets and turn them into a value-add to the ecosystem while driving incremental revenue. The revenue comes from usage of the network, not directly from the users. The implementation is based on an open architecture, delivering real-time targeting information in tags to all publishers, search engines, and advertising networks accessed by all the users on the operator's IP network.

The architecture is designed so that no personally identifiable information is ever used, and yet the real-time (techno-, geo- and demographic) data is more effective than conventional targeting technologies. This benefits both operators and advertisers, and generates incremental revenues for network operators from their existing assets, by selling online advertising networks reliable and accurate real-time market segmentation and media metrics.

OFF-DECK ADVERTISING: *ADMOB*

In 2006, following on Google's footstep, AdMob set out to become the world's largest mobile advertising marketplace. It focused on the vast underutilized WAP "off-deck" marketplace. While operators were trying to figure out the space, in a matter of months, they amassed so much momentum that on their one-year anniversary in 2007, they had already served 1 billion ads, the next billion took less than three months, the third less than six weeks, the fourth in less than four weeks, and onto when they will be serving a billion and some ads every hour. While the rest of the industry was debating, moaning, and huffing, a relatively young company already proved the viability of the mobile advertising model. And this was when they had 10 percent to 20 percent of their ad inventory unsold.

AdMob allows advertisers to reach their customers on the mobile Web and publishers to increase the value of their mobile sites. AdMob offers both advertisers and publishers the ability to target and personalize advertising to their customers in 165 countries.

AdMob is a mobile advertising marketplace bringing together buyers and sellers of mobile ads. Publishers place some code into their mobile web pages, and AdMob serves pay-per-click advertising directly to their users. For publishing partners, the revenue split is 75/25 in the partner's favor. For ad source partners, the split is 60/40 in favor of the partner. AdMob offers pay-per-click advertising on high quality, highly trafficked mobile web sites. Its personalization engine allows personalizing ads for each user based on their device, which makes it more likely that a user will click on the ad. The link can refer to the seller's own mobile site, or to AdMob's MobPages to promote products and services to customers. Publishing partners serve AdMob ads exclusively on their mobile sites. They are also required to provide links from their web site back to AdMob for interested advertisers.

Adsource partners source ads from AdMob but do not necessarily use AdMob ads exclusively. They may also source ads from other services or via their own direct ad salesforce. They are not required to direct advertisers back to AdMob. AdMob is based on a bidding system, so prices will vary from site to site and are in the range on $0.05 to $1.00.

Although most of the ads are published by relatively unknown publishers and companies, a good majority of the brands that want reach are embracing the off-deck model. Though the operators might argue the value of on-deck impression, from a reach perspective, there is just no match. While an on-deck impression can be highly personalized, that advantage might be short lived; for brands such as Coca-Cola, Adidas, and others who want to reach global audience with minimum friction, off-deck will be the solution. Imagine, trying to cobble together an on-deck campaign across 165 countries, practically impossible today.

Coca-Cola wanted to leverage web video assets for a global mobile ad. The intent of this campaign is for Coke to reach its audience by offering entertaining videos on their mobile phones. Further, the campaign has a strong viral component, as the consumer can easily share these videos with their friends. The campaign uses the AdMob platform to target video-capable phones, and places text and banner ads on those phones. A consumer who responds by clicking on the ad is brought to a Coca-Cola landing page (shown in Figure 7.2). On the landing page, they are offered the chance to view one of the "Bottle Film" short videos. These videos have been used previously in Coke's online ads, but this is the first time they are available on mobile. It is also

Figure 7.2   AdMob's Coca-Cola campaign.
Source: AdMob.

possible to download the video to their phone so they can watch it again later or show it to a friend without additional download time or charges. Finally, the truly viral part is that they can directly share the video with their friends by sending it via MMS.

According to AdMob, Coca-Cola reached users in 125 countries with 1.3 percent CTR and a 130 percent ratio of plays to clicks. Stats like this would be impossible to achieve in an operator environment. However, not all is good with off-deck mobile advertising. There is really no or little control over where the impression is being shown (Would Coca-Cola care if the impression is on a site with really objectionable content?); these impressions are heavily skewed toward Third-World countries where the value of the impression is lower than say in the United States or Western Europe.

Despite the shortcomings, the off-deck business of AdMob proved the attractiveness of the medium. In 2007, Medio Systems and Millennial Media introduced their off-deck solutions and the GYM (Google, Yahoo, Microsoft) brigade also started making inroads into this area.

Voice Solutions: *Bevocal* and *Vodacom*

People often forget that voice drives data usage both before and after the call. Some innovative companies have used the messaging or data traffic pre- or postcall to introduce ads with the data traffic.

Bevocal (acquired by Nuance in 2007) provides voice solutions to operators and have been using the customer service calls as a vehicle for providing relevant targeting. When customers call for any care-related query and are on hold, they are presented with offers related to content and rate plans:

> *By the way, we have a cool new Ringtones application where you can get the latest ring tones for your phone, would you like to hear more?*

or

*By the way, have you been doing a lot of surfing the Web
from your phone? You might be able to save some money
with one of our data packages. Would you like to hear more
about them?*

or

*I also wanted to let you know that you might be able to
save some money on phone calls if you switch to our <rate
plan> plan. With this plan, you'll also be able to check out
our feature packages in the <voice store>, for savings on
messaging, mobile-web, and night and weekend minutes.
Would you like to hear more about the <rate plan>?*

About 18 to 20 percent (up to 25 to 30 percent for rate plan
upgrades) of the users respond by saying yes to the offer. After
that, users are played a longer description of the offer along
with the costs and other information. About 14 to 16 percent
of the users who say yes to the offer go ahead and accept the
offer.[5] Offers work best before the main menu and after successful completion of a task such as checking account balance.
This response rate is several times higher than for other media
and indicates that if done right, it can yield significant benefit
for the advertisers.

Please Call Me is a service that a leading South African
operator Vodacom is running that makes an innovative use
of mobile advertising. It is designed to allow low-income
users to initiate calls without paying for them. The user
opens a USSD (unstructured supplementary service data)
session that sends a TXT message to the person they want
to call (users can send up to five messages a day). The service is open to both prepaid and contract subscribers. They
are not charged and the person is then able to call them
back. Vodacom attaches a 100-character advertising tag to
each TXT message that is sent—the service generates over
17 million messages a day.

Measuring the Impact: *Lenovo*

Lenovo launched what was probably the first U.S. Mobile WAP marketing campaign where measurement was a key focus area, and it was one of the first mobile marketing campaigns to test and measure branding impact. The campaign was successful at building awareness and purchase intent.

As shown in Figure 7.3, the campaign was fairly simple— a banner appeared on mobile web sites like *USA Today*; click-through took users to a WAP landing page where they could enter their contact information. The results were revealing (Figure 7.4): There was a 188 percent lift in brand awareness, 156 percent lift in product recall, and a 487 percent lift in awareness from the WAP landing page. The secondary and tertiary success indicators were 6.6 percent click-through, over two times better than the industry average. The goal of the campaign was to have the exposed audience shift the association of ThinkPad from IBM to Lenovo. Lifts in brand and product attributes were also witnessed, along with increases in purchase intent as a result of exposure to mobile advertising.

Complementing other Mediums: *HipCricket*

As discussed throughout the book, mobile makes other media digital and interactive and enhances the return on investment (ROI). In this section, we discuss mobile in parallel

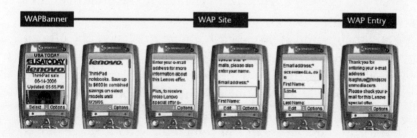

Figure 7.3 Lenovo's WAP campaign.
Source: Ogilvy.

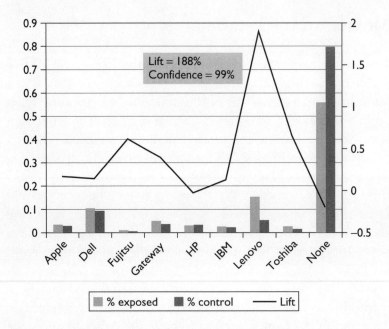

Figure 7.4   Lenovo's WAP campaign run by Ogilvy—Aided brand recall.
Source: Ogilvy, numbers from Third Screen Media.

with radio and TV advertising. Mobile enhances the ROI of campaigns running on other mediums.

HipCricket, a mobile marketing firm, ran a radio campaign for McDonald's in Seattle, where listeners of the local radio station KUBE-FM Seattle were prompted to text "QPC" to 97373 and receive a free offer to their mobile phone. In addition, all listeners opted into the station's mobile phone database received a push message telling them about the offer and the keyword to send to receive the offer over their phone. Consumer-listeners took that offer into their local McDonald's and showed their phone to receive the offer. It was a "one-day, buy-one, get one free" offer only good for the date stamped on the mobile coupon and was designed to push traffic and test mobile coupon redemption. Over 2,200 listeners texted in for the mobile offer in less than 24 hours. Based on the success of the campaign, McDonald's moved from one-day only advertisement spots to book campaigns twice a month for a year.

MOBILE ADVERTISING IN THE FAST-GROWING MARKETS: *CHINA* AND *INDIA*

As discussed, China and India will account for a majority of new subscribers in the next five years. Mobile will be the only way advertisers can touch most of these subscribers. Incumbent operators in these countries as well as the Internet brands are gunning for this market with hopes of big revenue streams down the line.

China

While the mobile data markets of China and India are still are just heating up, both markets have been active in mobile advertising. Some of the most innovative mobile campaigns have come from these two countries.

To promote the BMW 3 Series, 21 Communications launched an innovative mobile campaign. The goal was to offer BMW video ads and other branded content downloads through the mobile phone channel (wallpapers, text, video, and music) and to prompt customers to schedule test drives of the new 3 Series.

BMW banner ads and text links appear on China Mobile's Monternet and other portals that customers visit on their mobile phones (Figure 7.5). When customers click on the banners, they are transferred to the BMW branded 3 Series mobile site. Within the site, a Visualizer tool enables campaign participants to customize their favorite 3 Series with preferred colors and features right on their mobile phone. Customers can use the Click-to-Call feature to easily connect to the BMW call center for test drive appointment scheduling. The campaign resulted in over 500,000 unique visitors during the two-month campaign, 50,000 branded downloads, and over 2 million page views of the BMW mobile site.

Similar campaigns by 21 Communications for Adidas during Soccer World Cup and for GE during the 2006 Turin Winter Olympics reached over 500,000 users. Johnson & Johnson Vision Care ran various modes of mobile advertising

Figure 7.5   (a) BMW campaign; (b) China Mobile Portal advertising.
Source: 21 Communications.

that included a mobile coupon (getting a free trial part for Forte lenses) and user-generated content. In the first quarter of 2007, Coca-Cola extended its partnership with 21 Communications to include mobile video, mobile coupons, and branded content in its mobile campaigns and specifically get ready for the 2008 Beijing Olympics.

Sprite China launched a new music-via-mobile initiative that includes a joint promotion with McDonald's. The "Music in Every Sprite Bottle" campaign offers consumers free music content and other virtual products via the Sprite WAP site, wap.sprite.sohu.com. Pin codes printed on the underside of Sprite bottle caps can be keyed into the WAP site to allow consumers access to MP3s, ring tones, photos of celebrities, entertainment news, blogs, forums, and updates on the Sprite My Show talent show.

The community-oriented site features prominent interactive elements, including areas for user-generated content that may in the future include video. Sprite has worked with Internet portal Sohu, digital media planning agency Isobar, and mobile advertising agency 21 Communications on the China campaign. McDonald's, which is also going after a youth demographic through music, saw a natural fit with the promotion. They advertised the program on the back of its menus and at the counters of its restaurants across the country. Also, when diners purchase a McDonald's extra-value meal, they receive a scratch card with a pin code that allows them access to the WAP site. In a later stage of the promotion period, users received discounts for McDonald's meals via Mcoupons available on the WAP site. The coupons can then be redeemed with their mobile phones at McDonald's cashiers.

An advantage of the WAP drive is that it is very trackable. Every action at the site confirms a Sprite or McDonald's purchase, and consumer activity on the site can be monitored. Realizing the lucrative proposition, China Mobile and China Unicom, the two telecom giants have been running WAP ads for sometime with both banner ads and title ads in the mix.

India

As discussed, Indian wireless market has been booming since 2006 and will continue its unprecedented growth until 2011 or 2012. However, the ARPU levels remain at under $10 making it a tough market for mobile data services. TXT messaging services are practically free, so operators have long used TXT messaging to concatenate advertisements to the message. Brands have been actively testing the mobile media as well and for a lot of the campaigns, mobile is an integral part of the advertising campaign.

Reliance Infocomm is the leading operator in India and has been breaking new ground since its inception.

Figure 7.6   Cadbury campaign on Reliance Infocomm portal R-World.
Source: Reliance Infocomm.

Mobile advertising is no different. It has been active with several campaigns across both WAP and TXT. The campaign for Cadbury's chocolate shows the scale of the opportunity for mobile advertising in India (Figure 7.6). Exam results of various competitions and classes are a social event in India. Families and students look forward to the day when results are posted, and they rush to find out their scores and celebrate. Superior grades bring cheer and an occasion to distribute sweets. Tapping into that psyche, Cadbury's partnered with Reliance to become associated with the ExamResults application. Subscribers were shown an ad imprint before they checked the results, and if they succeeded, they were shown a congratulatory message. For one season alone, over 17 million users checked the results, which resulted in over 32 million ad imprints (the pass rate was 86 percent). U.S. advertisers would kill for these numbers, especially associated with joy, celebration, and social mingling. This campaign won the prestigious Cannes Lions 2006 award for Media Innovation and New Concept (see also Mahesh Prasad's opinion piece in Chapter 10).

There are also middleware companies and start-ups that have pyramid schemes (Figure 7.7) based on TXT mobile marketing. One such company is mGinger, which gives 20 paisa for every ad a user receives, 10 paisa for every ad

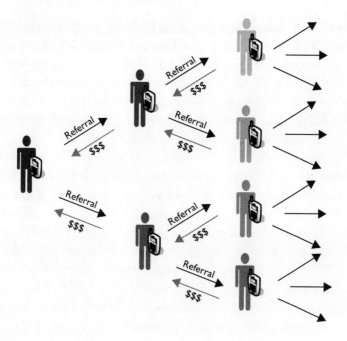

Figure 7.7   TXT advertising pyramid scheme.

the person's friend receives, 5 paisa for every ad the friend's friends receive—a user can accumulate Rs. 300 (approximately $7). The user has to register with some profile information that helps target the ads. Users can select the maximum number of ads in a given day with the default being 10.

Because of strong pressure on data ARPU (and ARPU in general), there is a strong market for mobile advertising; operators, however, are not well prepared to mine the opportunity with outdated backend systems. So, sophisticated targeting capability won't be available for sometime. Meanwhile, strong brands are eager to launch TXT and WAP mobile advertising campaigns.

Local Search Using Location: *NearbyNow*

In-store commerce is over half a trillion dollars in value in the United States, several times more than online, but not many solution providers have tried to bridge the gap between online and in-store. NearbyNow[6] provides technology and online marketing services to retailers and shopping centers, helping drive sales by converting online shoppers to in-store buyers. They use the poor man's version of location-based services driven by declaration of user intent. This way they didn't have to deal with the operators or limit their service to GPS-enabled phones.

Initially set up to drive traffic and sales to the malls, the effectiveness of the campaigns is in its simplicity. One by one, the company has collected the inventory for the malls (600K to 800K items in each mall) at the national and store level. For items that are on sale or need to be cleared or are part of a new test drive or promotion, mall goers are invited to TXT to "nearby" with a two-letter mall code (SF for San Francisco) for sales information. Shoppers then get a welcome message with a list of sales in progress and a request that users enter the brand or product they are seeking. In return, they get the list of stores with the said items including pricing and relevant sales information. For example, one could search for "Jeans" or "Levi's 509s" and get relevant results. Users might get a second ad saying, "Shoe sale at Macy's," which is a paid advertisement but the match is perfect for the user and for the advertiser.

Since TXT is the most common denominator across all handsets with almost all of the younger mall-going demographics using it, the interactivity has been remarkable. The response to special offers such as "free movie tickets" or "$25 gift cards for the first 10 buyers" can literally start a stampede indicating the power of mobile, interactivity, and context. NearbyNow has found that if they send two additional TXT messages per hour and make the ads contextual, users find the service useful instead of considering it spam. The real power is in the declaration of intent. By searching online or TXTing to get more information on the mall sales, 70 percent of the users end up in the mall within 48 hours having declared an intent to purchase as well as the mall they are going to visit.

The analytics from such a service are terrific. In real time, one can assess how many people are looking for shoes,

computers, and other items and retailers can tailor their offers
accordingly. Within the mall, approximately 7 to 10 percent
of the visitors use the service; this response is greater than
any other advertising medium. By end of 2007, NearbyNow
covered over 200 malls, and by 2008, the company is planning to cover 80 percent of the malls (approximately 600
malls). Did you know that the 25- to 45-year-old female age
group accounts for only 18 percent of the foot traffic but
55 percent of dollars spent? Over 33 percent of users are in
the 15- to 22-year age group, and they TXT seven to eight
queries on average versus two to three for the overall population. Did you know that usage of iPhone is higher in the
malls compared with other devices?

Retailers have a dashboard getting a real-time view into
what's going on right-now. As of 2007, this was still a batch
process done typically on a weekly basis but going forward,
this could be turned into a real-time shopper-traffic control
mechanism to drive sales and inventory. A cosmetic retailer
launched a new product in mid-2007 that they thought would
be a hit but during the first two weeks they knew something was wrong because the sales weren't picking up. They
launched a 2-for-1 promotion with NearbyNow, sending
an ad to consumers who were looking for beauty and cos-
metics products or women's apparel, and the reaction was
immediate—there was an 8 percent surge in sales. The campaign drove new customers in addition to regular loyal customers. In such campaigns, coupons also get forwarded onto
friends kicking the redemption rates by several percentage
points. Compare this with a coupon that prints in a newspaper read by 100,000 customers locally. The retailer has no idea
how many people read the paper; how many saw the ad; of the
people who saw the ad, how many were the target audience;
and of the target audience who read the ad, how many of them
will come to the mall to purchase This adds up to absolutely
zero accountability for the promotion, yet 40 to 50 people are
involved in it and a goodly amount of dollars are being spent.
Complementing or replacing such outdated methodologies
with mobile and online will drive more targeted users to the

stores, thus eliminating waste. Additionally, with digital, there is measurability and accountability for everything you do.

One of the future applications for NearbyNow is graphical navigational maps for mall directories that are cumbersome to read. People asking for directions or store information will be shown directions and a map also highlighting stores that have sales on items of interest. If you can control these dynamics in real time, it is nirvana for the retailers.

CODE-BASED ADVERTISING: NORTHWEST AIRLINES

Two-dimensional bar codes (QR codes) have grown in popularity in Japan and South Korea over the past year, showing up as thumbnails on magazine and newspaper ads. They work as a quick, automatic link between print and online media that don't require the customer to type in an Internet address or remember a special code. Looking at Tokyo provides a glimpse of what is in store for other cities around the world. The trend is that almost any object, machine, or advertising space can be reacted to and be a prompt to the consumer. Half of i-mode users use QR codes in Japan.

Northwest Airlines' QR code advertising campaigns (see Figure 7.8), seen in the streets and subways of Tokyo, tap into this future usage. In a city where new visions of tomorrow

Figure 7.8   Northwest's QR code campaign.

are unwrapped as eagerly as children unwrapping candy, it takes a lot to make a Tokyoite take notice and think. But the campaign achieved this by using QR codes in a way they had never been used before. Tests were taken from multiple angles and varying distances to a full-size outdoor billboard. The QR codes worked even when the ads were 10 meters (33 feet) high and viewed from across the road. With the technology already installed in people's phones, just waiting to be used, it was then a matter of getting the creative brief underway to develop an effective promotion that would draw in tech savvy Japanese consumers to interact with the world's largest QR.

Headlines on the mammoth QR code billboards enticed consumers to engage in an interactive "Guess the name of the city" quiz written in the style of Japanese senryu poems. The answers are all cities in the United States and Asia that Northwest Airlines flies to, North America being the biggest market for Japanese travelers. Prizes include e-coupons that count toward discounted fares and WorldPerks Bonus Miles. A further twist to the campaign allows consumers to

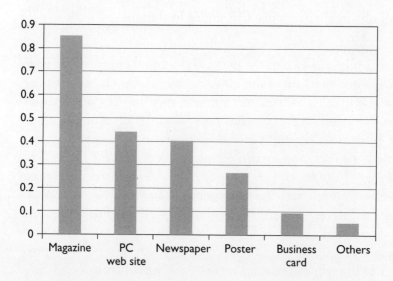

Figure 7.9   Percentage of users in Japan using QR codes from various mediums.
Source: Video Research, Japan, Mobile 2007 edition.

submit their own senryu poem about travel to the United States on Northwest Airlines. The best of these appear on the site, and people can vote for their favorites, bringing customers back to the NWA site time and time again. Poems can be submitted using the kanji ideograms (picture characters) found on the keyboards of Japanese mobile phones.

As mentioned, mobile makes other mediums interactive. In a survey done by Video Research, Japan reported in the Mobile 2007 edition, 83.6 percent of the consumers had accessed the mobile site from the QR code in other media (Figure 7.9).

MOBILE VIDEO: *RHYTHM NEW MEDIA*

In a survey done by Telephia in the first quarter of 2007,[7] data showed that mobile video audiences are primed for seeing ads on their phones. Video consumers had the highest recall of viewing ads on their phones compared with all data service consumers, with 55 percent saying they recalled viewing a mobile ad in the past 30 days (in comparison, TXT was 20 percent, while mobile Internet users scored 34 percent in the survey.

Mobile video clearly provides a much more lush user experience than some the other mobile channels. One of the first companies to exploit this new medium for advertising was Rhythm New Media (see also Ujjal Kohli's opinion piece in Chapter 10). Working with operator 3 in the United Kingdom, they introduced advertising for their "free category" content. The service was "zero-rated" meaning no charge for data, the customers didn't need a data plan, and the pay-as-you go customers were allowed to access the service when their credit ran out. The mobile video advertisements were in the form of small clips preroll and postroll of the content snack videos (for content from ITN, *Fifth Gear, The Apprentice,* etc.) as they called them, which were three to five minutes in length. Launched in March 2007, the service was successful. Within six months, they crossed the 1 million subscribers mark,[8] which was approximately 25 percent of their user base. Viewers watched three videos per day on average. The peak viewing times were around the morning commute (7:00 AM to 9:00 AM) and the late evening (8:00 PM to 11:00 PM), and the service is most popular among 25- to 34-year-old males and 18- to 24-year-old females. Most popular content types were breaking news and weather followed by horoscopes and movies.

The spontaneous ad recall rate was 17 percent with a 67 percent total ad message recall rate. Within the first three months, over 7.5 million streams were served. Frequency management allowed Rhythm to tune the number of times ads were shown to individual users very granularly.[9]

Rhythm also introduced a survey feature within the Electronic Programming Guide (EPG) where users could take surveys of the campaigns (Figure 7.10). Remarkably, within two to three days, the numbers of users needed to do a full demographics analysis capped out. Not only could the advertisers get more details (compared with regular TV campaigns) about their campaigns on mobile but they also get instant feedback from the users who actively participated even when no incentives were provided. Success of this offering prompted 3 to move some of their premium content offerings to this ad-funded service. Rhythm introduced another platform feature called "Companion Advertising" where brand

Figure 7.10   Rhythm's EPG survey.
Source: Rhythm New Media.

advertising and transactional advertising work hand in hand to maximize ROI for the advertiser. For example, if a user sees a brand advertisement for a movie in a video application when they are browsing on a portal or completing a survey on the EPG guide, they might be served with a discount coupon for the same movie, thus increasing the probability of click-through and ultimately doing a financial transaction.

Specifically, in May 2007, Lynx for Men, the Unilever men's deodorant, launched a new advertising campaign designed to increase awareness of the brand and to differentiate its products for men. Mobile advertising formed a part of this marketing campaign designed to communicate with Lynx's target customers in new channels previously unused by the brand. To reach the target market, the Lynx campaign used video ads on the Free Stuff video content area on mobile operator 3UK's Planet 3 portal. These video ads were placed with Rhythm's ad network using the media buying agency Mindshare. Looking at the results, the company found that there was 13 percent spontaneous awareness and 56 percent awareness of the brand. The correct brand message recall was 86 percent and 44 percent of the users felt more positive about the brand after seeing the advertisement.

An interesting finding from this offering was that brand advertisers were primarily interested in demographics-based targeting though other forms of targeting capability was available. Demographics targeting gave them enough to move R&D dollars to campaign dollars using this new vehicle. The brands that participated included Microsoft.

Also, one of the advantages of on-deck offering is that operators can truly offer zero-rated or completely free services that are fully subsidized. Off-deck offerings still incur data charge and require data plans. In the long-run, operators are likely to abstract this functionality and make it available to the ecosystem with internal mechanics in place to account for the cost of data delivery.

Similarly, high-fidelity mobile broadcast video and TV applications will offer a rich environment for both the consumers as well as the advertisers though we are a long way from having such services become mainstream.

BLUETOOTH-BASED ADVERTISING: *BLUECASTING*

Bluetooth and infrared are cheaper versions of location-based advertising that marketers and brands can use to distribute mobile content. Bluecasting, a company based out of the United Kingdom has been pioneering several campaigns for major brands around the world. Its kiosks are becoming an attractive option to marketers within retail environments and public spaces like airports.

Instead of the user noticing the ad, the ad notices the user, and the relevant content is pushed to the user's device. The types of file supported are txt, gif, jpg, animated gif, wav, rmf, mp3, mp4, ring tones, rm, 3gp, mp4, jar, vcard, and others.

As shown in Figure 7.11, the idea of Bluetooth advertising is to educate or invite the user to open up their Bluetooth connection to receive content. This campaign for Land Rover,[10] was a minidocumentary with a stunt, behind the scenes clips, and interviews to the phone for users around Times Square in New York City. Bluecasting has run campaigns for great brands such as Coca-Cola, Audi, BMW, Apple, Motorola, Canon, BBC, Harrods, Nokia, Volvo, Virgin Mobile, Sony BMG, UBS, IBM, Microsoft, and Samsung. Cisco extended its famous TelePresence marketing campaign using Bluetooth. With the phrase "Welcome to the Human Network," Cisco Systems is engaging the passengers at Pearson International Airport in Toronto. Working with OgilvyOne, Cisco's advertising agency in Toronto, and Clear Channel Outdoor Canada, three different videos were beamed to the users, each one telling part of the Human Network story.

Samsung used Bluecasting to spread the word to thousands of consumers in New York's Times Square as part of

Figure 7.11   Land Rover's billboard ad fitted with Bluecasting.
Source: Filter Worldwide, 2007.

the U.S. launch of the new high-definition Blu-ray video format. IBM used the solution to send latest scores, XML feed, and animated content to the visitors during Wimbledon. BMW used the technology to push promotional videos of BMW Z4 Coupe with thousands of downloads per week.

However, not all is good with Bluetooth advertising. In addition to the device challenges, security issues, and paranoid operators, it can also be problematic to broadcast information to a large audience. Microsoft experienced this problem first-hand at the TechEd 2007 conference when hordes of users tried to download content all at once bringing the system to its knees. With interference and congestion, the speed might get worse than a dial-up, so make sure that the system is con-figured to handle peak loads.

Also, for Bluetooth the file transfer protocol (FTP) fea-ture must be installed on the device. Some U.S. operators have intentionally omitted that Bluetooth profile on their handsets. Also, it requires some knowledge of how to use Bluetooth (turn the device to discoverable). All these factors limit the addressable market for a Bluetooth-enabled campaign. Meanwhile, infrared delivery is slow and less reliable. In addition, there is a significant privacy issue. Bluetooth-based advertising should be opt-in and not blind-push to devices in the vicinity. Without permission, such campaigns will be considered spam and are unlikely to succeed.

ADVERTISING BASED ON NEAR FIELD COMMUNICATIONS (NFC): *NTT DoCoMo*

NTT DoCoMo has been trailblazing new applications and services using mobile devices since the introduction of i-mode in the late 1990s. In September 2005, NTT DoCoMo, Inc., and its eight regional subsidiaries announced plans to offer an information-capture function, called *ToruCa* in the *Osaifu-Keitai*. [11] DoCoMo's Osaifu-Keitai platform for mobile wallet services has taken Japan by storm in less than three years. Now a major offering from the company, Osaifu-Keitai turns DoCoMo phones into powerfully convenient tools for payment applications and services that build on the i-mode mobile Internet platform. ToruCa will enable users to obtain information by simply waving their phones in front of dedicated reader/writers installed at restaurants, theaters, music stores, arcades, and other establishments. When users buy a CD at a store using the Osaifu-Keitai, they can simply wave their DoCoMo phone in front of the store's reader/writer to retrieve extra information about the CD, the artist, and possibly a promotional coupon offered by the artist's recording label.

The ToruCa service enables users to capture information into their mobile phone with ease, using the mobile phone's various interfaces (FeliCa, Mailer, Infrared, etc.). With the captured information, users can perform an in-phone search, manage contents simply and easily with the sort function and exchange information hassle free with fellow

Figure 7.12   ToruCa life cycle.
Source: NTT DoCoMo.

ToruCa-compatible mobile phones. Also, by pushing the
"details button," users can capture even more detailed information (see Figure 7.12).

As discussed in our five-points framework for mobile
advertising, viral functionality is critical for any mobile advertising strategy and campaign. ToruCa has this in built into the
system. Any coupon or information captured via ToruCa can
be easily sent to other friends in the community via Infrared,
mail, or memory transfer (see Figure 7.13).

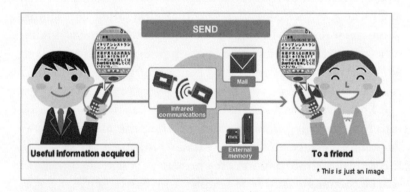

Figure 7.13   Viral capability of ToruCa.
Source: NTT DoCoMo.

To deliver the services to the customers, as well as to manage the promoting campaigns and enhance their customer loyalty, NTT DoCoMo and Japan McDonald's established a joint venture in July 2007. The company invested a capital of JPY 300 million, 70 percent from McDonald's and 30 percent from NTT DoCoMo. By introducing ToruCa, McDonald's will be able to cut production and distribution costs as it will be issuing fewer paper coupons to Japanese customers. Japan McDonald's has approximately 3,800 outlets and it is estimated that 140 million customers purchase its products annually in the Japanese market.

McDonald's issues approximately 30 million paper coupons per promotional campaign in newspapers, leaflets, and so on. In a huge and dynamic market like Japan, this requires a lot of time in terms of preparation and is very costly. For the time being, McDonald's is planning to continue issuing paper coupons and gradually shift to ToruCa.

In addition, with the introduction of iD, a credit card platform developed by NTT DoCoMo, McDonald's will achieve faster payment transactions in its outlets. It is estimated that if the service time can be reduced by 30 seconds, this will increase sales by 5 percent. Therefore, if the use of Osaifu-Keitai (mobile-wallet service) becomes widespread in McDonald's outlets, it will benefit both the company and the customers.

Also, it will enable more effective customer relationship management (CRM). NTT DoCoMo has been aggressively marketing the CRM capabilities of ToruCa as mobile marketing enables a more sophisticated promotion, allowing the companies to market by outlets, products, and different customer groups. For instance, a restaurant located in a building's basement floor, on a rainy day might send messages to the customers located in the building such as, "It's raining! Forgot your umbrella? We are located in the basement floor of C building." Through the partnership with McDonald's, NTT DoCoMo is expecting to increase the users of ToruCa.

It requires a commitment from a large player to invest in the infrastructure directly or through partnerships. NTT DoCoMo partners with nontraditional players like 7-11,

Tower Records, banks, and stores to make sure the infrastructure is there before the devices with specific functionality like ToruCa come into the market. North American and Western European markets typically don't follow that strategy and hence have been behind in implementing mobile payment and NFC-based mobile advertising strategies. In fact, in the United States, it is Visa that pushed for Contactless NFC adoption through a wide range of trials in 2006 and 2007.

The Visa mobile platform is a set of mobile services and enabling technologies that will allow banks and mobile operators to develop new mobile payment services for individual markets. Visa believes that value-added features, such as loyalty applications, ticketing, security alerts, and account management in addition to payment services will create a more compelling consumer experience and therefore better business opportunities for member financial institutions, mobile network operators, merchants, and others.

To enable innovative trials and go-to-market strategies for mobile payment services globally, Visa has been actively fostering collaboration between leading mobile and financial industry partners, including handset, Subscriber Identity Module (SIM) card, device management, mobile messaging, and over-the-air vendors, to develop a mobile platform that has the flexibility to meet the business and technology needs of banks and mobile operators in a variety of markets.

In a recent Visa survey of 800 mobile phone subscribers who also have a debit or credit card, 57 percent said they would be interested in getting a phone with mobile payment capability. Of those who expressed interest, almost 90 percent said they would be willing to pay more for a device that offered mobile payment capability. Almost two-thirds of respondents between 18 and 42 would consider switching wireless service providers if their current provider didn't offer mobile payments. And 58 percent of this group would be prepared to switch card issuers to gain this capability. By a factor of five to one, consumers would prefer to have mobile payment purchases appear on their credit or debit card statement rather than on their wireless bill.[12]

GROCERY STORE ADVERTISING: MODIV MEDIA

Grocery store advertising and marketing is a big business. Companies like Proctor & Gamble (P&G), Unilever, Kellogg, and others. Millions of dollars are spent capturing what P&G calls the "First moment of truth"—the first moment that the customer decides to buy a given product. Consumer brands face such moments of truth millions of times a day. Several factors go into play when a customer decides to pick an item from the aisle to pay at the counter. It could be brand association and loyalty, it could be discounts and coupons, it could be the positioning of the item, perhaps packaging, or maybe a friend's recommendation to try it out. But, like traditional marketing, grocery marketers typically have no way of gaining the complete picture of the consumer. A P&G customer might be buying products for hair care, skin care, baby care, fabric care, and dental care, but it is often hard to link the consumer to these purchases and even if the information on individual purchases is gathered, it remains in silos of the organization that typically don't talk to each other.

Such a situation is ripe for innovation. Grocery chains have been pushing loyalty schemes to track customer purchases for years, but companies like Modiv Media (formerly Cuesol) are planning to change that. They have combined technology and information to create customer-interactive solutions that empower retailers to communicate with consumers on an individual basis and influence in-store purchasing behavior. The Cart Companion application helps customers save money and use their time more efficiently in the store. With functionality that can include targeted marketing at the point of decision, self-scan in the aisle, specialty department ordering from the cart, and personalized location-based coupons, the Cart Companion is designed to increase customer loyalty and basket size, and reduce operational costs. Since the system is location based, the information is delivered to the customers at the time and location where they are ready to make a decision. By offering shoppers personalized location-relevant (location tracking

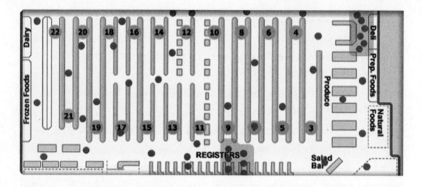

Figure 7.14   Keeping track of grocery carts or devices in the store using Bluetooth.
Source: Modiv Media.

is done based on Bluetooth as depicted in Figure 7.14) offers, retailers benefit from increased basket size. The Cart Companion application also offers retailers a real-time solution for viewing store traffic, flow, and congestion. The Cart Companion technology enables store personnel to monitor and alleviate delays in deli and the front end.

The application can be deployed via a cart-mounted table manufactured by IBM, or via a handheld device. As customers walk through the aisles, they get a personalized marketing message based on their shopping history.[13]

Based on its ability to track every shopping cart through the store, and map purchases with traffic patterns, the system enables retailers to understand and affect consumer shopping behavior. The technology uses infrared location beacons that are installed in the ceiling. The second component is a small tracking device that is attached to each cart. These tracking devices receive location identifications from the beacons and immediately transmit them and cart identification to the system. The server collects the data and initiates or feeds various applications, including:

- *Post hoc analysis:* Linking trip to Point-of-Sale (POS) transaction databased on checkout time, and mapping shopping behavior to purchase behavior, which results

in a better understanding of purchase-behavioral cau-
sality and store layout.

- *Real-time store operations:* Viewing all cart location status in the store, monitoring deli and checkout lines,
forecasting front-end workload, sending alerts for
staffing, and so on.

The same technology could be used to capture so much
of the "state of mind" of the consumer that will impact how
advertising takes place for consumer items. With the advent
of camera phones (and bar code readers in the phones), a
shopper can scan the product or the bar code and get coupons,
additional information on the product, competitive pricing
information, simple surveys that capture "the first moment
of truth,"[14] send information to other sources—devices, lists,
or friends—and so much more. Even with such technical
advances, it is important to provide value to the customer in
return of data gathering.

THE NEW CURRENCY: *FREE*

Since the murmurs of mobile advertising became louder in
2006, several FREE business models have emerged. The
idea is simple, users watch ads; they get rewarded with subsidized and free content. For people looking for reach, the
FREE business model works whether it is downloadables,
free subscription, free messages, free this or free that. A trial
run by Vodafone showed a 60-fold increase in downloads
for free but ad-injected downloadables, 10 times more than
a subsidized piece (price was reduced by 66 percent) of the
same content. In this section, we discuss case studies that
thrive on the FREE business model, which many people
think is where the mobile content industry is going anyway.

Mobile games played an important role in testing this
business model since its inception in the mobile industry.
Companies like Greystripe,[15] Mobilerated.com, Mobile
Vision, and others have focused on putting the ad network

and technology platform in place that allows them to put interstitial ads before and after the game. The ads are richer, typically occupy the whole screen, and are hard to ignore. The more compelling the game, the more people play, and more ads can be served as a result. Sometimes brands like DHL issue completely branded games and content: Users could download the Tetris-like game "Stack-it" that let users shift DHL labeled boxes to fill empty spaces. This was part of DHL's "Customer Service Is Back in Shipping" branding campaign.

One of the mobile campaigns conducted by Coca-Cola in 2006 was related to the launch of its "Happiness Factory" ad campaign, which featured a beautifully animated ad shown in cinemas and on TV. In France, Coca-Cola decided to pre-cede the launch of the mainstream advertising campaign with a mobile campaign, building a dedicated web and WAP site from which mobile users could download a video clip of the ad. Also on offer was other mobile content based on the ad, including wallpaper and a dedicated game. The three-week prelaunch mobile campaign attracted about 60,000 downloads.[16]

Mobile games is not the only category being funded by ads. Mobile TV and video will be primarily funded by advertisements in the future. U.K. operator 3 announced in June 2007 that its ad-funded mobile video service, which went live in April of the same year as the first of its type from a U.K. operator, has already seen over 6 million streams of video content from its customers. The success of the service, which wraps demographically targeted advertising around free-to-view video content, validated the first video ad package of its kind.

Virgin Mobile's Sugar Mama campaign to give airtime for time spent watching ads online was the first such campaign by an operator in North America. Virgin Mobile is a youth-centric MVNO and is always tinkering with innovative programs to keep its customers engaged. The idea for Sugar Mama was relatively simple; consumers can watch ads from prominent brands like Microsoft, P&G, Apple, Pepsi, Sony,

Nintendo, and others. The program was extended to include Qtime where users could fill out surveys about brands, products, or services to get additional minutes and also Textime, an opt-in service to receive exclusive offers and discounts. It was an effective way to leverage the traffic to Virgin Mobile's web site into something fun, engaging, and rewarding for the consumers.

In the first year of operation, an average of 1,000 new customers signed on to participate each day, earning over 9 million minutes of free airtime. Average CTR was 5.5 percent with some of the successful campaigns reaching over 21 percent CTR rates. Further, 33 percent of the users provided additional optional psychographic information.

IDLE SCREEN ADVERTISING: *MOBILE POSSE*

The idle screen is the Holy Grail for advertisers. Instead of waiting for the user to initiate contact, advertisers can push relevant ads and content to the screen that the user is going to see. The idle screen is the prime real estate for providing access, search, discovery, and advertising of mobile services. As active idle screen solutions become a standard feature of most mass-market handsets by around 2009 or 2010, we will see increased focus on capturing the users' attention on the active screen. The concept goes further and picks idle usage time on the phone: When a person is on hold, or when dialing a number, or receiving a call, or downloading content, the real estate can be used to present relevant information (advertisements).

Mobile Posse, a U.S.-based start-up had good success with a 5,000 user trial they ran in 2007.[17] Different pieces of content like weather information and offers/coupons were sent to the phone when it was idle. Consumers found the information useful, and there was a high level of engagement. The click-through rate was 10 percent to 20 percent, even just for informational content like current weather information. The number of consumers who went into the application to

check for the offers was even higher, with a total engagement rate of 40 percent to 45 percent of the base engaging
with the application in one way or another. For offers like
photo printing coupons, the CTR was higher, with redemption rate up to 10 percent (overall redemption varied from
2.5 percent to 10 percent depending on the offer). The surprising finding was that 80 percent of the trial base asked
for more offers a day (which were limited to 4 or 5 during the day), and the satisfaction rate was over 90 percent.
About 84 percent of the users said they were more likely stay
with an operator that offered such a service, and 80 percent
said that they would recommend this service to a friend (see
Figure 7.15).

For the advertisers, the targeting capability was available around demographics (gender, age group), zip code,
and the time of day when they wanted to send the promotion or information to the user. Users have the ability to fill
out their preferences and interests online, which helped in
making targeting better and more contextual. Mobile Posse
takes into account both the implicit and explicit preferences
to target the offers to a given mobile subscriber.

This and other early experiments with idle screen confirms our theory that the value in delivering targeted and
contextual advertisements and information to the idle screen
is an area for great innovation and competition.

Figure 7.15   Idle screen solution by Mobile Posse.
Source: Mobile Posse.

B2B Mobile Advertising: *Vodafone*

In the first quarter of 2007, Vodafone Netherlands introduced a unique variant of mobile advertising. It introduced a service for two segments of the enterprise market—insurance resellers and pharmacists. Users were offered access to free professional content, combined with ads, on their phone. Based on opt-in, the insurance agents receive ads and relevant free content from the Dutch Insurance Network, enabling them to have instant access to relevant content or financial accounting models. The pharmacists will receive ads and free relevant content from a healthy-care publisher. Such a program could easily be extended to other professional groups.

Other Noteworthy Campaigns

We discussed a range of campaigns and business models in this chapter. Table 7.2 lists some other noteworthy campaigns.

As is apparent from the variety of campaigns across the globe, advertisers are using different channels within mobile to interact with traditional media as well as create new creative campaigns to engage the customer. If done right, the resulting engagement is higher than anything we have seen with other mediums. User experience is key to any campaign design. That is what will make campaigns viral. Ease of use and ease of sharing should be key ingredients of any campaign. Permission is key to all push campaigns. Without securing the consent of the user, campaigns fail and are subject to regulatory and legal oversight.

Mobile will be the only digital way to reach many subscribers in developing countries like India and China because these devices are their single most important connection to the world. In fact, some of the most innovative campaigns and business models are coming out from these countries. India launched the first in-application (mobile) advertising in 2003. Companies like Google and Yahoo are keen on

Table 7.2 Other Noteworthy Campaigns

By Country	Service	Operator	Brand	Enabler	Impact
United States	Mobile News Service (gomobile.msnbc. com)	Independent	MSNBC	Action Engine	CTRs were double the Web rates.
					Consumers were using the service to access content in excess of 20 times/user/month on average.
	Promotion of show *Barbarians*	Independent	History Channel	Enpocket	Of those impacted by the *Barbarians* campaign, 40 percent watched the History Channel.
					88 percent read the message, and 12 percent forwarded the message or showed it to a friend.
					58 percent of participants said they were more likely to watch the History Channel as a result of the project.
India	Airtel Live	Airtel	AirFrance, ICICI (bank)	Erpocket	AirFrance offered Summer fares with location-based discounts; generated 32K in 50 hours.
					ICICI—7 percent CTR.
					20 percent of users visited microsite to submit details.
United Kingdom	Raise awareness to hazards of drunk driving among 16- to 25-year-olds	Orange	Zerotracas.com	ScreenTonic	More than 700K ad views in 2 weeks.
					6 percent CTR; traffic increased 10-fold during campaign.

	Service	Operator	Brand	Enabler	Impact
Germany	First House	Independent	Delta Lyod	MADS	5 percent CTR (goal was to drive traffic to mobile site and generate leads).
	Orange Wednesdays: Two-for-one movie ticket	Orange	Orange with advertising partners	Flytxt	6M orange coupons were issued.
Argentina	7UP Sweepstakes	Independent	7UP	Mobile Computing	There were about 200K responses to mobile coupon offer to win an iPOD (10 percent redemption rate).
By Industry	**Service**	**Operator**	**Brand**	**Enabler**	**Impact**
Auto, Electronics, and CP	Samsung Funclub (Engage Samsung phone owners through MMS campaign)	Independent	Samsung	Enpocket	Response rate was 15 percent with conversion rate of 2 percent.
Music and Entertainment	Mobile News Service (gomobile.msnbc.com)	Independent	MSNBC	Action Engine	CTRs were double the web rates. Consumers were using the service to access content in excess of 20 times/user/month on average.
Retail, Apparel, and QSRs	Coca-Cola campaign	Vodafone	Coca-Cola	ScreenTonic	Traffic to Coca-Cola's site "We all speak football" increased by 600+ percent during the campaign (targeted at 12- to 29-year-olds).
Travel	Banner ads	Independent	Embassy Suites	Go2	Five-month campaign generated 55K clicks and $3.2M in revenue.

using mobile as the channel for increasing digital advertisement revenues in these two countries.

New channels such as NFC, barcodes, and mobile video will evolve over time. While they have shown significant traction in Japan and South Korea, the infrastructure elsewhere is just beginning to get deployed.

Operators should look at different business models to structure their role in the ecosystem. Most of the "do-it-alone" efforts have failed; joint ventures and spin-offs have worked in Japan and South Korea, while China and India remain ahead because of investments in content production operations. The business model of FREE is becoming prevalent across various mobile advertising channels—TXT, applications, games, and video.

On-premise deployments provide the potential of leveraging operator's data about the customer. Case studies have consistently shown that when such profile data is used, CTRs jump 10 to 20 times. Off-deck provides significant reach compared with on-deck. While the quality of ads is suboptimal, reach compensates for the lack of profile targeting or measurement capability of such systems. With Internet brands entering into the mix, off-deck advertising will start to resemble on-deck in a few years.

NOTES

1. David Verklin and Bernice Kanner, *Watch This, Listen Up, Click Here* (Hoboken, NJ: John Wiley & Sons, 2007).
2. What? Never heard of it—exactly our point.
3. Recorded at Ogilvy Verge Summit, September 28, 2005.
4. Interview with John SanGiovanni, Eric Hertz, and Jim Cooley, May 2007.
5. Interview with Kevin Stone and Martin Cheng, Bevocal, July 2007.
6. Interview with Scott Dunlap, August 2007.
7. Telephia Mobile Advertising Report, Survey Analysis, Q1 2007.
8. As a reference, YouTube took eight months to cross the 1 million mark (Compete, Inc.), though it got the next million in one month,

and the net 19 million (reaching 20 million) in just eight more months.

9. Interview with Ian Foley and Ujjal Kohli, Rhythm New Media, July–August 2007.

10. You can see the videos at www.bluecasting.com/newspages/landrover .html.

11. DoCoMo announced in March 2007 that users of its Osaifu-Keitai compatible handsets had doubled to over 20 million in the previous 14 months—astonishing growth for a service launched in July 2004.

12. John Coghlan Keynote Speech, CTIA Wireless 2007, Orlando, Florida, March 28, 2007.

13. IBM and Ahold ran a trial of this technology in the United Kingdom and found the revenue increased by 75 percent in the top-shopper segment and increased visits for the lower shopper segment.

14. Instead of relying on surveys, companies can use wireless to capture the "second moment of truth," when consumers use the products and form opinions about them. They are much fresher in their memory at that time rather than an e-mail response a month later.

15. On August 23, 2007, Greystripe announced 14 million downloads of its 800 free mobile games on Gamejump.com and distribution partners in under 12 months.

16. Mobile Media, Informa, January 26, 2007.

17. Based on interview with Anurag Mehta, Mobile Posse, August 2007.

8

Technology—The Lifeblood of Digital Advertising

In the old media, it has always been about creative elements of the advertisements and promotions, something that captures the users, attaches it to the subconscious mind, and at key moments, influences at the point of sale. The new media is a transformation from older forms of content and types of communication networks into all digital content transmission over the Internet and mobile networks. Growth in consumer use of new digital devices is beginning to gradually decrease viewing, listening, and reading time away from traditional TVs, radios and newspapers.

As we slowly migrate toward the digital world, technology is becoming as important as the creative piece—especially in three areas: *understanding the user, contextual targeting, and measurement of results*. Bill Gates extolled the virtues of software in entertainment, media, and advertising at Microsoft's annual Strategic Account Summit in May 2007: "Software is going to really revolutionize not only advertising, but the whole way people consume media, the way they communicate, and the way they create."[1] The role of software and technology in advertising is to make the thousands of potential consumer advertisement exposures[2] (to the consumers) in a day become more relevant, more useful, more actionable, and help the head of the advertising food chain—the advertisers—influence purchase intent. At the end of the day that's what matters the most. Advertisers care less about the medium and more about the result.

Until very recently, measurements and ROI metrics were superficial in pure technical terms. Much better tracking capability across mediums has created the opportunity and the responsibility to make advertising count.

As we discuss in Chapter 9, the future of digital advertising is not about one medium but about an integrated experience across mediums. In an Internet Protocol (IP) world, the digital advertisement can be targeted, adapted to the user, and forwarded, thus increasing its reach manifold.[3] In an all-IP scenario, whether it is IPTV or broadband Internet or 3G mobile, user experiences will be connected by the IP cloud in the backend. The shift has already started with significant initiatives around triple- and multiplays. In this chapter, we discuss the technical architecture needed to enable *ambient advertising*, meaning relevant and useful advertising in an IP-connected environment. It doesn't mean that users are inundated with advertisements but that the advertisements and promotions they are already exposed to are relevant, useful, and provide value to the user. Technical integration enables optimization of the reach, ad campaigns, and measurement capabilities across mediums.

TECHNOLOGY EMPOWERING ADVERTISING

In a survey conducted by Booz Allen Hamilton, a consulting firm, a good majority of the marketing executives indicated that return on investment (ROI) analytics, consumer insights, and media and messaging are the three top issues they continuously grapple with (see Figure 8.1). This also highlights the role technology will play in the evolution of advertising both in mobile and in an integrated platform era that ties TV, Internet, and mobile together.

At its most basic, advertising is gaining exposure to customers in order to send them messages that will influence their behavior.[4] All things being equal, the less it costs the better. Advertising objectives range from supporting a brand ("image" advertising) to triggering a sale ("direct response"

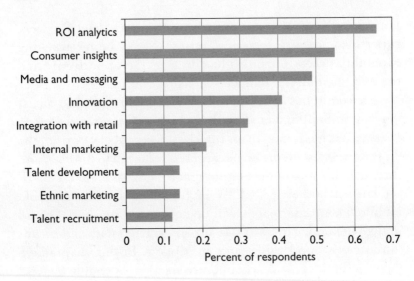

Figure 8.1   The key issues for marketing executives.
Source: Booz Allen Hamilton.

advertising). And broadly, some advertising aims for reach (maximum exposure or number of real customers) and some for purity (relevance and quality of information). If you have something everyone wants, you want to send your message to as many people as possible, but if you're selling hot dogs, you are unlikely to spend much for targeting vegetarians.

Successful mobile advertising requires reach, purity, and analytics. As discussed earlier, analytics involves matching users' interests—implicit and explicit, context, preferences, network, and handset conditions—to ads and promotions in real time. It does not mean just bucketing users in a group and giving them a number but understanding them in every way possible and customizing every interaction, imprint, and promotion to the closest degree possible.[5]

The key to making sense out of all the data gathered is the seamless integration capability that can take data from disparate sources and in different formats, and then prune and store it in the data warehouse for further processing. Once the data warehouse is cleaned and ready for consumption, it can be then be used for different purposes.

Reporting is the obvious one. Operators, content providers, and aggregators are all interested in finding out more about the customers, the content and products, and how they are selling. Trends that might emerge from mining the data can help in monetization and future planning of the services, applications, promotions, and advertising. Reports can be customized by groups and user levels and the results from these reports can be fed back into some of the engines such as promotions and advertisements.

The analytical system needs to have the capability to digest all the user data, summarize it, and update the master user profile. This functionality is essential to provide the rich segmentation that is at the heart of recommendations, campaign and offer management, and advertisements. The segmentation engine can help cluster users into affinities and different groups based on geographic, demographic or socio-economic, psychographic, and behavioral characteristics.

Finally, the context engine combines various inputs and uses location and other contextual information to package information before it is pulled or pushed to the consumer. This is true of all application areas such as portals, storefronts, local search, mobile search, off-net access, and other applications. This means that the context engine (the technology that knows what to serve you when) must be able to provide customer info very quickly. Key performance attributes will be required—when you are loading an ad into a phone browser, you won't have time to execute a complex query to a relational database and then formulate a result. Data that powers the user profile has to be loaded into a highly efficient store or even better, should be stored on the phone and updated regularly.

User profile also provides input into the churn and operations and management (O&M) system that helps provide customer care a better picture of the user and hence predict churn earlier so some corrective measure might be applied in time. In fact, user profile information can be monetized many ways by making it more accessible to the ecosystem via services architecture. If it enhances the user experience, everyone wins.[6]

Only by tying the data services architecture at multiple points and most importantly at the user profile level, can the full potential of mobile advertising be realized.

THE GENESIS OF THE SILOED APPROACH

As mentioned, operator technical architectures have evolved as a function of business evolution. As the applications got introduced, so did the number of business and technical silos. While the 1990s were about the advent and growth of TXT messaging, this decade has seen the rapid-fire introduction of new services, from multimedia messaging (MMS) to broadcast video in short succession. While the voice services architecture has evolved over three decades, data services picked up steam over the past five years.[7] Due to service evolution and the desire to time the market, most of the mobile service delivery environment has been vertically integrated wherein the functions within the silos cannot be reused for existing or new data services. Typically, most services operate in isolation from a user point of view; even the user experience across such applications or storefronts[8] can be different. Service providers may end up having many players managing these individual storefronts with the primary linkages being authentication and billing systems. The inability to reuse or integrate functions not only has impact on user experience but also on the cost and the implementation of a competitive road map. An example of silo architecture is shown in Figure 8.2.

After TXT, MMS was introduced; this meant a new vendor implementation. Then ring tones and wallpapers came along, again with a new set of infrastructure vendors. With better handsets and networks, mobile games became more relevant, and yet another set of vendors was introduced. This was because, at inception of any of these categories, the start-ups focused (as they should have) on a specific niche in the market. With the advent of the iPod,

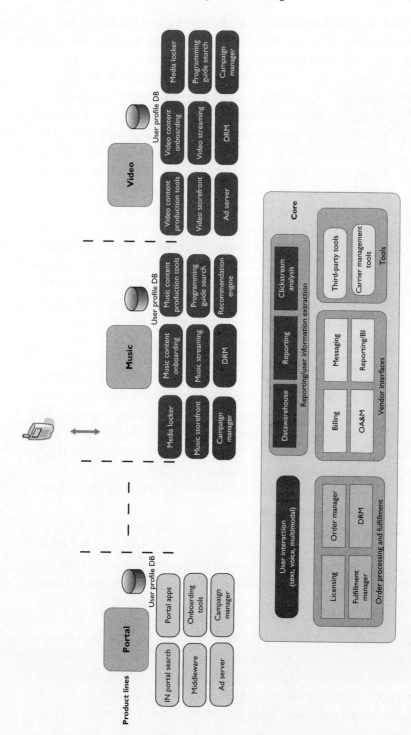

Figure 8.2   A stovepipe deployment.
Source: Chetan Sharma Consulting.

OEMs started focusing on MP3 phones, and while the numbers dwarfed iPod sales in 2006, it also meant introducing another vertical silo in the network infrastructure. Unicast video services, such as the ones from MobiTV and others, got consumers excited and a good majority of service providers rushed to provide such services to the consumers. Since these players only focused on mobile TV and streaming, it meant yet another block of complexity in the network. Then came user-generated content and social communities, mobile search, and now mobile advertising. The desire to be the first to launch meant the introduction of new services without tying them together via an integrated platform.

As shown in Figure 8.2, the core architecture is typically made up of interfaces to billing, operations, some elements of digital rights management (DRM), licensing (though under several implementations these typically go hand-in-hand with the respective content categories). The new services typically carry the entire subcore with them and especially the user profile information, so the portal doesn't always know what music the customer is buying, the video platform doesn't know what ring tones the subscriber just paid for, and so on. This leads to the missed opportunity to bundle content or upsell, cross-sell, or even get relevant recommendations. This is starting to change with the introduction of mobile search capabilities into the architecture, but even here, the results might be based more on metadata hits than on actual behavioral data.

The explosive growth in content also meant that thousands of stock keeping units (SKUs) were being added on a daily basis, which made the task of user navigation and content discovery next to impossible. In fact, if operators would just clean the current user vertical interfaces to make the discovery process simpler and more efficient, there could be a 5 to 10 percent jump in content sales within each of the major silos. Although such an approach would be an improvement, it would be extremely shortsighted. It is time for the industry to step back and look at the data services in the context of the long-term evolution and not just short-term tactical patchwork. The revenues are significant enough that the same discipline that has been courted to voice architecture must be embraced for data services. This will help maximize efficiency and profits, empower the ecosystem, increase the data attention span of a mobile user, and help introduce new services into the market without significant organizational, technical, and business disruption to the service providers. The impact of such an approach will show up in revenue matrices such as reduction in churn, increase in customer life-time-value,[9] increase in usage and hence in revenues.

Pros and Cons

The dilemma of vertical versus horizontal integration is not a new one. In fact, many industries experience this challenge. The vertical integration is generally less disruptive and allows faster introduction of products and services in the markets. The unified approach is better strategically, while siloed architecture might win the day tactically. Although it might be easier organizationally and technically to introduce a new application or content category in the mix, this also means further alienation from the universal customer view. The vertical strategy might get the new category into the market quickly, but the launch also means that the ability to cross-sell and upsell effectively are next to none. The opportunity to bundle or to develop time-sensitive promotions is also limited. This approach might help get the customer in the door, but it is typically hard to keep them in the store.

Though the vertical slapstick approach might work in the short term, it is not a viable option long term. With a few vendors, it might be easy to manage the business,[10] but with increasing numbers of content providers and solution vendors in the mix, it is hard to manage the process cost effectively, let alone steer service level agreements (SLAs) and business goals. The breathtaking pace of introduction of new services is also not sustainable. A study done by the consulting firm Accenture noted that to generate an additional $10 in average revenue per user (ARPU) through mobile data services, operators need to roll out a minimum of 500 new, creative, and attractive services each year.[11] While one might disagree with the numbers, it is clear that the current model of increasing ARPU by introduction of new services alone, doesn't work. Most consumers have a certain threshold of spending; more services don't necessarily translate into more ARPU. The key is to maximize the potential sale using proven mathematics rather than guesswork in war rooms and enhance the user experience to make customers keep coming back for more.

The key alignment across all the applications needs to take place in three key areas:

1. *Process and management:* The process flow and management of day-to-day operations needs to be in sync such that common functions are moved into the core architecture while the application-specific elements that can't be moved are handled on a one-on-one basis. All content onboarding should follow a similar process: The same workflow should be able to tackle different forms of content across different applications; the DRM component should be able to tackle ring tone, graphics, music, and video; and the promotion management should tie all applications and all content.

2. *Technology:* Components such as device profiling, transcoding, ingestion, locker, content management, licensing, messaging, subscription management, provisioning, fulfillment, and other type of functions should be part of the core architecture.

3. *Universal user profile:* This is the most important component of the new analytics-driven architecture and the one that is the most complex to implement. All applications and services should talk to a common user profile. This initiative will experience the most resistance, yet without it, our whole thesis of competing on predictive analytics falls apart. It might seem that the "explicit data"[12] collected from the user

might be sufficient information to be applied against all applications and services. In this day and age of "family plans," however, it is exceedingly difficult to generalize user behavior and preferences change over time,[13] and specific targeting becomes a useless exercise. Hence, the need for a universal user profile.

Simply put, companies' ability to communicate with and support their customers is only as effective as their access to consistent and accurate customer data.[14]

If history is any guide, the failure by access-based ISPs to collaborate on developing a single advertising platform has cost them much of the increasingly large revenue streams that online advertising delivers. With the threat from strong and fast-moving brands, mobile advertising could go the same way unless operators move quickly to establish an industry-wide platform for mobile marketing services. While the telcos sit exasperated seeing the market cap of Google bypass them one by one, the debate of Net neutrality and the attempts to rewrite history won't yield much progress. Operators do have an opportunity to aggregate inventory across platforms, offer a compelling solution to the advertising industry, and leverage user information to its own advantage.

INTEGRATED SOLUTION OFFERING

An integrated solution or a unified platform is not a new concept. Our industry has discussed this under the umbrella of "Service Delivery Platform."[15] The emphasis, however, has been on combining the technology components into core architecture to enable function reuse. This section extends that discussion by encompassing the user profile elements. The user profile is used to determine which offers, content, and services should be packaged and presented to the user.

The behavioral analysis of user activity should impact the experience not only within a specific content area or activity but across all user interactions. One can increase the probability of customer action, indeed acceptance of an offer or sale, by understanding interdependencies of behavioral elements, hit rate for offers and promotions.

The secret of achieving a good marketing ROI is simple: Give customers more of what they truly want and less of what they don't. In the journal article, *"Knowing What to Sell, When, and to Whom,"*[16] the authors illustrate as to how the understanding and tweaking of the behavioral parameters can increase the hit rate probability significantly which has immediate impact on revenues. By applying new statistical methods based on the work of Daniel McFadden, Nobel Prize winning economist, researchers could predict specific purchases by a specific customer at a specific time about 80 percent of the time. Such an analysis is possible by having a unified architecture in the first place so one has a comprehensive view of the subscriber within the operator network.

The unified approach has several key advantages:

- Discovering hidden patterns
- Getting the forecasts right
- Identifying key influencers
- Lowering acquisition costs and higher lifetime value
- Bundling and long tail discovery
- Accurate targeting

A unified mobile data services platform[17] is shown in Figure 8.3.

The integration is at three levels:

1. Technical components based on a service-oriented architecture enable each system module to be extensible, upgradeable, and removable to optimize the open service architecture of the future mobile systems and networks. Full discussion of such architecture is beyond the scope of this chapter. The principal benefits are modularity that drives efficiency and decreases costs, better security, better testing and fewer defects, better scalability, manageability, and reusability of investment.

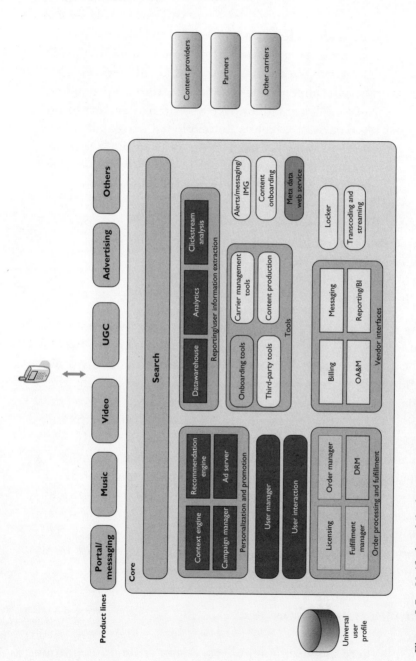

Figure 8.3   Unified mobile data Services Platform.
Source: Chetan Sharma Consulting.

2. All service offerings are integrated by a "mobile search" layer. This also includes voice and phone-related content such as features on a phone (How many times have you struggled to find the menu item for turning off roaming?) or voice content like address book.
3. The most important integration is at the user profile level. Most implementations have a separate user store or profile database, which is not exploited across all content offerings; as such, there is revenue leakage due to missed opportunities to not only enhance user experience and help find content, but also cross-sell and advertise.

A services-based integrated platform will go a long way in setting the foundations for the next 5 to 10 years of mobile data evolution.

Challenges

As the mobile industry matures, customer retention, cost optimization, and customer lifetime value increase become the key drivers for improved revenue and sustainable profitability. Operators have relied on two to three key suppliers to manage their voice network infrastructure; however, data side of the house presents a completely different picture. A good strategy would be to treat the mobile enablement platform as a strategic investment, and build and grow on such an approach. While there are some technical and business challenges, immediate and the most complex is organizational. Executives fear rocking the boat and current stream of work to juggle the longer-term strategic objectives. This requires vision, execution, and the ability to integrate information across functional areas on an ongoing basis.

GIVING USERS CONTROL

While there has been a lot of discussion around integration on the back end, there has been little discussion around user control of advertising. Without having the subconscious and physical control over the advertising that comes their way, the chances of mobile advertising realizing its full potential are limited. Users should be able to configure and control the ads based on their presence, device, context and location, preferences, moods, community, needs, and desires. One should be able to turn on ads when users want to receive information about fast food or turn off ads when on vacation or turn on which applications or services one would want to share the location information with. The success of mobile advertising depends on making the users feel that they are in control. Doing anything else will stunt the growth. The need for a strong user-control framework will vary with geographics. Users will also likely only tolerate ads if they are given something in return. Users are already paying operators a lot to get content. They'd be more likely to take the time to configure their profiles for ads if they are encouraged by free ad-supported content that they want.

The expectations will be higher in Western nations, cultures that are sensitive to tradition, and social etiquettes like Japan and Korea and less in developing countries like India and China where the younger generation has been brought up on TXT messaging, and mobile advertising has been part and parcel of receiving subsidized rates for mobile data services. With better technology, however, people will be ignoring these ads a bit less.

It will be important to provide user control for:

- Configuring tastes and preferences
- Configuring the destination—application, machine, or person
- Configuring context, presence, preferences, interests, and location
- Configuring when they want receive ads
- Configuring who to receive ads from and who to forward to
- Configuring one-click forwarding of advertisements and promotions

- Configuring turning off and on advertisements as a subset filter or on a global basis
- Search capabilities to discover advertisements and ad-subsidized content

The preceding needs to be wrapped up in a very simple, easily accessible, one-to-few-clicks user experience. If it is cumbersome, it won't be used. There should also be a companion online or IPTV interface that allows for more granular configuration if the user is up for it. For a majority of the users, the sense of control will accelerate embrace and adoption.

TRUST-BASED PRIVACY FRAMEWORK

In the digital economy, trust is the bedrock of relationship between consumers and brands. We trust that companies we are dealing with have policies, procedures, and practices in place to protect personal information. While we expect the corporations to roll out terrific products, any direct interaction with them assumes that your private information is not up for sale (at least not without your explicit authorization). Any damage to that trust cannot only damage the brand's reputation but open it up for lawsuits, government oversight and legislation. If the trust is gained, customers will be more willing to share their tastes, intent, and desires explicitly.

Companies should work diligently to design their campaigns around the following basic rules:

- Be absolutely transparent.
- Listen to your customers.
- Give control and access to your customers.
- Don't apply the same rules for all consumers. Calibrate accordingly.
- Provide strong value—monetary, convenience, efficiency, timeliness, social currency.

- Implement clear and simple policies and procedures.
- Put adequate processes and technology in place.
- Ensure your partners adhere by the same principles.
- Be aware of local laws and customs.

Are You Listening to Your Customers?

In a survey conducted by Harris Interactive in mid-2007 (Figure 8.4), to the question of what incentives will help overcome the barriers of mobile advertising, consumers overwhelmingly pointed to control as the defining feature of mobile advertising. Over 67 percent said the ability to opt out, over 55 percent said the ability to choose the type of advertisement, and almost 50 percent wanted to choose the number of ads received in given time. Other important factors were choosing specific times when ads would be delivered. Only 12 percent said that nothing can lower the pain. This confirms the thesis we have been discussing throughout the book: Give customers the control and they will respond. Give customers relevant content and they will become addicted. Win their trust and they will tell their friends about it.

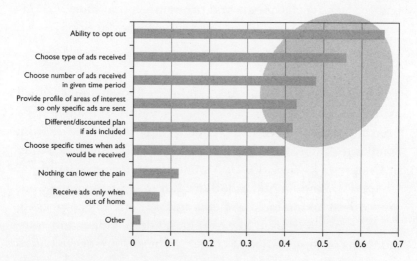

Figure 8.4   Incentives to overcome barriers of mobile advertising. Based on a survey conducted by Harris Interactive, 2007.

User-Controlled Trust Framework

The devices and services up to 2008 haven't really focused on trust-based computing. While everyone has focused on releasing a dizzying array of applications, services, and price plans, very little thought has been put into a trust-based framework on the device that helps users control how the outside world communicates to them. In 2006, we started seeing some basic launches of mobile Presence services, which allow users to control (as in the IM environment) who, when, and how the outside world communicates to the individual. A person might grant full communication access to a close group of friends, family, and colleagues 24/7 while giving limited exposure to people not in their address book. The user might further curtail the access list on vacation. We need a similar model for mobile advertising (see Figure 8.5). Consider mobile advertising as an external entity that is trying to have a conversation with the user. Depending on the users' state of mind, they may or may not be interested in receiving any advertisements.

A person might only be interested in food- and beverage-related promotions and advertisements during lunch hour or on vacation and will consider them an intrusion and/or ignore the advertisements and promotions that have no context. This is independent of the network they are on.

Cache and Carry

To make the loading of ads less painful for the consumer as well as the network during peak times, several companies have been adopting an advertising-cache model. Technologies from companies such as Action Engine, Zumobi[18] (see case study in Chapter 7). MediaFLO, Mobile Posse (see case study in Chapter 7), and Digital SideBar differ in implementation but are focused on minimizing clicks and waiting time, especially for multimedia content like graphics, audio, video, and combinations of these forms of content. The ads are downloaded during off-peak hours based on service and user preferences and displayed and rotated as the user is navigating within

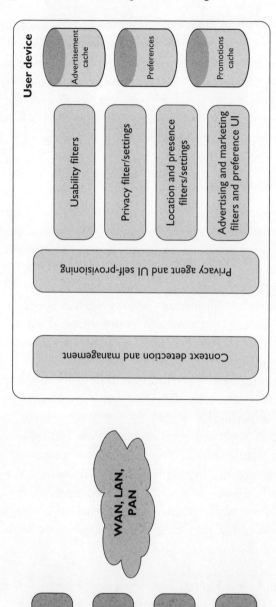

Figure 8.5 A trust-based framework to manage user privacy.

the application. For most of the implementations, advertisements are not a unit that can be superdistributed, but in the future we expect that advertisements will be treated just like content that can be easily shared with a user's community of interest. It also requires good client technology. The client will need to connect with the network to upload information about ad views and ad interactions.

Context Awareness

We briefly touch on the role of context engine in Figure 8.8 shown later in the chapter. As we move from a stovepipe architecture to an integrated and autonomic component architecture, what users see on the device will be all context driven including, and particularly, advertising. The system will comprehend from various inputs context with respect to application, component, service, environment, and so on while applying the rules based on application, service, components, user, and community to present the most useful user interface at that given moment. The functional, operational, and management aspect of the application, device, and network will be handled accordingly.

Context is any information that can characterize the immediate relationship between a person, place, or object that is relevant to the interaction between them.[19] We are in the very early stages of truly understanding what context means to mobile applications, services, and the user experience. The variables that influence context can be broadly divided into following categories:

Private context variables: These variables are private to the user, the community, and environment around them. They are measured and monitored by the sensors or the mobile device. In most instances, the device will be processing this information with the help from the remote server.

User context: Attributes describing user's activity, position, presence, status, and calendar.

Device context: Attributes describing device capabilities, battery, CPU usage, and memory.

Network context: Attributes describing network status parameters like link status, quality of service (QoS) availability, bandwidth, and topology.

Environment context: Attributes describing the environment such as background noise, temperature, and light.

Community context: Attributes describing the status of people, friends, and community surrounding the user.

Public context: The information related to these variables can be retrieved without knowledge about the identity of the user such as traffic jams, date and time, events related to user's preferences.

Context awareness could be both proactive (things are proactively figured out and relevant content is pushed to the user) or reactive (based on user interaction, content or relevant information is pushed to the user).

So, how is context relevant to advertising? Context is useful for both content-related advertising (advertising that is associated with specific pieces of content) and content category (e.g., banner ads on a portal; interstitials before, during, or after application runs on the device; and promotions and offers such as ads for a Hawaiian vacation package in December for a user in Seattle or London) or for not sending ads when presence of the user is set to "meeting with the boss." (Well, some might still choose to receive ads and be entertained, but, you get the picture.)

The key is for the application to have implicit knowledge of the user's environment and task goals. The ambient connectivity ecosystem should continuously learn about the user's world and adapt the databases, applications, and services to the same. There will be some preferences that the user will explicitly mention, but they should be inferred from user behavior so that needs can be predicted and help in information fetch and task completion.

As the user moves between home, office, car, and outdoor environments, the device, the associated networks, and the relevant applications are aware of the movement and need to present the relevant information for that very moment to the display so that the user can interact with minimal friction.

You Say Idle, I Say Active

The role of the idle screen or active screen in defining future user experiences as well as the hub of clever mobile advertising is going to be important. The ability of the user to flip the phone, and look at the most relevant content combined with most relevant advertisement is what advertisers dream of. This personal, one-to-one, zero-touch interaction is not afforded by any other medium. While the opportunity to deliver value to the consumers is enormous, the idle screen is also a sacred place for the consumer—only the most relevant and important items surface to the top; the rest are relegated to being clicked further down or need to be discovered via search.

Figure 8.6 shows T Interactive service from SK Telecom that allows users to include news, alerts, recommended content, and applications on their home screen with easy access. The figure shows the cover of mobile *MelOn* magazine that is delivered to idle screens automatically; the user can browse all articles and pictures without a network connection.

Figure 8.6   T-Interactive service from SK Telecom.
Note: There is a similar service from KTF, its main rival.

From an advertising perspective, idle screens will be used both for advertisements related to content and for direct promotions in the form of offers and coupons that are based on highly relevant targeting. It is going to be promoted by both small and big operators. In fact, the smaller operators will try to be more proactive about it than major markets. In the United States, Alltel with Celltop and an obscure regional operator Revol Wireless in Ohio were the first ones to fiddle with idle screen, the latter specifically for advertising. The opt-in program allowed users to provide some demographic information (age, gender, and zip code), and the relevant offers were sent to them. The ads appear on the screen of the subscriber's phone when the phone is not in use. It attracted advertisers such as Pizza Hut. Over 75 percent of the subscribers signed up with only a 1 percent opt-out rate.[20]

Because advertisers (and operators) have no room for error, the value of segmentation, relevant targeting, and user experience in delivering advertisements becomes imperative. We discuss this in detail in subsequent sections.

ANALYTICS-DRIVEN UNIFIED FRAMEWORK

Most of the traditional advertising relies on outdated measuring methods to understand user behavior. It is not because of lack of desire but due to lack of capability. Diaries, memory, and surveys are inefficient because they rely on what people say and not on what people do. An analytics-driven framework takes the explicit preferences and needs into consideration but really hones in on the implicit behavior and interaction, for that is what defines the individual.

Pay Attention to What I Do, Not What I Say

Cost of acquiring a new customer: $350. Cost of handset subsidy: $2B/year. Cost of building out the 3G network: $6B. Cost of acquiring the spectrum: $4B. Giving customers what they want: Priceless. Our industry spends so much time, energy, and resources on things that don't matter to customers and very little on understanding those customers—their tastes, needs, and dislikes. But if you had a change of mind set, how would you do it? Asking customers about themselves doesn't work, at least not all the time.

Inordinate resources are poured into figuring out the "code" of a demographic before launching any major product or initiative. Conventional wisdom is that by understanding the code, brand messaging can be appropriate tailored to deliver the maximum return that translates into sales. By no means is the in-depth, one-on-one customer research a complete waste but it is incomplete and takes too much time for this digital age. There is rarely a feedback loop that self-corrects a campaign in real time or improves the understanding of the segments. In his book, *The Culture Code*, the brilliant cultural anthropologist Clotaire Rapaille wrote, "There is a remarkable freedom gained in understanding why you act the way you do."[21] Indeed. But how to do it? Experts like Rapaille and others spend countless hours with participants of studies and research projects talking about their likes and dislikes, dreams and fears, but is that adequate for the cracking the code in this age?

In a piece on recommendation engines for the *Wall Street Journal*, Jason Fry wrote, "It's bizarre to expect Amazon to ignore the trainloads of *Star Wars* stuff I've bought from it, or to somehow detect that I thought all those Boynton books were insipid even as I kept buying them. When it comes to describing us as customers and consumers, recommendation engines may do the job better than we would. As Mr. [Greg] Linden puts it, 'In some ways watching what people do can be more accurate than asking people what they do.' In other words, we lie—and never more effectively than when we're lying to ourselves."[22]

To put this theory to test, we analyzed the user interaction and profile data for over 120,000 users on a movie site.[23] For all given users, both implicit and explicit profiles were created. Implicit profiles were based on user action or event (e.g., browsing, previewing, purchasing, or playing activity), while the explicit profiles were based on user input of either filling out profile surveys or rating of an item. Any duplicates were taken out (e.g., if user visits the same item multiple times; the count is still one for that particular event). In looking at the user behavior in aggregate, 63 percent of the events correlated with implicit behavior, whereas only 26 percent correlated with explicit behavior—they were based on what users said they liked. Eleven percent of the events were common to both the profiles. In looking at the data on a per user basis, the differences in what people say versus what they do are apparent. Approximately 70 percent of the users behaved according to their explicit profile less than 20 percent of the times (count of events) and over 51 percent of the users behaved according to their implicit profile over 80 percent of the times (see Figure 8.7).

The differences are stark for low usage users, which make up the majority of the population; up to 63 percent

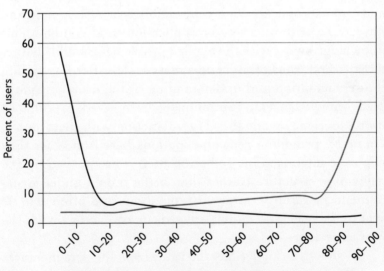

Figure 8.7   Differences in explicit and implicit user data.
Source: AgentArts data, Author analysis.

of the users behaved according to their implicit profile over 80 percent of the time.

Thus, making assumptions based on what users tell you is a failing strategy. Explicit user data should not be completely discounted, but it needs to be augmented with implicit data on an ongoing basis because users' behavior and preferences change over time through acquired taste, discovery, and recommendations from the social network. This refined intelligence should then be applied to each user interaction and user experience strategy.

Integrated Mobile Data Platform

The highly integrated mobile data services platform is key to rapid monetization of future mobile data services. The technical architecture of such a platform and the business processes that govern them should be driven by *predictive analytics*. The goal of the framework is to capture the behavior and interests of users while they are browsing, shopping, and interacting with a variety of applications and content. This knowledge mixed with the explicit profile helps build characteristics and traits of users on a mass scale. After fine-tuning the segmentation and understanding of the users, the gathered knowledge can continuously be applied to enhance user experience while they are interacting with their mobile phone by providing recommendations based on what they might be interested in. Topics of interest are pushed up the navigation structure (rather than being buried under layers of menu hierarchy), targeted promotions and offers can be sent to the user, and mobile advertising can add value to the user experience.

As shown in Figure 8.8, the value from the data increases as the analytics get more and more embedded into the technology and business processes of data services. The ultimate nirvana for the service provider (and the consumer) occurs when the user's desires and content offerings reside in harmony, fully aware of each other and fully adaptive to the user's context. Building such a platform is hard work and

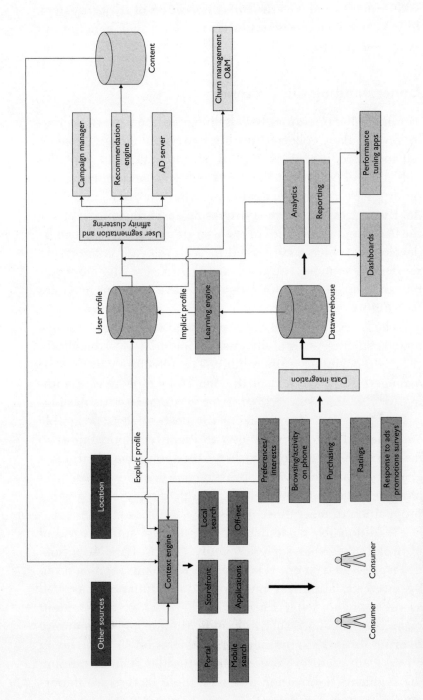

Figure 8.8 High-level analytical framework.

takes time. It involves the full cooperation of the ecosystem, so it is not just the operator or the user that benefits but everyone in between.[24]

Understanding the Customer

Traditionally, operators have segmented their users primarily on the data collected during provisioning: age, gender, zip code, credit profiles, and so on. However, this provides only a small picture of the user's behavior and more importantly gives minimal insights into what the user is likely to do. By understanding the purchasing and browsing habits of the user, implicit profiles of the user or group of users can be developed, which can be used to push relevant content and services. The more you understand the users, the more significant impact this knowledge will have on your revenues (see Figure 8.9).

These segments can then be studied with other strategic models such as profitability, usage potential, possible credit risk, and customer vulnerability. These factors can then be managed in the context of the operator's objectives: retaining profitable customers, growing customers with the biggest potential, and optimizing the costs of less profitable customers. By doing so, they can identify opportunities to make a difference in the market. Once you have identified a group of customers who appear to have common needs, you have to determine whether you can profitably offer a value proposition to meet those needs.

Traditionally, customers are segmented into a handful of broad categories such as Family, Youth, Late Adoption, Enterprise, and so on. It is essential to look at segmentation by interests, affinities, age groups, and functions, as well as subsegments when fine-tuning the message and content push. New segments such as Family Monitoring, Community Sharing, Instant Communicators, Generation M,[25] and many others help identify growing opportunities. Understanding the segments' motivation and why these factors are important helps match content with users.

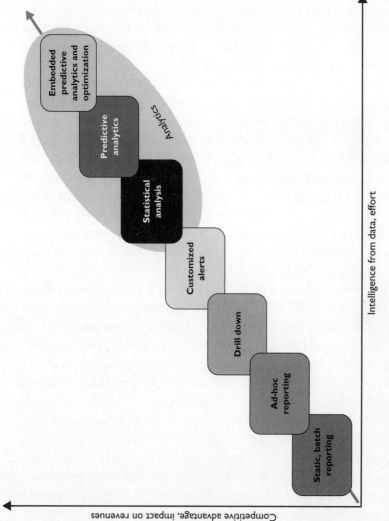

Figure 8.9 Impact of analytics on competitive advantage and revenues.
Note: A similar model is discussed in Harris Davenport, *Competing on Analytics: The New Science of Winning* (Boston: Harvard Business School Press, 2007).

SEGMENTATION

The days of mass market advertising and marketing are numbered. The fragmented consumer base is no longer interested in one size-fits-all products; they demand that marketers design and create offerings customized to their specific needs. With the cost of production greatly reduced, businesses find it profitable to target more and more specialized subgroups of consumers through niche offerings.

Traditionally, operators have followed common segmentation models such as (1) segmentation by size (e.g., large corporations, small and medium enterprises (SME), Small office and home office (SOHO), residential customers), (2) segmentation by technology (e.g., GPRS, EDGE, WAP, TXT, and so on) and (3) segmentation by billing.[26] Marketers have used these basic techniques to guide programs and campaigns. In the subscriber-saturated world, however, these methods are woefully inadequate, especially as services need to be personalized and the acquisition and retaining of customers become paramount. We need to move from these 4 to 10 segments comprising millions of subscribers to hundreds of segments with 100 to 1,000 subscribers that help you model the preferences and behavior of the population.

The concept of consumer segmentation is based on the idea that the large markets comprise many subgroups. Each subgroup, or segment, has different characteristics, such as demographics, lifestyles, work habits, social networks, preferences, product requirements, or consumption habits that could benefit from different product features or marketing approaches. These differences suggest that the greatest profitability can be achieved by developing multiple strategies to address the unique characteristics of each individual segment rather than by putting the soccer mom and the globe-trotting executive in the same bucket. In the online world, decreased development costs combined with technology that allows for greater customization drives many ventures to focus on narrowly defined targets—often many at the same time.

Each target population has specific needs that can be addressed in a product or service offering. In many cases, a product focused on the needs of a specific segment can be brought to market cheaper and faster than one designed to have broad-based appeal. One of the primary objectives of segmentation is to identify subgroups that may be more profitably targeted than the mass market. Segmentation can also be part of a multiple segmentation or multistage strategy. In a multiple segmentation strategy, a few key segments are picked and their independent needs are developed simultaneously. In a multistage strategy, a primary segment is targeted for early adoption or for alpha users, with other groups slated for later efforts after the brand has developed a core following and a solid customer base. Good segmentation technology and processes not only enable recommendation and advertising capability along with the refocusing of data offerings but also empower traditional functions like customer service, billing, churn management, and subscriber acquisition.

YIELD MANAGEMENT

So, you have done your segmentation, you have your inventory, but how do you maximize ROI given the various variables and inputs. You now have the extremely complex task of trying to optimize revenue, customer experience, partner revenue, promotion impact, segment propensity, individual behavior, and system resources—and all of this in real time. The concept of yield management has been around since the late 1970s when American Airlines introduced the first yield management system; it allowed the airline to dynamically adjust fares based on inputs of historical and current booking patterns. Since, then other airlines and other industries have copied the inventory management system. Yield management is all about revenue management or, if you are customer focused, experience management. Given the various inputs, how do you optimize the output to maximize return? In the advertising world, it translates into maximizing the revenue from selling its ad inventory. The concept is the same across various channels. Publishers try to sell their inventory at different pricing levels based on the segmentation and size and types of ad units. Some inventory is premium, like an operator deck or content/application from Disney; whereas others are more commodity type, like user communication or plain browsing. The more targeted the ad, the higher the price it can command as the lure of response from the user is higher. The challenge remains the balancing act of selling the inventory at the highest possible price while minimizing your unsold inventory.

The online inventory is sold on a CPM basis, and the user site navigation for many years has been around page views but is changing slowly to duration or time spent and total sessions. So, the task of the yield management system is to maximize revenue/page view, revenue/session, revenue/minute, revenue/user, revenue/ad, or revenue/campaign. In the mobile world, we are just starting to tackle such issues. Though the initial wave is more focused on the online derivates of maximizing revenue, different metrics will inevitably will come into play around duration, session, level of engagement, and viral capacity of campaigns. We discussed some of this in describing our five-points framework earlier (see Chapter 3).

For mobile, the yield management system also needs to ask: How does this impact the user experience? What if users choose to turn off ads for a specific period or only turns off ads for a specific category or specific brand? What if they only allow ads forwarded to them by their friends? How would the yield management system take into account user preferences on an individual basis? How does it impact inventory and how is that managed? When does the network deliver ads—during downtime or in real time? How and when do you deal with perishable inventory? What happens when you combine mobile and online with a common user profile? And then extend it onto three screens to include TV? How do you optimize? It is a multidimensional problem with an ever-growing number of dimensions, the complexity of which we have yet to appreciate.

Over time, though the accuracy and impact of mobile advertising will be apparent, the complexity of yield management systems will go beyond anything we have seen today. This is for a simple reason—there are more variables to manage while keeping the goals of many parties in mind. Managing such complexity in real time will be a competitive advantage. It requires years' worth of data to master the black art of yield management, so any serious player should already be collecting and analyzing data for sell-through rates, demand patterns for targeted buys, user behavior, segment behavior, market behavior, segmentation impact, CPM effectiveness, engagement effectiveness, and campaign ROI.

A Word about Frequency Management

Mobile empowers frequency management. The ability to track the frequency of exposure on a per user basis is invaluable. In traditional advertising, advertisers have a convoluted view of how frequency might affect their return on advertisements (ROA). To reach a particular demographic, advertisers blanket the ads by attaching the ad to a particular time slot or show. They have limited knowledge of the viewers—how many times they might have watched, how many times they skipped over, how many times they didn't react, and so on. Mobile enables all these deficiencies by providing the capability of tracking the exposure per user, so you don't under- or overexpose. In addition, you will have a good idea about what the user is doing with that ad—especially, if they forward or tell their friends about it. Previously, this was just not possible. Though the siloed solutions can provide the capability for each mobile medium, it is important for the solution providers to tie the mediums (TXT, WAP, mobile video, etc.) together so you know which medium worked the best for a given campaign and you can control the frequency across all the mediums.

In an all-IP world, as discussed in Chapter 9, you would have the capability to track exposure across different mediums such as TV, Internet, and mobile. That, of course, would be advertising nirvana.

We covered quite a bit of ground in this chapter. From the impact of convergence on advertising to the need to move away from silo architecture to a unified framework, we discussed the issues around analytics, segmentation, and user experience. As we look into the next five years, new content applications such as broadcast video, idle screen, user-generated content, community, and mobile search will continue to be refined. The functionality available with these applications, such as the sharing and tagging of data, will also increase the demand on the mobile entertainment platform to adapt to the growing needs of the market. To stay competitive in this rapidly evolving and challenging marketplace, service providers must move from siloed point solutions to integrated unified platforms that maximize their returns from the declining services and better prepare for the technical and business challenges in front of them. The vast potential of mobile data services in general and in mobile search and advertising specifically can't be realized without a retooling of the fundamental approach to deploying services, engaging partners, and serving users with the best possible *analytics-driven contextual user experience.* This chapter outlined the evolution of data services, discussed the need for a unified mobile data services approach, and laid out the basics and the merits of a *services-oriented analytics-driven framework.*

The technology will increasingly play an important role in designing and executing advertising campaigns. The platforms will help unify the campaigns across various mobile mediums like TXT, WAP, video, and idle screen, so the complexity and nuances of the mobile world are shielded from the managers who run the campaigns for the brands.

NOTES

1. www.microsoft.com/Presspass/exec/billg/speeches/2007/05–082007 MSNSASBillg.mspx, accessed December 7, 2007.
2. American Association of Advertising Agencies,"How Many Advertisements Is a Person Exposed to in a Day?"www.aaaa.org/eweb/upload/FAQs/adexposures.pdf, accessed December 7, 2007.
3. To reach 10 percent of a given segment, one might need to target just 1 to 2 percent of the segment; if the application is well designed

for being "sufficiently contagious," it will spread itself much faster and will have higher value, interaction rates, and response rates because the ads will be coming from their friends and family and not advertisers.

4. Chetan Sharma and Victor Melfi, "Sell Phones, What Will Make Mobile Advertising Tick?" *Wireless World Magazine* (Part I, January/ February 2007; Part II, March 2007). These articles can be accessed at www.chetansharma.com/msandmm.htm.

5. Analytics and data mining are not free of issues. In fact, one could be walking into a legal minefield. Depending on the region, the regulations for privacy and fines for violations can vary significantly. Security of the profile information is another element of concern. As was evident from the AOL mishap last year, companies need to guard this information carefully or they could open themselves up for litigation. However, the problem is not with analytics but with how the information is used or abused. In any case, policy control is another element that needs to be consistent across all content applications and services.

   In the early days of a developing market, too much segmentation and targeting is also counterproductive as targeting might result in a very small population of users who might not be of any material interest to the advertisers.

6. Speaking at the Intel Capital CEO Summit in May 2007, Ram Shriram, the founding director of Google offered this advice: "Don't focus on a business model—focus on the best experience for the end-user." The point being—if the experience is good, everything else follows. Google is a good example of this thesis.

7. The evolution has varied depending on the geography. Scandinavia and Western Europe saw the explosion of messaging in the 1990s. Since 1998, Japan and South Korea have taken over in terms of mobile Internet and subsequent data services.

8. Storefronts refer to the digital store for buying digital goods such as ring tones, graphics, music, and video games.

9. Customer Lifetime Value = NPV[Lifetime Estimate $\times$ (Future Revenue − Cost)].

10. Relying on just one or two vendors also has risks. By becoming too dependent on a small number of vendors, service providers lose leverage; if the technology is embedded into the daily operation, it is hard to remove and insert a new vendor midstream. Billing is one such function where operators face consistent pressure of being locked in. Such a risk can be mitigated by a more open service-oriented architecture, where it is easy to replace and add modules from various vendors who all adhere to a common set of a application protocol interfaces (APIs) and standards. Service providers should drive such an architecture.

11. Accenture, "A New Model for Mobile Data Services," www
.accenture.com/Global/Services/By_Industry/Communications/
Access_Newsletter/Article_Index/MobileDataServices.htm,
accessed December 7, 2007.

12. Name, marital status, gender, zip code, some preference data, credit
check, type of phone purchased.

13. Studies have shown that even when users explicitly indicate preferences of one artist or genre over another, the actual buying patterns
or the declaration of intent may be different. Additionally, the
generic data loses relevancy as the user gets introduced to new content, artists, and communities.

14. Jill Dyche and Evan Levy, "Reaching a Single Version of the
Truth," *Customer Data Integration* (Hoboken, NJ: John Wiley &
Sons, 2007).

15. For a list of white papers on the subject, please see www.moriana-
group.com/sw1635.asp, accessed December 7, 2007.

16. V. Kumar, R.Venkatesan, and W. Reinartz, "Knowing What to Sell,
When, and to Whom," *Harvard Business Review* (March 2006).

17. The need for user profile integration goes beyond mobile. With
consolidation in media, cable, and wireless industries, large players are coming out with triple, quad, and many play offerings. The
integration will be needed not only for promotions and marketing
but also for services and applications that transcend a given delivery
medium.

18. In fact, Zumobi adheres to a strict 90 to 10 percent philosophy with
application going to the network only 10 percent of the time and
the content and ads picked up from cached 90 percent of the time.
Similarly, for MediaFLO's video, clipcasting, and datacasting applications; some of the content and related configuration elements are
cached and presented to the user when appropriate.

19. Telektronikk 1.2007.

20. "Ohio operator innovates with idle screen advertising," *Fierce Wireless*
(May 22, 2007).

21. Clotaire Rapaille, *The Culture Code: An Ingenious Way to Understand
Why People around the World Live and Buy as They Do* (New York:
Broadway Books, 2006).

22. Jason Fry, "Under the Recommendation Engines' Hood—The
Choices Engines Make for Us May Be More Accurate Than We'd
Like to Believe," *Wall Street Journal* (June 12, 2006).

23. The data was provided by AgentArts, one of the pioneers in the
recommendation systems for online and mobile industries. The company was acquired by FAST in Q2, 2007.

24. An example is analytics or reporting information for content providers. Today, content providers know the success of their offering by

the size of the check in the mail. Even some of the big brands have no idea about users or how their content is being consumed. The lack of feedback process hampers the growth and increases the cost. This severe lack of the basic data is forcing many to build analytics systems of their own.

One of the most basic lessons from the success of i-mode in Japan was the empowering of the mobile ecosystem. Even when the operator controlled the various elements of the ecosystem, they let the contributors to the ecosystem—big or small—succeed, or fail on their own merits. It led to innovation, tapped into insatiable demand, and the rest, as they say, is history. This case study is well documented in Mari Matsunaga, *i-mode: The Birth of i-mode*, 2001 (Matsunaga led the initiative) and also discussed in Sharma, Nakamura, *Wireless Data Services: Technologies, Business Models, and Global Markets* (Cambridge: Cambridge University Press, 2004).

25. Yankee Group defines Generation M—mobility—as a generation caught between Generation X and Generation Y. It is loosely characterized by media, marketing, millennium, multitasking, and the focus on me, myself, and I; members are between ages 18 to 34, *Wireless Carriers Are Missing Out on Generation M*, January 2007.

26. Tomi Ahonen, Timo Kasper, and Sara Melkko, *3G Marketing: Communities and Strategic Partnerships* (Hoboken, NJ: John Wiley & Sons, 2004).

9

What Comes Next?

Advertising is entering an exciting era of major digital innovations. Online advertising has laid a lot of critical groundwork for mobile in terms of education, definition, measurement, and results. Even though it took over 10 years for it to become a truly vibrant industry (see Chapter 2), the lessons learned have proven vital for the "always on, always connected" age. It is not about the debate over the death of the 30-second spot but about how the digital era transforms consumer behaviors and the media and advertising industries behind that behavior. The technology advances of tomorrow will define the growth of this new industry. Random research and development (R&D) will turn into sustainable mobile advertising budgets for the advertisers; SMS campaigns will turn into a more visual multimedia experience for the consumers; the agencies with new tools in hand will become more creative and interactive with their consumers; the technology enablers in the ecosystem will keep pushing the boundaries of perfecting the user experience and performance; and the mobile advertising industry will shed the cocoon of cautious optimism to reach the transcendent state of contextual nirvana. In this chapter, we look at the trends that are likely to have a major impact on the mobile media ecosystem and future mobile user experiences.

A DAY IN THE MOBILE LIFE OF . . .

Since this is the generation that will drive the major trends and impact mobile media and advertising the hardest, let's look at a day in the life of this future mobile media grazer.

Although it is almost impossible to predict exact day-in-the-life scenarios—it is clear that everything that looks totally amazing today will look normal tomorrow.

. . . an Eighteen-Year-Old in 2012

Maria Stephenson wakes up around 8:00 AM because she hears her favorite song coming from her mobile phone. As she looks at the wall, she sees an analog-style clock projecting on the wall from her phone. She immediately grabs her messaging hub, er, uhm, her mobile phone and checks her TXT, IM, and her favorite social networking site. She finds some interesting gossip and forwards it to a small group of close friends.

While eating breakfast, she sees a new music video on the plasma television and hits ** on her phone to download the video, complete with a recommended playlist set to her phone. She immediately gifts it to her brother as it is restriction free. The video comes with a promotional offer for a concert that weekend that might be too great to pass up. As she is looking at the promo, she gets a message from a friend recommending that she should check out a specific playlist on an Internet radio station, which she immediately does. She listens to the station from her phone as she eats breakfast. She tags the playlist in her main list for future sharing with friends.

As she gets ready to drive to class, she asks her phone for the latest real-time traffic on her specific route. The traffic comes back with a predictive map, which changes before her eyes in near real time on the car screen as a wreck just happened. The map suggests an alternate route, which she takes and gets to school on time. She also notices a coupon for a discount tank of gas if she gets a tune-up at the gas station down the street—the mobile agent on the phone makes a reservation. She asks for $50 from Dad to go into her electronic wallet.

While she is in class, someone puts a pool of $20 per student together to prompt the class clown, Don, to rip off the grumpy science teacher's toupee while he sits at his desk. Don does, and the teacher, stunned speechless, jumps up and screams before hightailing it out the room—hairless. Soon, all the world can laugh at it. Maria takes a mobile video of it as a joke. She immediately posts an automatic mobile upload on her social networking site. Little does she know, but the video is so funny that it will drive over a million and a half downloads in the next 24 hours. Tomorrow, Don gets $560, is kicked out of school with the video as the witness, and Maria will be semifamous for 37 seconds of video directing.

As Maria leaves school, she goes mall trolling with five friends. As her phone has a global positioning system (GPS), she asks it to "find an open parking stall close to Nordstrom," and it does. She pays for the stall with her mobile phone. She and her friends walk to the mall and through the front door, where a Reactrix display is projecting a puzzle from Haagen-Dazs; solving it will give her coupons for two vanilla cones. Tempted by the stunning visuals, Maria looks up the answer on her mobile, enters it, gets the coupon transferred to her phone and redeems it from a nearby stall. On the way to another store, they see a promo poster for Halloween #27 and take a photo of the mobile bar code to win free tickets, which they get back in near real time. Maria sends one of the tickets to a friend with a TXT and asks her "LtsGt2gthr @ Lucy's 4 food 2Go." She sends walking directions to the restaurant to her friend right after the ticket is sent, with a voice command. They found the restaurant by asking the phone by voice search to find "the best Italian dinner under $30 a plate in walking distance. serving Italian food."

At 7:00 PM, she gets a message from the parking meter that the time is up, asking and if she would like to extend the time. Maria presses the 1.5 hr icon and gets more time on the stall.

While at dinner, her friends play with a dating site that looks at music playlists to identify compatibility. They find some matches and send out TXT invites immediately to join them for dinner as they are known to be nearby. While at dinner, she gets a phone call from her grandmother, a near-miss inconvenience in her day of data.

When she gets home, she logs into her computer and gets a new promotion from the same concert promoters that sent her the earlier promotion. She is seeing ambient advertising in action, which is good because she loves these deep discounts for her favorite band, An Army of Me. From her computer, she downloads a video lesson of tomorrow's class to her phone. She also downloads a few new MP3 files to rip, remix, and mashup, and send to her friends. She can do that because she rents songs for a monthly fee with remix rights. She goes to bed by setting her phone alarm by voice to wake her up at 6:00 AM with the new remixed MP3 played on the phone.

Even a $50 iPhone would fail with this crowd. In this world, they chat; they blog; they share pictures; they make videos on their phones and share them; they share music; they rip their own MP3 files as ring tones and they share them; they link with each other in intricate mobile webs; they swap effortlessly between different online identities; they listen to Internet radio from around the globe; they argue on mobile friendly wiki discussions; they speak into their devices to find stuff; and they click their camera phones to interact with brands. The iPhone today does not allow any of this. The mobile device for this eighteen-year-old is not a smallish personal computer in her hands, it is a new, highly connected, communications oriented social networking device—and it makes phone calls.

Maria and her friends are still just basically worried about school and goofing off with their buddies after school. All that this cool new mobile technology would enable in their lives is stronger connections to their friends. If it fails in that area, it will have failed totally.

AN ALWAYS ON, REAL-TIME ERA

In 1991, Mark Weiser, in his seminal article, "The Computer for the Twenty-First Century,"[1] described ubiquitous computing as a "world in which humans and computers were

seamlessly united." The article opened with "The most profound technologies are those that disappear. They weave
themselves into the fabric of everyday life until they are
indistinguishable from it."

Though often talked about and often-touted by visionar-
ies, the *always-on* term and its derivatives have been overused since the late 1990s. But the initial vision laid out by
Weiser is starting to emerge as pieces of it are starting to fall
into place in consumer friendly ways. With progress in the
networks, middleware architecture, and the mobile devices,
we are entering a new era of an always-on, real-time access
consumer experience.

We have seen tremendous growth in the mobile industry
in the past five years and if progress in Japan and South
Korea is any indication, we are on the verge of some truly
major changes in mobile consumer experiences. Though there
are likely to be a few significant new breakthroughs, benefits will come mostly through great integration-innovation in
networks, middleware, and devices. Such integration innovation will enable the rapid development of diverse applications by multiple entities and to be used with new devices
that enable simple, elegant user experiences with these
applications.

We generally view tomorrow through the prism of today.
In this section, we briefly consider some of the innovations
that will force us to think outside the box.

Connected Devices Everywhere

Mobile technologies and services will evolve to provide
consumers with tools to access information on the go, enjoy
entertainment on demand, stay connected with the social
fabric of their lives, and make the device a necessary utility
to control that activity. This will be done by enhancements in
software like web services, contextual agents, active screens,
instant discovery, and semantic search. It will be complemented by hardware improvements such as miniaturization
of electronics, multimodal input capabilities, longer battery
life, biometrics authentication, and UI projection features.

It will be delivered across future networks with advances such as automatic best network transition, contextual profiling, gigabyte download speeds, and all IP multimedia capabilities. This combination will enable users to interact with information like never before and will present a perfect platform for the advertising industry to be creative and effective in an age of ubiquitous computing (Figure 9.1).

Multiple types of mobile devices, some without voice, will extend the principle of "harnessing collective intelligence" from the Web to mobile. Intelligence, location context, and other context can be captured with a mobile media device and collectively, they can extend the value of future, interactive web sites. A series of mobile developments will enable this connected device scenario. Mobile widgets will make it easier to create mobile mashups and mobile web sites will all drive heavier consumer engagement for mobile as a connected device to the Web. Consumer-friendly mobile sharing, rating and reviews, music recommendations, and many other community-based web sites will be interconnected with mobile, thereby extending the value of those communities exponentially with mobile inputs. Maps and directions, with context based special offers, will be sent to mobile phones from 411 or 118 voice call services and to new classes of music devices that happen to contain a global positioning system (GPS). Music and playlists will synchronize from the phone or a personal music device to a massive hard drive in the car trunk for a road trip. Payments via mobile devices will be commonplace, exceeding other payment methods, and will provide universal, easy to use, secure, and cheap payment services.

In the near future, mobile devices will be equipped with electronics that will let users project the device UI onto walls or conference room screens. Say goodbye to the 10-pound projector that doesn't talk to the computer! New technologies such as PicoP from companies like Microvision, shown in Figure 9.2, will redefine how users interact with mobile media, how advertisers perceive mobile devices as a branding platform, and how technology companies take advantage of this new paradigm of device UI.

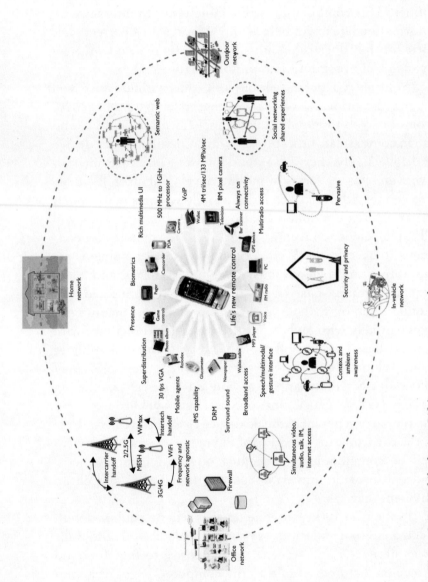

Figure 9.1   Mobile device: Life's new remote control.

Source: Chetan Sharma Consulting. Some of the images were adapted from Qualcomm and Motorola.

Figure 9.2   Microvision's PicoP technology enables device projection.
Source: Microvision.

These visually stunning, portable experiences will require no physical infrastructure and enable brand-new social interactions that will have a high impact on mobile advertising. Adding interactivity within these new projections, like the ones you see in COEX Malls in Seoul, South Korea, from Reactrix Display, will take brand awareness and interactivity to new levels. The images are projected on the floor or the wall and users can interact with them (Figure 9.3); for example,

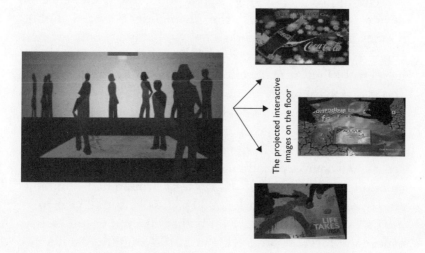

Figure 9.3   Reactrix interactive images.
Source: Images assembled from Reactrix.

the projected image could be of a soccer field and if the users mimicked kicking the ball, sensors would detect that and kick the ball with the same speed and in the same direction as the user intended it to be.

Such sophisticated devices can interact with users devices using Bluetooth and other devices so that they can transfer digital goods, gifts, information, or coupons to users who stopped and interacted with these fun displays.

All of this will be consumer friendly and enable new forms of engaging media and advertising, and it will all be interconnected with mobile devices as the future glue that ties it all together. Mobile devices will be everywhere and will be highly connected with each other through intelligent, semantic interactions.

The Impact of Alternate Devices

Mobile advertising to date basically refers to mobile phones. That's understandable; after all, there are about 3 billion of them roaming around the world and that magnitude of exposure is compelling. But it's important to recognize that other mobile devices present looming market opportunities.

The industry has long talked about the imminence of device convergence—that the distinction between mobile phones, music players, and so on will likely become extinct. But it may not be necessary to sit back and wait for that to happen. In fact, it may reflect good business sense to think about making your move now.

Personal navigation devices (PNDs) have just begun to catch on in the United States. The market tripled in 2006 to 2.9 million units according to Canalys Research. That may seem small compared with mobile phones but it's a bigger circulation than *O, The Oprah Magazine* by around half-a-million. And *Oprah* packed in nearly 2,000 pages of ads that year ringing up over $282 million.[2] Not bad at all. And if you look at everyone's forecast for PNDs in 2010—around 40 million— it starts looking like a valuable circulation opportunity. And how many of the expected 45 million cars in 2010 will have built-in telematic systems? What about ultra-mobile portable computers (UMPCs)? Portable music players?

The point is to look at the market more broadly than as mobile *phone* advertising. It may be more valuable to look at mobile in terms of the user *state* versus a particular device. And the user state is simply the need to communicate and/or access information and content while "mobile"—that is, away from their stationary computer. When we look at the consumers' needs in that situation, independent of the device, we begin to get a sense of how large and interesting this market can become. Beyond communicating with others, there are plenty of times in a day that we wish we could access information—directions, product information, restaurant information, or movie listings. And as we speak, the number of devices positioning themselves to meet these needs is growing. The market for mobile advertising may be well served to focus on exposures generated from devices other than the mobile phone, particularly since that ecosystem, as discussed, isn't exactly making it simple to facilitate a great market opportunity.

MOBILE IS, AFTER ALL, A VOICE INTERFACE

It has been encouraging to see the renewed interest in voice recognition technology. It at least shows we're beginning to admit that the current mobile interface isn't satisfying consumers and thus inhibits the potential for mobile advertising. Triple tapping on the small screen makes it hard to find anything on a mobile phone, particularly while truly mobile. Voice seems like a possible solution.

Speech recognition technology has been around for almost a century. The first commercial success was Radio Rex, a 1911 toy celluloid dog. When the user called Rex's name, he jumped out of his tin doghouse. Rex was held inside by an electromagnet, the circuit for which included a metal bridge. That bridge was tuned to a resonance matching the vowel sound for the word, *Rex*. So when you called his name, the bridge would vibrate and break the circuit releasing Rex from his magnetic restraint. No kidding.

In terms of underlying technology, there was nothing new until the 1960s. No kidding.

While things have gotten remarkably more sophisticated since then, current speech recognition is still fundamentally limited relative to the needs of the mobile consumer. Good examples would be recent attempts at "enhanced 411"—using a voice interface to access information beyond phone numbers such as weather, traffic, and stock prices. While voice-411 has really improved over the past couple of years, the experience quickly erodes when you add multiple content types. We find ourselves getting lost in voice-menu trees. It can take over two minutes to find a single stock price. And if you added a commercial to the experience, it would only get more frustrating.

Why is this?

Current voice recognition technology is based on an acoustic model that translates sounds into analog form and then matches them to a dictionary of known words. The problem comes from background noise and phonetic variations such as accents and utterance imperfections like *um, ah*. Remember the old party game, telephone? If we go around the table and whisper a phrase from person to person, it always comes out jumbled. Without any context for the phrase, the phonetic variation overwhelms the experience. It is fun at parties but not on a mobile phone.

With these inherent challenges, voice applications guide the user conversation by limiting choices. The application constrains the possible utterances coming in (Would you like news, sports, stock prices, weather, traffic?) to help the match rate. And more often than not, users find themselves traipsing through command menus.

So while the technology has become incredibly sophisticated, its conceptual roots are pretty similar to Radio Rex— we utter a single *command* and hope the celluloid dog comes out of the tin house. But for mobile applications to become simple enough so that adding a commercial message is plausible, we have to get away from the command and control paradigm. People do not use voice-phrases to communicate, they use *language*.

Nested menus are a vestige of the computer graphical user interface (GUI) that seems to work when we're sitting down with a keyboard and large screen. But when we're physically mobile with a small device, it falls apart. And even if we replace the keyboard with our voice, if the underlying logic of the conversation flow is still one of nested categorical menus, then it doesn't create a satisfying experience.

New technologies, from companies like VoiceBox Technologies, are being developed around conversational voice search capabilities. These new approaches take the output of traditional voice recognition software and put it through algorithms that model the human brain versus the ear. It allows the user to ask questions across many topics without having to declare the topic or jump into a new application or menu. And the technology polices the ongoing conversation versus just individual phrases, finding contextual clues that help figure out the speaker's intent.

The user experience is radically different than that of traditional voice recognition technology. The user, not the machine, starts and controls the conversation, which can jump naturally across topics. And we are not held hostage to learning a fixed set of commands. The difference in mobile usability is significant. Innovations such as these can greatly accelerate mobile advertising by making mobile device navigation easy enough to leave some "cognitive space" for commercial messages. And, by minimizing nested menus, screen real estate is freed up for advertisements.

THE INTERACTIVE MOBILE WEB

As these new generations of devices appear with faster and faster new processors, new screens and interfaces, and high-speed networks, they will soon be leveraging the Internet in a fundamentally stronger way then they are today.

Over the years, a tremendous number of innovations have led up to the collective group of capabilities that define the current Web 2.0 services. But Web 2.0 is not a product and it is not a service either on the Internet or in mobile variations. The concepts define a powerful new landscape, and you can't make money building a cool new landscape in media or advertising. Marc Andreessen summarizes it best:

> *After an initial phase of the Web as a medium, in which lots of people attempted to make the Web look like a newspaper, or a magazine, or a TV channel, we as an industry have recently been collectively developing a much clearer idea of what the Web is really like as a medium in and of itself. This has led to broad realization of a set of design patterns for how Web services and Web companies often get built and used.*[3]

The design patterns of new Web technologies enable rich, but simple user experiences. Microformats provide a formalized approach to add commonly used semantics, such as contact details, location, event information, and reviews to a mobile application. More importantly, microformats are open, decentralized, built from the bottom up, and are self-organizing. They work in all of today's Web browsers and will work in most of tomorrow's mobile browsers. They can be aggregated and assembled according to personalized ad hoc points of view and will unleash the wisdom of crowds. Communities of like users interested in their subject can now tag an item of interest and the power of the community scales the knowledge of that tag. Imagine tagging mobile media to create a favorites list to share with your friends via TXT. The idea sounds absurd in today's world of closed storefronts— but it will be a must-have in five years. By applying keyword tags like indies, chillin', bad, hot, lovespirals, jamming, moody, vintage '05 rock . . . well, you get the idea. If you liked chillin' music, it would be easy for you and your friends to find those tracks. You could rate, review, and tag new music and save, send, and share the tag lists virally with your phone. Imagine the power of contextual advertising in this mobile world.

Mobile widgets will be another key to the distribution of a new generation of mobile applications. They will also provide a totally new way of exposing advertising to consumers. Although widgets are a good way to personalize content, share photos, or make music recommendations, they can be used for much more. Creative advertisers could build a widget for a target demographics' favorite sport. As widgets are interactive and possibly viral, they could see heavy usage and heavy sharing and sending among the targeted audience. The widget turns into digital candy. And it gets embedded into many mobile web sites for fans of the sport. The end result is that the widget is shared, extended, and takes on a life of its own in that community of interests, replete with advertisements.

Widgets enable more advertising and put more control over that advertising in the hands of the widget creator. In the near future, millions of widgets will show up everywhere. Old media companies, like television web sites will distribute widget-based content. Community-based sites are all beginning to support widgets. The Web is about to get hit with a widget firestorm and mobile will benefit from this.

Microformats and widgets are only a few examples of new design patterns and dynamics that are becoming permanent on the web, yet just beginning to appear in mobile. Some patterns and dynamics will appear faster than others in mobile media and some may never appear at all. But all of them will affect mobile advertising and reach into new audience segments. Richer, more dynamic, yet simpler user experiences along with new ideas and capabilities will combine to drive new levels of mobile user experiences. This, in turn, will drive fundamentally better consumer traffic into mobile media and open new doors for mobile advertising.

CONVERGENCE: FROM AN ADVERTISING VANTAGE POINT

Convergence is an often misused and overused word. It has been used in every possible context and probably in every new technology discussion. From an advertising point of view, convergence is really in bringing audio, video, entertainment, messaging, Internet access, and voice together across Internet, cable, and mobile. It is by tying the same user across these three channels with common user profile that one can evolve the advertising industry to the next level. AT&T's "3 Screen" Strategy[4] and similar initiatives are all about bundling services to increase the lifetime value of the customer and reduce churn.[5] As the competitive pressures are increasing, cable/MSOs, Telcos, and wireless operators are planning on offering triple and quad plays either through direct investment (like Verizon investing in fiber-to-the-curb) or partnerships (like Sprint's partnership with cable companies) or acquisitions (like NTL acquiring Virgin Mobile in the United Kingdom). Bundle awareness is growing. Consumers are increasingly comfortable with nontraditional providers. There are different permutations and combinations available for cable/MSOs, Telcos, and wireless operators.

The Arrival of Ambient Advertising

The capability to have an integrated view of users, advertising campaigns, and their results will be unprecedented and eventually change the advertising industry as we know it. While this new age in advertising has conceptual roots in efforts such as the *Reader's Digest*'s unified customer promotion systems of the 1960s (see Chapter 1), today's technology is creating a world of integrated consumer contact management on steroids.

The players who can sew such integrated platform capabilities together for advertisers will hold significant competitive advantages. This will also accelerate consolidation and alignment across the three mediums into three or four major players in all major markets.

While the benefits from the convergence of TV, Internet, and mobile are obvious from an advertising point of view, the implications are enormous and go beyond mere product bundling. It is more about understanding user behaviors across these mediums and using that knowledge to adapt the targeting of ads based on user interests, profiles, and context. Measuring the effectiveness and ROI across all these mediums will be mandatory.

The idea of an integrated offering goes beyond just streamlining these silos, to actually tying the user experience and commerce together across platforms. It doesn't matter where the transaction or the session gets initiated, the other elements in the network are fully aware and ready to respond to how a user or a group of users may move in and out of a network and jump from one device to another in completely different physical environments. Users could purchase an ad-subsidized movie on the mobile phone on their way back to home, switch on the TV and the movie would be ready to play, with the relevant ads appearing at appropriate times. One could then record, interact, and respond to the content, share and forward, and continue the engagement online or on mobile. The friction between silos, the network components, and user experiences would diminish (see Figure 9.4).

Mobile Ad Stitching in Real Time

In the future, we will take targeting and creativity to a new level by individualizing mobile ads in real time. Right now, even in the most sophisticated analytical-driven mobile advertisement systems, segments are chosen and matched with the relevant ads, but not much is done to differentiate the message and visuals within the segment. In the future, we will take various user profile and context variables and pull-together an advertisement that is specifically tailored to a narrower segment down to a segment of one. There may be two users in the segment who fall in the same demographics but differ in tastes—one has a taste for international travel, speaks five languages, and loves golf, while the other just got married and is into NASCAR. The advertising platforms will take the nuances into account and refine the message by considering their preferences and tastes for an automobile ad. The vehicle could be shown near a golf course in Scotland versus a NASCAR track in Charlotte,

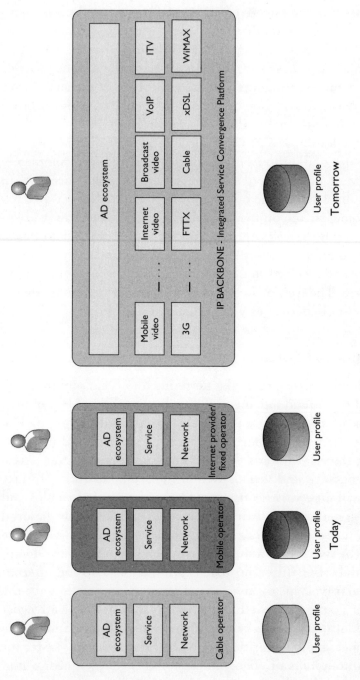

Figure 9.4   Convergence: Move toward an all IP infrastructure.

North Carolina; the spokesperson could be Tiger Woods versus Jeff Gordon—all prepared in real time. Such personalization will have a profound impact on how users consume advertising and react to the brands.

So, What's Holding Us Back?

While technology is capable of enabling a vibrant world of integrated consumer contact management across devices, including mobile devices, getting there is not inevitable. Ironically, this is not a technology challenge but rather one of the industry structure and vision.

Industries do in fact restructure: When was the last time you went to a travel agency? Fundamental change can be driven by a variety of factors such as shifts in demand, the emergence of alternatives, changes in the basic power relationships of key players, or new opportunities. Sometimes the change is an evolution; sometimes it's a revolution.

TWO VIEWS OF A MOBILE ADVERTISING EVOLUTION

During the congressional hearing on the subject of 700 MHz in the United States, FCC Chairman Kevin Martin testified:

> *A network more open to devices and applications can help ensure that the fruits of innovation on the edges of the network swiftly pass into the hands of consumers. Consumers would be able to use the wireless device of their choice and download whatever software they want. . . . Wireless consumers in many other countries face fewer restraints: for example, they can take their mobile phones with them when they change operators, and they can use widely available Wi-Fi networks—available in their homes, at the airport or at other hotspots—to access the Internet.*[6]

The subject of openness has led to fierce and passionate debate over the past couple of years. Operators argue that they have to maintain the user experience and service quality and can't let rogue applications mess with that while others argue that operators stand between them and innovation on the biggest user platform world has known.

Each country and region has tackled this issue differently. While in Japan and South Korea, the monopolies have controlled the ecosystem very tightly with the government's blessing, they have put a lot of R&D dollars into innovation as well as openness. Though they control the specs of the devices and network to the very minute details, they have let the content and applications ecosystem proliferate and have benefited immensely from it. As discussed, NTT DoCoMo tried to replicate the model in other parts of the world but failed miserably due to the lack of similar ecosystem dynamics of the network, devices, and content. In Europe, operators have already given up on control and are much further ahead in opening up their network for access and content. Ingo Schneider, VP at T-Mobile said in an article in the *Wall Street Journal*, "The walled garden approach didn't work with AOL. It's not going to work for mobile either."[7]

North American operators have been the most zealot guardians of their bastions, although cracks have started to appear. In July 2007, Sprint and Google announced plans to collaborate on WiMAX Mobile Internet Services by providing open standard APIs to partners and developer community to create customized products for WiMAX devices. Features such as location, communication, and search will be available to exploit. This was to spur the demand for Sprint's nascent WiMAX investment and is an indication of the path operators will have to take to differentiate and survive in the long run.

In this section, we discuss the impact of the two approaches on mobile advertising.

Rapid Revolutions in the Open World

If you study the mobile market evolution over the past 20 years, two facts are inescapable. First, as markets mature, flat rate "all-you-can-eat plans" inevitably creep in. Second, the time cycles for operators to recoup their infrastructure investments are shrinking with each new generation of technology. Without a doubt, the future of mobile revenues is in applications, services, and software. The earlier operators grasp this inevitable market march and enable third parties to participate in it, the better prepared they will be for the future. We see a multifaceted definition of "open" in this context:

- *Open device capabilities:* If WiFi, Bluetooth, or similar capabilities are available, users should be free to use them as they desire.
- *Open access for mobile consumers:* They should be able to go anyplace they want on the Internet.
- *Open media and communications around that media:* Consumers should be able to *cut and paste,* link, send, and share almost any piece of media on the mobile web from their mobile device.
- *Open platforms and operating systems for developers:* They should be able to exploit features and functionality available on the devices.[8]
- *Open consumer payment methods:* Application and media vendors should be free to choose the methods of payment from their consumers. Standards for mobile payments should be opened up to create critical industry mass and momentum.
- *Open mobile advertising:* Publishers should be free to control and choose all aspects of advertising on their properties.
- *Open user profile and contextual information:* Deliver on the promise of targeting by abstracting personally identifiable information, opening up the contextual information about the user when appropriate, and adopting a completely transparent privacy policy.

Such an ecosystem will empower the entrepreneurs to keep pushing the boundaries of technical and business innovations to make mobile media and advertising a sustainable, vibrant, and scalable industry at a much faster pace. User engagement will be much higher, mobile media revenues will dwarf any forecasts made to date, and advertisers will invest in repeatable multimillion-dollar campaigns.

The single biggest challenge around "open access" will be the balance between the benefits of openness and the need to ensure security and privacy of an individual. This balance needs to be calibrated on an individual basis because one policy doesn't fit all. If you get down to it, the real battle in mobile advertising is for the "user profile"—who has the best user profile for the highest number of unique individuals around the world? Who controls this information and has a direct relationship with the customers? Who updates this profile on a regular basis? Who mines it for user experience and mobile advertising dollars? And who abuses it by going overboard and undermining the user trust? (See how one can use privacy as a competitive strength in Chapter 8.)

At a Snail's Pace in the Closed World

The demise of walled gardens is inevitable—it is the pace at which it might happen that is in question. It is not that the operators don't see the implications; they are just uncertain how to play in the new ecosystem that looks so different from the voice world. If, instead of enabling the ecosystem, they end up strangling the growth by throwing too many roadblocks, innovation will suffer. Almost all the innovation happens outside the walled gardens today. The best thing a operator can do is bring the innovation in-house and leverage it. Advertisers will try out the medium but realize the complexity of implementing large-scale repeatable campaigns and the budgets won't move outside the market experimental budgets. In this scenario, industry will have to wait till the smart phone penetration reaches an inflection point and customers are educated by the market to try out new applications and services beyond the operator portals, at which point, their grip on the ecosystem will start to loosen.

This shift is inevitable, but it will happen at a slower pace in this scenario.

Evolution or Revolution: Which Will It Be?

While mobile advertising is exciting to marketers in terms of its unique capabilities in the media mix, there is a risk of its potential never being actualized. Again, *markets need to be made.* If the industry takes the snail's pace route, marketers' attention may shift to the next big thing before mobile advertising has a chance to establish its value as a medium.

What is the potential for the revolutionary acceleration of mobile advertising? What could trigger dramatic change? Is there a tipping point in sight?

As we've discussed, the technology doesn't seem to be the problem. Networks have improved dramatically. We see hope in solving the problem of the mobile device interface through creative uses of technologies like voice.

If rapid change is experienced, we believe the trigger will not be any new technology but rather a change in the power dynamics between large industry players and entrants. And we believe the movers will be those who fundamentally rethink the mobile communication industry through genuinely embracing an advertising-enabled business model rather than a service-utility model.

OPERATORS VERSUS ONLINE ENTRANTS—WHO WINS?

During the last quarter of 2007, there was significant discussion around "open access" with some of the major players like Apple, Google, Verizon, AT&T, and Sprint announcing initiatives or intent toward a more open ecosystem. Two massive industries—communications and media—are clearly at loggerheads. How this battle unfolds over the course of 2008 to 2009 will define how users will consume media, entertainment, and information.

Media companies and mobile operators think about customers differently. Operators are focused on subscriber acquisitions while media companies are fanatic about audience acquisitions. Media companies do not care about the black box between the end user and content. Service providers care deeply about the boxes between the content and subscribers. Operators think of adding a few hundred thousand subscribers a month; media companies think of acquiring millions. Therefore, while a large operator might have 50 million to 60 million subscribers with room to grow to 70 million, online brands have audiences of over 500 million unique visitors. In the Telco 2.0 world, where service providers aspire to become media and entertainment brands, shouldn't they be thinking like media companies? Shouldn't they be more focused on audience acquisition strategies—selling their goods beyond the confines of today's existing barriers?

If we look at the strategic canvas in the mobile data industry,[9] we will notice that operators have a huge advantage over online brands at this time (Figure 9.5). The horizontal axis captures the range of factors the industry competes on and invests in, and the vertical axis shows the level of advantage for the industry player.

As shown in Figure 9.5, mobile operators have a huge advantage in the current landscape with superior reach, and the capability to segment and profile users. Their current influence over the ecosystem is a magnitude ahead of online brands. In other areas of user experience—content, service cost to consumers, and being quick to market—online brands have a stronger strategic footing and they will use these factors to close the gap in the other areas.

If mobile operators can use their existing strengths to their advantage, online brands will struggle to get a grip on their audience strategy for some time. This shift in mindset (and subsequent execution of the resulting strategy) will have a direct impact on any viable mobile advertising strategy. Advertisers look for an audience, precise targeting, and measurement. If operators can offer that, then advertisers

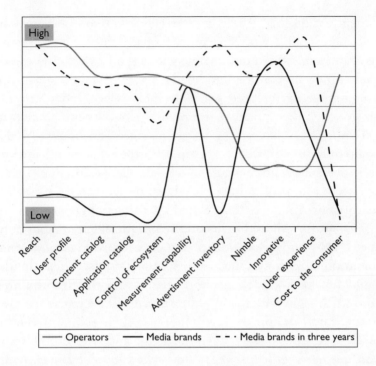

Figure 9.5   Strategy canvas of competing factors in the mobile data industry.
Source: Chetan Sharma Consulting.

will come to them, but, if three years down the road, online brands have three times the audience; it does not take a rocket scientist to figure out what happens next.

Dumb Pipes Equal Huge Value

Too much ink has been wasted on the equation of being a dumb pipe. Dumb does not imply little or no value, in fact it implies exactly the opposite. For operators, nothing is more insulting than the insinuations that they are to become bit pipes and reduced to the utilitarian task of keeping the streets clean while the media companies zoom past them in their Ferraris. Operators must realize their unique value propositions, accept what they are great at and what they are not good at, and structure their monetization strategies around that realization. The growth of the nascent mobile advertising industry is largely dependent on this. While it is conceivable that operators can become mobile advertising powerhouses, the evidence points us elsewhere. Operators and agencies are the exact opposites of each other in culture and media savvy. Mobile operators are engineering focused and extremely conservative in their approach to the critical operational aspects of running a voice network. They have to be to retain voice consumers. Media companies, in contrast, come up with the most creative ways to express a brand message in a media landscape that would burst the brains of the very brightest network operators with its consumer nuances and related myriad creative intricacies.

Operators should focus on the unique elements that only they can provide—location, presence, user profiles, platforms for applications, devices, and network APIs. They should build business models around abstracting this information so that the ecosystem can enhance the user experience and usage. Such an approach will increase their competitiveness in the media ecosystem, keep the usage and ARPU levels up, and get more entrepreneurs and users involved in moving the industry to its next milestone.

Such an ecosystem will empower the entrepreneurs to keep pushing the boundaries of technical and business innovations to make mobile media and advertising a sustainable, vibrant, and scalable industry at a much faster pace and will help deliver on the promise of "open access" quicker than any of the spectrum battles.

Organizational Cultural Issues May Be the Deciding Factor

It may be easy to say that carriers would be better off "embracing openness." But in reality, it is difficult for any large, established industry to rethink itself. This is understandable from a basic, commonsense perspective of organizational culture.

Anyone who does business in the carrier world today can quickly identify with how embedded the basics of the business model are in the industry. It is difficult to explore new opportunities, let alone radical ones, when those assigned to that task do not have the internal influence held by those who represent the traditional business—especially when the traditional voice business drives most of the revenues.

And it's understandable that the carrier culture would not be expected to easily embrace the concept of openness that we think may be required to unlock the huge latent industry value inherent in mobile advertising. Their gardens are walled for a damn good reason: They have spent billions of dollars hauling, tilling, fertilizing, and managing the soil.

Most of us have spent enough time in the new economy to forget that until quite recently, basic communication technology, broadly defined, has been very asset intensive. In a single day, we may find ourselves playing chess with someone in Bucharest, buying Christmas gifts while sitting on the couch, or webcaming with our daughter at Waseda University in Tokyo.

In the old economy, many of us may remember calling a U.K. operator from a pay phone and waiting for them to call back with a phone connection to the United States. It wasn't as simple as it is today, and it certainly wasn't free. It involved a lot of stuff like copper wire, optical fiber, and switches.

In contrast to the carrier experience, new economy companies like Google built their businesses on the Internet—which they didn't have to pay to build. So they do not have to be protective of any huge upfront investment in the pipes, routers, switches, spectrum, and voice channels.

If the potential of mobile advertising is dependent on an industry rethink, it's hard to imagine the carriers as the change agents. So are we destined for a snail's pace and have to hope that marketers will give up on mobile? Is the type of revolutionary change we believe necessary to catalyze the potential of mobile advertising even possible?

Such revolutionary change has happened before: Remember the discussion of Frank Munsey in Chapter 1? He was the guy who in 1893 was bold enough to actually lower the price of *Munsey's Magazine* to 10 cents and position the circulation as the core asset of the business. In so doing, he paved the way for the magazine industry to see itself differently, as more of a business than a public service.

And it has happened more recently: Google presents an interesting parallel. Its founders, like the early pioneers of the magazine industry, had *social* objectives. Magazines before Munsey aimed to inform and entertain; Google aimed to make all the world's information equally accessible to all through the Internet. The profit objective was initially driven by investors.

And we've all seen that the social and profit objectives are not mutually exclusive. In wedding improved web search, which met social goals and exposed user intent to advertisers, Google has shown, just like Munsey, that the ability to monetize the exposures is often a more lucrative way to look at the business.

Thus, players like Google may have an organizational culture advantage, which we'd argue is never trivial. This is simply because exploiting the potential of mobile advertising does not require them to *rethink* their business but rather treat it as an extension of their core strengths and organizational raison d'etre.

The Forecast Calls for a 95 Percent Chance of Revolution

The seeds of significant industry change are now being sown as we write this book. As 2007 came to close, the industry was introduced to Google's Android, positioned as the first complete, open, and free mobile platform in the making. And the related Open Handset Alliance, committed to working with Android, is over 30 strong, including T-Mobile, Sprint Nextel, NTT Docomo, China Mobile, Telefonica, Telecom Italia, HTC, Motorola, Samsung, Qualcomm, and Intel.

Nokia is another change agent candidate. Their recently announced Ovi internet-services project, supported by Vodaphone, combines Nokia's mapping and music services. Add a social network around that, and they have the essence of a new consumer software strategy.

And what about advertising? Nokia, who has invested heavily and built ad server and analytics systems, has made hints that Ovi will include geo-targeted advertising capabilities. While the initial Android plan includes no direct advertising component in the platform, Google is quick to point out that consumers will be able to access advertising the same way they do on the Web.

In addition, there was significant movement on the U.S. 700 MHz spectrum auction—the last beachfront property auction in the wireless industry. The very fact that Google got involved forced operators to publicly state their position on "open access" and start thinking about their place in the new ecosystem.

The winner of the spectrum will be required by the FCC to let consumers use any device and any software on the network. The openness requirements themselves were largely the result of Google's significant lobbying efforts.

While how these events will play out is unclear, we think that there are significant structural forces at work that will drive industry change. We believe that the potential we see in mobile advertising will help drive these structural changes. The revolution has begun. The pace has been slow, held back by carrier cultural inertia. The pace of change has been picking up steam, and once it gets momentum, it is going to be a torrid sea of change. The biggest beneficiaries will be consumers, who will be exposed to almost free, breakthrough new mobile media experiences.

The Business of Mobile Advertising

We have talked quite a bit about the impact of technology on the advertising business, but how does that change the way business is done? Would advertising sales teams become irrelevant? Would the media buying process be a thing of the past? Would the handholding be eliminated by automated processes? We think not. While a lot of the traditional functions will be automated and there will be more accountability, building and maintaining key relationships will always be a high-touch effort.

Competitive advantages will come from adaptation to the new digital landscape and utilization of new tools. Data gurus will be the new rock stars at the center of the picture, not at the fringes. They will sit center stage with the creative types. Mobile will be required knowledge at every digital agency, not just the cutting-edge shops. Mobile campaigns will have standard metrics, measurements, and high levels of verifiability and auditability within the industry. Digital is already demanding these changes on the Internet and that will roll into mobile at a rapid pace.

As long as the media models are priced at a flat rate with all-you-can-eat consumer pricing, the advances in devices; power cells, displays, input approaches and other areas will allow a massive expansion in consumer usability and usage. The big "if" in the models is around pricing and enabling consumer sharing to create the magical sufficiently contagious effects needed for massive adoption. This could have a tremendous effect on the business of advertising because this combination would have a truly massive scale impact to get to the right level of consumer eyeballs to be interesting for a brand.

Finally, we believe we will see new forms of advertising pricing emerge in mobile and interactive television that make a CPM approach look dated and stale. Engagement is measurable—especially when the ads can be separated from the media as in mobile and interactive TV. This engagement visibility, combined with mobile interactivity making older media, such as print, radio, and television, come alive with new measurability, will put mobile as a key spoke in the new digital wheel of media spends in the future.

In his book, *The End of Advertising as We Know It*, Sergio Zyman, former CMO of the Coca-Cola Company, had a key message: *"There is only one rule: advertising must sell."* Advertising is all about selling *more* and building lifetime relationships with customers who keep on buying *more*. These goals won't change in the future.

Mobile has a significant possibility of winding up as the first screen—not the third screen as it is called today. The technology advances around the device and the networks are marching forward at torrid paces. We are headed into a true, always on, real-time era. Mobile may well become the core hub of that daily usage and it will be centered on three key screens; the computer, interactive television, and mobile.

We see massive potential for mobile advertising in this future view. But we have lived through the ugly issues of storefronts, application distribution, pricing, digital rights management, and many other issues. Those issues can all be overcome, but the friction they create in the system is loud and deep. The complexities they cause are unnecessarily confusing to the advertising agencies and brands. But when the barriers are removed—the progress will be amazing and the pace will be incredibly fast. The business of mobile advertising looks incredibly bright when you look at it without all that friction.

NOTES

1. www.ubiq.com/hypertext/weiser/SciAmDraft3.html, accessed December 14, 2007.
2. Folio, January 18, 2007.
3. Marc Andreesen, blog.pmarca.com, "Why there is no such thing as Web 2.0," June 5, 2007.
4. http://att.centralcast.net/3screen/, accessed Dec 14, 2007.
5. While convergence of Internet, cable, and wireless is a worthy cause few players can pull this off. From the network side, AT&T, Telecom Italia, SK Telecom, and Telefonica are players with all three pieces. From the content side, companies like Disney are ideally suited with products and services already in place across the three mediums and capability to track things on each of them.
6. Kevin Martin's testimony prepared for the Subcommittee on Telecommunications and the Internet, Committee on Energy and Commerce, U.S. House of Representatives, July 24, 2007.
7. Li Yuan, "Breaking Down the Walls of Phones' Web Gardens," *Wall Street Journal,* August 2, 2007.

8. There are some caveats to openness; for example, if the location or presence information is implemented on operator's network and every application started to request them in concert, it would bring the network to its knees and escalate the cost of implementation and maintenance. Thus, some rules and conditions need to be put in place to ensure network integrity and fidelity in the short term. In the future, alternate implementations like location from the device or presence query fulfillment from other sources will negate such burdens on the operator networks.

9. The strategy canvas was made popular by *Blue Ocean Strategy: How to Create Uncontested Market Space and Make the Competition Irrelevant,* by W. Chan Kim and Renee Mauborgne, (Boston: Harvard Business School Press, 2005). The strategy canvas is both a diagnostics and an action framework for building a compelling blue ocean strategy or strategies to build new marketplaces and industries. The canvas captures the current state of play in the known market space. This allows one to understand the factors the industry currently competes on in products and services and the areas of investment by players in the industry.

10

Perspectives

Throughout this book project, we received tremendous support for our research. We conducted scores of interviews with executives and playmakers from major markets. This chapter brings together views of experts and mobile advertising thought-leaders from across the value chain around the world.

OPPORTUNITIES FOR MOBILE ADVERTISING

Richard Saggers, Head of Mobile Advertising, Vodafone, and EMEA Chairman, Mobile Marketing Association (MMA)

The strength of mobile to connect brands to customers has long been recognized—and the development of mobile advertising gives the industry a real chance to harness that power to everyone's benefit.

At Vodafone, mobile advertising is a key part of our strategy. It sits squarely in the mobile-plus space we seek to occupy, taking our services beyond mobile telephony to meeting our customers' total communication needs and creating mobile advertising revenue streams that tap into our large customer base.

Why do we see this as an opportunity? First, the market exists: 89 percent of brands say they plan to use mobile advertising by 2008. European customers' media consumption was 95 percent traditional against 5 percent online in 2000; today, those figures are 84 percent and 16 percent.

Second, we've already made the Internet accessible to mobiles. Customers want online access whenever they choose. Through our mobile Internet and Vodafone live! Portal, we have a mobile experience that mirrors their personal computer experience.

It follows that there are synergies between online and mobile advertising that we want to make available to the wider community—especially tapping into key segments such as youth, whose traditional media consumption is declining.

We believe that mobile advertising has a huge and very exciting potential, not least because of its targeting capability; the fact that it can reach key customer segments more effectively than traditional media; and the ways in which it can enable brands to interact with customers.

That's the opportunity. Our challenge is to make sure mobile advertising has clarity, consistency—and underpins our reputation of quality and trust.

Our Approach

There are three key elements that reflect and support our approach to mobile advertising:

1. *Aim:* Our aim is to pool our expertise and create an innovative mobile advertising business that enhances the customer mobile experience. Giving customers access to what they want and the content and experiences they are familiar with online is crucial. We're creating a depth of offering by working with a number of high-profile partners, including search engines and social networking sites.
2. *Experience:* We have already launched mobile advertising commercially on Vodafone live! in Germany, Italy, the United Kingdom, Spain, Czech Republic, Australia, and Egypt; on messaging services in Italy, and Czech Republic; and on applications such as games in the United Kingdom, Greece, and Italy. This gives us valuable early experience as the fledgling mobile advertising market grows in pace and volume.

3. *Insight:* We have learned much from a number of consumer trials with leading global brands.

Insights from Trials

These trials, using different channels and approaches to understand user response and reaction, inform our approach to mobile advertising. We've found that customers will accept advertising if it is short, unobtrusive, and relevant to them in a service and/or usage context, but they expect something in return.

Like most Internet sites, we display advertising on the Vodafone live! Portal. However, for other forms of advertising involving, for example, MMS/SMS (short messaging service) to customers, we ask for customer consent first. Their reward for engaging with brands via their mobiles will be some benefit in kind, such as subsidized or free services.

For example, offering customers free games resulted in significant levels of download but reduced levels of activation compared to subsidized and full game prices. Subsidized games featuring advertising are the most attractive option.

In another trial, we ran a pre- and postroll advertisement for a *Big Brother* television clip. In 2006, this was available for 35p per clip but in 2007 we used the sponsored model with advertisements. The uplift was more than 50 times the expected result.

We had similar success with sponsored messaging in South Africa's "Please call me" service. Clearly, advertising-funded content unlocks a new level of content activity and we have started to commercialize this in a number of markets.

The trials also showed us that users want interactivity and that the youth segment (18 to 30), in particular, like the viral capability: they want to forward advertisements and promotions to their friends. Our approach to mobile advertising is to maximize those opportunities for customers.

We have our own content that we can publish through our Vodafone live! Portal, as well as through third parties.

Our Role in the Value Chain

Much of the value mobile offers to brands is unique to our medium, such as the consumer relationships and insights that provide genuine targeting opportunities to engage with consumers. This is particularly important at a time when media fragmentation gives brands a greater challenge than ever before in communicating effectively with their customers.

Targeting across age, gender, and location allows us to put context into the advertising—and return data to advertisers to help their media planning and measure return on investment by using mobile as the key response path.

Mobile delivers multiple platforms for advertising campaigns. As well as allowing for different formats, it allows frequency capping and the ability to storyboard advertising, both of which are mobile-specific.

Timing is also high in the mobile value portfolio. Advertisers can time their customer touchpoint, exploiting impressive brand engagement opportunities at the time customers make their buying decisions. Other advertising media cannot offer such a close customer relationship, making a strong case for advertising to be seen as the glue that holds together other media and supports spikes of activity.

Setting Standards

We believe strongly that mobile advertising demands a mobile industry approach. While competition is taking place between mobile operators and mobile publishers, there is an overlaying competition of mobile as a medium with other channels, such as television, print, radio, and Internet for a share of revenue from advertisers.

To earn the confidence of advertisers, brand owners, and the agencies with which they work, the mobile industry must have the consistency and operational framework that has been built up in the online world. Customers must, equally, have confidence in us if we are to retain our reputation and their trust.

Vodafone is a thought leader in developing standards, guidelines, and best practices across a number of areas in our business. We play a leading role in the GSMA Mobile Advertising Programme, the Mobile Marketing Association (MMA) EMEA Region, and the MMA EMEA Mobile Advertising Committee, which we co-chair.

MMA members and the mobile industry at large have developed the MMA Mobile Advertising Guidelines to encourage the growth of the mobile advertising industry. These have been amended just recently and published as the MMA EMEA Mobile Advertising Guidelines (http://www.mmaglobal.com/emeamobileadvertising.pdf).

We support wholeheartedly the MMA's goal of ensuring that as this advertising market develops, consumers not only experience a positive mobile advertising experience but also are treated equitably by all in the value chain.

This is a young industry that will—and must—evolve as best practices and technologies change. The most critical areas where we need to set industry standards are:

- Capabilities and creativity (e.g. animated banners, new banner formats)
- New mobile advertising inventory (e.g. SMS, MMS, applications/clients, mobile content)
- Effective targeting (e.g. to increase value and consumer relevance)
- Acceptable serving and execution (e.g. privacy, consent, content standards, frequency)
- Measurement and transparency (e.g. market assessment, delivery reporting, and metrics)

As an industry, we need standards not only for our own and our customers' benefit but also to make it easy to buy mobile advertising collateral.

Advertising agencies will not deal with multiple tools across multiple channels. They want—and as their partners we must give them—collaborative standards that ease their buying process, provide verifiable results, and build credibility for the mobile advertising channel.

Summary

To me, the prize for a mobile industry that works together proactively to create stunning brand advertising opportunities that make the most of mobile's value is straightforward. Mobile advertising will be a recognized choice for advertising dollars, with marketers seeing it as a natural option for brand and product communication.

I believe that mobile advertising is a very exciting opportunity for Vodafone, just as it is for advertisers, all our industry players, and consumers. It has the potential to be the glue between multiple channels and gives agencies a fantastic opportunity to develop creatives that maximize mobile's strengths, qualities, and potential.

The industry has to come together to make this happen. This opportunity is ours to deliver. Only then will all parties realize the benefits and the power of mobile advertising to make targeted, meaningful, and rewarding connections with consumers.

MARKETING NEEDS INNOVATION, CAN MOBILE HELP?

Syl Saller, Global Innovation Director, Diageo

As the world's largest premium drinks company, Diageo manages category-leading brands including the likes of Guinness, Johnnie Walker, Smirnoff, Tanqueray, and Baileys.

A unique feature of the drinks business is the heritage, provenance, and long history of our brands. Guinness is coming up to its 250th anniversary, Bushmills is turning 400, Johnnie Walker is over 180 years old and even Baileys, a relative newcomer was launched over 30 years ago. How many brands do you know are that old and still so vibrant? Innovation in our industry, should emphasis heritage, dialing up quality credentials while making sure we send the message that we should be consuming better quality, not greater.

How does a product brand last that long? I think there are at least two things that have to happen—the ability to selectively innovate on a brand in line with its heritage, but perhaps more importantly the ability to continually engage the consumer in new ways. As the corporate Global Innovation Director at Diageo, I'm constantly challenged by both.

We are reluctant to tamper with the core architecture of our brands and that puts more pressure on our marketing techniques to evolve in a vibrant and relevant way. If their objective is to articulate and engage consumers in the brand, they must align themselves to changes in consumer behavior and in particular their changing media consumption habits.

And this is why new media constantly evolves. If people are watching television, we marketers have to understand that medium. If they are on the Internet, we have to do the same. And every large marketing organization has people dedicated to understanding and testing new media as they emerge.

Four years ago, a friend asked for my professional opinion, "What do you think of mobile marketing and advertising?" "What's that?" I replied. After that initial scare, I sent him to speak to our New Media people and, luckily, they had more to say than I. The point is at that early in the development of the medium, parts of our marketing organization were busy testing mobile marketing campaigns, but it hadn't yet hit my radar screen because it wasn't yet established. Implementing effective new media campaigns take time.

Four years later, I definitely know what mobile marketing and advertising means. It seems to be a lot more developed in the United Kingdom, Europe, and especially Asia, than in the United States but I am seeing many signs of steady growth in the United States.

Intuitively, mobile marketing is a very compelling medium to marketers. It generates a great number of exposures, it's capable of personalization and targeting, and it's measurable. In addition, people carry it with them and knowing someone's location and being with the consumer at the point of influence is pretty interesting.

And more important, it has the attention of the new consumer. While it's clear that people are brand conscious, it's also clear that it takes more than a glossy image to articulate the brand statement to them. This is the generation of multitasking, multimedia—always connected. It takes more to get their attention. You have to go from a passive or interruption message to a more active and sometimes permission-based experience. You have to *engage* people in an interactive and inclusive brand relationship.

So, for example, Guinness is currently running an interactive campaign asking consumers to vote for the pub they think serves the best pint of Guinness—an SMS text competition offering a chance to win a weekend in Dublin. Now anyone who's ever been here understands that the pub scene is an integral part of life in the United Kingdom. Engaging the consumer right in the pub, the actual point of consumption, is a compelling way to interactively engage them in the Guinness brand.

Using SMS marketing, be it opt-in outbound communications or inbound text response, has proven to work well for us; but we are also innovating in various more interesting forms of mobile marketing.

In Japan, Guinness faced a distribution challenge: Only a small number of the 500,000 outlets in Tokyo stock Guinness. So we developed an application called Guinness Navi where consumers can scan a QR bar code on our ads using their camera phone. A GPS then pinpoints their location. They then see a Google Maps page that shows them the location of the nearest Guinness outlet and provides directions. The success of Navi plays to the secret of mobile marketing—to provide relevant and useful services to consumers on the move.

Also in Asia, Johnnie Walker has tapped into insights relating to Asian men and recently launched an innovative digital personal assistant offers various organizational services to consumers through your mobile phone.

We are increasingly seeing consumers who get their first Internet experience on their mobile phone. To this end, Smirnoff has recently launched smirnoff.mobi—a mobile phone web site platform designed specifically for consumers on the move. This site contains useful information such as bar guides and cocktail recipes and is proving extremely popular in terms of visits and consumer interaction. We have conducted a successful trial using mobile spot advertising to drive traffic to Smirnoff.mobi.

In Great Britain, Smirnoff successfully conducted a trial using Bluetooth transmitters at their unique Electric Cabaret events to provide consumers with exciting opt-in video content to take away with them.

Finally, we're also aware how using mobile marketing presents challenges because it represents a particularly personal device to most consumers. We don't ever want to be seen as intruding on consumers, so we are careful to always adopt an opt-in policy on our outbound communications. Given our commitments to responsible marketing, we have developed an industry-leading Digital Code of Practice that governs our responsible, legal, and best practice use of all mobile marketing efforts.

Managing brand vitality over long periods of time requires strategic innovation in both product development and product marketing. Mobile media has some distinctive capabilities and is something all marketers are watching closely. Our job is to test; the job of those driving the new media is to create innovative capabilities and to articulate their potential value. Our interests are aligned—figuring out ways to meaningfully message to and truly engage consumers in places where they're spending their time.

CONSTRAINING YOUTHS IN THE MOBILE GATEWAYS

Ian Stewart, Senior Vice President, MTV Networks International

The world has never been more accessible; virtually via television, the Internet, and now through mobile media, or physically because of cheaper travel. People are curious to experience the new and exotic, to absorb cultures from around the world, and to integrate this into their globally infused lifestyles. A fascination with interesting themes and concepts from other places is a solid trend and one we expect to have around for many years. Combined with sub-sub genres of music, niche media, cut-and-paste fashion, multiple youth tribes, international film, an explosion of the arts, the media can't keep up with the splintering and fusing of pop culture, and the globalization and localization of it. Consumers are reaching out everywhere for everything: It's an information and ideas explosion. Mobile media is a key part of this dynamic.

There is also a major generational shift moving forward about how technology, including mobile media, is engaged and used. This is a very different technology perspective from what we see in the older crowds—moving from new—to having it—to having had it. This generation doesn't notice the technology around them. Teens, and in particular preteens, have grown up with computers in the classroom, their homes, and for many, their bedrooms. They have mobile phones in their pockets and their content is digital. This is their world. They know no other paradigm. In our surveys, we have noticed the most marked difference in the 8- to 15-year-olds, where full technology is something that's handed out to them in their everyday life. For mobile media and advertising, this will be a major theme.

The second big theme is that, more so than ever, there are many things young people can do with technology around communication, community, and media. It is really the connection side of things that young people are the most excited about. We think that we've got to get cool media to young people, but they are also incredibly interested in the social networking side. Who's online and what goes on with whom in that place? Broadband, Bit Torrent, MP3, P2P, 3G, TiVO, PVR, IPTV, blogging, podcasts, bluejacking . . . the technology is almost irrelevant. Everyone is now "six degrees" or less apart, and by-and-large loving it. It is the ability to connect and keep in touch with their friends, and to make new friends that is the most exciting thing about technology. They spend more time on IM, chat, blogs, and TXTing than any other digital applications.

The third major theme we are seeing is that young people can access everything digitally; music, friends, information, media, and entertainment. An amazing claim, but youth believe that because of the Internet there is no question they can't answer, no content they can't acquire, and no person they can't find. This has huge implications on everything from learning (a shift from memory to acquisition skills) to entertainment (something for everybody but fewer common threads). Within this trend, the role of media is becoming a social currency—if it isn't worth sending on, is it worth anything at all? Digital media has taken on a new value to this "forwarding culture" generation. The things they discover and collect are stored and forwarded to friends, partly to entertain and partly to show how good a find is; a new popularity currency of sorts.

But we are in an integral time with mobile right now where the online applications and online usage now have exploded to such a point that mobile has to play quite a bit of catch-up to get to where youth are online. Mobile is still constrained by youth with handsets that are complete with 3.5G cameras, music players, Bluetooth, always-on high-speed Internet, and most importantly, with the operators sort of packing it up at an affordable price. Apart from South Korea and Japan, the operators haven't got the flat rate, all-you-can-eat, pricing models figured out yet, so young people can't fully max out their phones to keep up to speed with what they are doing online.

Mobile consumer frustration hits because people can do something on one medium but can't do it on mobile. As an industry, we have come a long way with legally sharing media. That is a great thing because young people are experiencing new media virally, sharing content. Online it is working very well and is leading to much more exposure, new trends, and new media. Online you have the chance to find out what the films are, the trends, fashion labels, travel trend information. The phones aren't keeping up with that facility to forward media and content. It is constrained at the gateway. We don't see a lot of young people forwarding content on their phones. For the most part, the phone doesn't even have cut-and-paste yet, a critical underpinning for viral effects with new media.

If mobile media were made affordable, subsidized with advertising, and enabled for viral effects at the gateway level, young consumers would create massive, new, dynamic mobile markets throughout Asia—far bigger than they are today.

What if, in the future, you blinked and suddenly you could do 10 times more than what you could do today with mobile? What if you could remix MP3s and share them virally from your phone? What if you could take a mobile photo and one-click it to your moblog and send an SMS to all your friends automatically? What if you could rent a set of songs for your mobile phone for a month and share the playlist with your mobile friends? What if this were all flat rate, all-you-can-eat, affordable pricing for young consumers and subsidized with advertising? This is all real—in South Korea—and we should look to that dynamic market as a bearing point for the future of mobile media and advertising to get through the current market fog.

MOBILE IS THE CONNECTIVE TISSUE TO OTHER MEDIA

Joe Doran, General Manager, Microsoft Advertiser and Publisher Solutions Group

We believe that mobile holds tremendous potential as a marketing channel, but also recognize critical issues that are preventing the channel from reaching its full potential. We're working hard with industry partners to solve challenges such as campaign scale, measurement problems, the difficulties with carrier walled gardens, and lack of standardization. Our different groups are looking to break down barriers by developing a channel-agnostic adserving and analytics platform that can support mobile and other emerging channels like VOD. We're looking past the short-term limitations and working with clients to construct strategic road maps for fully embracing what's possible today while laying the groundwork for what's coming 12 to 18 months down the road.

We look at mobile as the connective tissue between other media channels. It excels at building bridges with other channels and other media. It is the ultimate remote control for your life. It's easy today to look at things like WAP banners or SMS as isolated media channels, and they can be effective that way. But the real power is building bridges from the static out-of-home to the phone; from television or radio to the phone; from print to the phone; from in-store media or packaging to the phone; and so on. The phone becomes the central hub of marketing channels. We're not quite there yet, but that is a powerful evolution and it is much closer than most people think.

Think about it. My phone is always in my pocket. Forget AmEx—I don't leave home without my phone. It's always on and it is perhaps the most personalized gadget in my life. A simple text message to a shortcode quickly turns static media channels into fresh new digital platforms for interactive campaigns. That billboard or print advertisement, enhanced with a simple SMS short code becomes a gateway into a much more engaging advertising experience. In that sense, mobile is the ultimate activator. And it changes the very nature of advertising because the consumer has opted into the campaign. Suddenly that's not advertising anymore. It's content that's of interest to the consumer. It brings interactivity to media that used to be static, and with that interaction comes a level of accountability that simply did not previously exist.

To accurately navigate this massive amount of data, we look to centralized platforms that can help us assimilate and understand this data.

Authority Shifting Drives Strategic Changes

Consumers are in control of digital media. And they've got nearly unlimited choice due to explosion of content and fragmentation of distribution. In that world, the old models of interruption and grabbing attention begin to erode. Marketers need to stop buying or grabbing attention, and they need to start *earning* attention. You earn that attention either with great content or by providing tremendous value. We think that's true of all media, digital or not. And the remarkable thing about mobile is that it is so much more than another channel through which you can try to earn that attention. As the connective tissue and ultimate universal remote, it will play a critical role in carrying the attention you've worked so hard to earn from one place to the next.

Media Measurability: Lessons from Other Emerging Media

We recognize that the connective tissue approach suddenly makes media performance far more transparent than at any time in its previous history. Mobile as the media hub takes the accountability that marketers have come to expect from online, and applies it to offline media like billboards, television, and print ads. One of our key roles is to help customers with the data extraction, analytics and performance optimization of a campaign. We equip them with the intelligence around the campaign so that they can wrap their consumer insight around that core dataset and optimize the campaigns. When it comes to mobile specifically, we apply some of the same thinking that has driven our dynamic insertion and data innovations on cable TV/VOD platforms. We learned a lot as we navigated the complexity of that ecosystem, and the mobile ecosystem can look surprisingly similar—both are highly regulated and dominated by a few large players who ultimately own the data and the subscriber relationship. Whatever the source, we are in the game of getting as much granular data as technically possible from the owner of the data. At the end of the day, the advertisers want to know that somebody saw the ad and ideally that they took some kind of action or that the ad had some kind of impact. With mobile becoming the connective tissue to other media, suddenly you might have a measurement of how somebody interacted with the ad, or viewed the ad. Out platforms are about separating the advertisement from the content so that it can be dynamically served and optimized, and then enabling interactivity—both of which provide tremendous market value.

14 Flavors of Data

However, none of this is going to be able to reach its incredible potential until there is far more standardization of what those response mechanisms are going to be. We have these incredibly powerful metrics from other channels— impressions, click-throughs, post-click tracking, reach, frequency, brand exposure duration—all of which can help an agency or advertiser to maximize their return on ad spending. But with mobile, we have 14 different flavors of campaign data. To resolve these piles of inconsistencies coming out of the various mobile silos, strong standardization is required. Until there are significant resolutions in that area, mobile could wind up being stuck in between testing and big budget campaign potential. These standards must transcend carriers and technology players, and present a united front to the media community. Until the industry can begin to thread that together and provide a united front in the form of the third-party ad-serving model, it will be in between massive success and experimental budgets. We need these standards to facilitate the marketplace with both the buy and sell transactions. We will see a massive marketplace here only after we get to unbiased, standardized, manageable metrics enabled in third-party technology.

MOBILE ADVERTISING IN INDIA

Mahesh Prasad, President, Reliance Infocomm

Mobile advertising is a new concept that is catching on in India as much as anywhere else in the world. For the past five years, we have been trying to break into this area and educate the market, the advertisers, and gauging the tolerance level for various forms of advertisements from consumers. There are a couple of ways to look at advertising—intrusive and nonintrusive.

Most of the mobile advertising today is somewhat intrusive. If you look at mobile advertising, the usage that has the largest penetration is SMS. Using SMS, people are primarily doing promotion with the consumer's consent—banks, insurance companies, and others are trying to get in touch with the consumer, are sending their offers, which are akin to promotion offers sent on e-mails. That's the most primitive and pervasive form of advertising both in India and other parts of the world. The second form is the banner ad placed on the home page or the WAP landing page or subsequent screens. The third one is advertising served within the application (e.g., banks advertise on financial applications). Fourth is the most nonintrusive form of advertising. We were the first one in India, to create Brandzone (an application that is available through the carrier portal) where we showcased the top brands in the country when they were interested in launching a product or advertising a product or generate leads. This is the most consumer engagement-friendly and noninterruptive model. However, the number of exposures is relatively small compared with SMS blast or banner advertising, but it is the most effective in terms of ROI.

Mobile Campaigns at Reliance

We partnered with LML Motorbikes who wanted to launch a new motorbike series and make the product information widely available. LML zone was created in early 2005. In addition, customers can download related content such as wallpapers. This application provided a lead generation vehicle whereby a customer can fill out a form, give explicit consent, and schedule a test drive. This increases awareness and generates targeted leads nationwide. On average, five to six brands showcase their products in any given week. Several banks, investment companies, and automobile companies have used this service and engaged users who come on their own and engage themselves. Since we didn't want to diminish the value of mobile advertising and didn't want to commoditize, we chose the revenue model of fixed fee with the advertisers.

We started our first advertising campaign with the Cricket World Cup in 2003. We took advantage of the fact that a lot of consumer brands want to advertise during the World Cup. We brought in LG Consumer Electronics; they wanted to introduce their brand into the market (at that time LG and Samsung were not household brands in this market). They felt that there was an opportunity to convey the message of LG as a consumer electronics brand. Reliance launched a cricket application (probably the first in-application mobile advertising in the world). We would update the scores, provide ball-by-ball update, and integrate the sponsorship message within the application, which could be changed by the ad server. At that time, we were a free service and got lots of visibility for the advertisers. The service was free to the consumers but we had revenues from the advertiser. We were able to demonstrate in India that there is a revenue model for mobile advertising (it was not a barter) and advertisers saw the value. We were getting 13 to 14 million hits on a 10-million subscriber base on a daily basis. Our recent campaign with Cadbury also got tremendous response with over 31 million impressions delivered to 5.5 million users in 10 different languages (see the case study in Chapter 7).

The mobile advertising is taking new shapes; for example, using voice portal, play a song, dial a tune. We have integrated across SMS, WAP, Java/BREW apps, and Voice. An area where the industry needs to get better is profiling and targeting. Today, many things have been talked about in terms of data mining and customer relationship management (CRM), but the data that an advertiser is looking for is quite different from that provided by the data operator. The operator is concerned about address, telecom usage patterns, type of tariffs and revenues, types of services—a lot of this data is available. Advertiser are looking for demographical data and are not interested in telecom consumption patterns; they are interested in age, education levels, gender, and targeting by geography (Bandra versus Navi Mumbai within Mumbai). The level of targeting is minimal today—mostly intuitive or behavioral matching. If someone is browsing apps for pre/postnatal care in the women's world section, most likely it is a new baby family; if the user is in cricket, it may mean the user is a sports buff, and so on.

Summary

Mobile is better than Internet advertising since more targeting information can be used for mobile. First, we want to get to the most sophisticated data mining model and provide slicing and dicing of data to the advertisers so that they get completely targeted information and influence the user at the moment of decision or action. Most are looking for call-for-action on mobile, which traditional advertising media don't provide. We want to get better at data profiling so that advertisers get the most bang for their buck. Second, we want to expand advertising to all mobile mediums to cast the widest net. Finally, we want contextual interactive advertising to take center stage. So, if a person is using certain products, it is the best time to introduce relevant ads with a call to action. Since the user is in the mood to consume the product, the chance for contextual call-to-action to get a response is much higher compared with intrusive banner ad advertising when the person is not in the mood to consume or purchase.

The ultimate nirvana is tying all of our properties across Internet, TV, radio (we operate the biggest FM radio network in the nation), and mobile. Integration from a media-buying process will be there but tying the four channels together for the advertiser and the consumer will take time. In terms of the ecosystem, companies like Google and Yahoo are just surfacing in the Indian market. I don't see competition from them, but we will have to work together. We need each other in developing this market and industry. They need us as much as we need them.

DELIVERING THE RIGHT AD AT THE RIGHT TIME

Marianne Marck, Vice President Engineering, Walt Disney Internet Group

Disney is at the forefront creating rich media experiences for broadcast, online, and mobile. Whether providing mobile games throughout the world or delivering full streaming television episodes online, Disney delivers content created for the way customers want to experience it. As our customers consume more digital media online and on their mobile devices, an ad-based approach for providing free media is gaining in popularity and effectiveness. Delivering advertising effectively across the three screens (broadcast, online, and mobile) presents many technical opportunities and challenges. Here I discuss two of the technologies that play a role in optimizing ad delivery: targeting and inventory management. I also offer insight into how lessons learned from online targeting and inventory management apply to mobile.

Delivering the Right Ad to the Customer

To get the most effective advertisement in front of a customer, our advertising system has to use whatever information is available to determine the best ad to serve. Evaluating this data to determine the best ad for delivery is called targeting. Targeting can use many data sources such as the type of content shown with the ad, a customer behavioral profile, a customer segment, or a customer zip code. Every time an ad is served online or on a mobile device, targeting can be used to select and serve the best ad, thus optimizing the opportunity to reach customers in the most effective way.

To sell these optimized opportunities, aka "targets," our salesforce must know how many ads it can sell. Inventory management involves estimating the number of ad impressions that can be sold for each target to provide the advertising salesforce a forecast of availability. This data is used to determine what is available to sell during a given time period.

Targeting and inventory management are two technical capabilities that are constantly being refined in the online advertising world. These capabilities also have direct application to the mobile advertising environment with a few twists.

Target Data Source Development

The development of data sources to be used for targeting creates rich opportunities and some challenges. Mobile and online environments generate a significant amount of data on customer interactions. Developing strategies to manage the data, apply it effectively, and protect customer privacy is critical. Understanding the customer in both online and mobile environments provides an opportunity to customize targeting across these environments. What is known about the customer in the online world can be used to target on the mobile device and visa versa. Tying online and mobile data together in a customer profile enables cross-environment targeting.

Several interesting challenges arise when undertaking to unite mobile and online customer data. First, the ways in which customers are identified and can therefore be made known to an advertising targeting system are not always consistent across online and mobile. On the mobile side, users are generally known by a subscriber id. Online, customers are generally known by a login name or a global identifier that is placed in an encrypted cookie or registration record. It is important to have an identifier or key that can work across both environments so that the data gathered from online and mobile can be joined together into a single profile. It is also important to have an identifier that allows targeting to occur anonymously. This means that the mobile and online divisions have to work together on their identification and data management strategies. Both must adhere to privacy protection policies, protect children, and adhere to legal requirements.

Another challenge lies in driving the performance for targeted ad delivery. For advanced targeting, we don't know what ad to serve until the customer makes a request for online or mobile content. Then the right ad has to be selected and delivered almost instantaneously. This means that customer-centric targets must be optimized for look-up. A customer segment, geo code, mobile content code or any other targeting data source has to be looked up in milliseconds so that the related advertisement can be inserted and sent back to the customer's web browser or device.

Today, we typically sell advertising in the broadcast, online, and mobile environments as distinct and separate opportunities. Targets that are developed for online ad opportunities such as geo targets, behavioral targets, and content targets, are separate from mobile ad opportunities, which are primarily content and sponsor driven. But as we continue to develop richer targeting data sources and refine the ad system targeting capabilities, we will provide more consistent advertising targeting across the three screens. The mobile and online targets can be combined, and ad opportunities that are working well in the broadcast environment can be extended to the same target audiences in online and mobile.

The mobile environment also creates new targeting dimensions. One new dimension is on- and off-deck presence. If a media content provider is featured on a carrier's deck, advertising campaigns will likely be adhering to the advertising controls dictated by the carrier's on-deck requirements. Advertisements featured on the media content provider's mobile deck will be considered off-deck and the content provider can control the sale of ad inventory at this location with no restrictions. Another mobile targeting dimension can be provided through location based services. Knowing where the mobile customer is currently located can provide more effective local advertising. Just as in the online world, the challenge in targeting mobile ads is in knowing how many ads you can sell for each targeting dimension. Inventory management gets more complicated as more targeting dimensions are added.

How Many Impressions Can Be Sold?

Targets can be created from many sources. A big challenge (and glorious fun for a statistical modeler) is the development of accurate forecasts of available ad inventory for each target. This requires an understanding of traffic patterns and site usage by the predefined customer targets. It also requires that mobile and online inventories be accurately estimated. Our ad sales reps have to know how many impression deals they can sell in a given time and they can't do it without accurate forecasts. Mobile adds some new challenges, as standards for tracking mobile page views and standards for tracking mobile ad impressions are still evolving. Caching, robot filtering, client side tracking—techniques that are generally standardized in the online environment—now need to be well understood in the mobile environment to enable accurate and trackable delivery of mobile advertising.

Many of the techniques for ad targeting and inventory management that have been refined for online can be applied directly to mobile. For example, customer targeting schemes and segmentation strategies can be reused across environments. The good news for the technologist is that there is a rich problem space here ready for the application of existing technologies and the creation of innovative solutions.

GLOBAL MOBILE ADVERTISING MARKET DEVELOPMENT AND THE INTEGRAL ROLE OF GUIDELINES

Laura Marriott, President, Mobile Marketing Association (MMA)

What role do standards or best practices play in the mobile marketing and advertising industry, and how do we efficiently create the best practices by which our industry adheres?

Imagine if mobile marketing methods and advertising inventory used to reach the mobile audience differed widely across operators, publishers, and mobile devices. Imagine how local and regional differences would add further complexity. Can we realistically expect to see marketers designing and executing large-scale campaigns using mobile as a medium if this was the case? Imagine a brand having to contact at least three wireless operators in every country in the world to deploy their mobile advertising campaigns? It is probably not going to happen!

In response to the complexities of our mobile industry, the MMA and its membership seek to simplify market entry for all in the ecosystem through the development of standardized guidelines and best practices. The MMA members and the mobile marketing and advertising industry at large have developed the MMA Mobile Advertising Guidelines (http://www.mmaglobal.com/mobileadvertising.pdf) to encourage the growth of the mobile advertising industry and widely adhere to them. It is our overall goal to ensure that as the mobile advertising market develops, consumers not only experience a positive mobile advertising experience but are also treated equitably by all in the value chain. Widespread adoption of the guidelines also allows brands to quickly and efficiently deploy mobile advertising campaigns using a consistent set of creative material across networks and countries, thereby creating a ubiquitous mobile media environment, easy to do business with.

Most important in establishing best practices is ensuring appropriate representation from the companies and individuals in the ecosystem. Representation is important for knowledge and awareness and to ensure adoption of the guidelines once they're published. All participants involved in the process providing knowledge, feedback, and collaboration across industry participants has been an important factor to the success of the mobile advertising guidelines worldwide. Mobile advertising stake holders include marketers (brands), agencies, wireless operators, technology enablers.

There is a delicate balance between guidelines and best practices agreed on internationally and their fine-tuning and promotion toward implementation within the individual markets. The elements are complementary and together create the level of trust necessary to grow this industry. MMA supports global, regional, and national structures to stimulate the consistency required.

Best practices will change and technologies will develop as this young industry grows. Consequently, guidelines are dynamic and are subject to continuous enhancement. The MMA mobile advertising committee maintains an ever-growing list of aspects to be addressed in their future releases, thereby building on the ongoing commitment to innovation of all parties involved in the ecosystem. The MMA mobile advertising guidelines are reassessed and launched every six months, given the fast pace of growth in the mobile industry. An iterative best practices development process, which progresses in incremental stages, helps maintain focus on manageable additions while ensuring earlier modifications are successful before later stages are launched.

Best practices are a first step in building a sustainable business and help to underline the importance and maturity of an emerging industry. Best practices help all industry participants know and understand the baseline rules that, in turn, ensure consumers are treated fairly and have a positive overall experience. All this will ultimately grow the mobile medium as a valuable and exciting channel.

Once the mobile advertising guidelines are published to the industry, each company in the value chain implements them among its staffers and evangelizes them to the broader industry as a whole. Communication also occurs between each company and its respective vendors to ensure all are advised of guideline changes. Communication, evangelization, and adherence are critical to broad scale global adoption.

The guidelines and best practices that are published today are only revealing the tip of the iceberg. Mobile advertising inventory being offered is growing rapidly, as is the underlying technology at arm's length of the consumer. While advertising text and image banners have been introduced in many markets already, the race for growth is now developing along some distinct evolution paths:

- Capabilities and creativity (e.g., animated banners, new banner formats)
- New mobile ad inventory (e.g., SMS, MMS, applications/clients, mobile content)
- Effective targeting (e.g., to increase value and consumer relevance)
- Acceptable serving and execution (e.g., privacy, consent, content standards, frequency)
- Measurable and transparent (e.g., market assessment, delivery reporting, and metrics)

Providing well-accepted guidelines at a demanding pace will remain the MMA's and the broader industry's challenge for the foreseeable future.

The MMA, along with key leaders from the industry, is developing mobile advertising guidelines for mobile web, text messaging, downloadables, search, mobile video, and television as well as MMS. As the industry matures, the MMA will continue to define formats, guidelines, and best practices for all emerging technologies.

The MMA has a long history in establishing the rules of play for the broader mobile marketing and media industry. In the United States, the MMA's two foundation sets of guidelines, the Code of Conduct for Mobile Marketing, and Consumer Best Practices for Cross Carrier Mobile Content Services (CBP), launched in 2003 and 2005, respectively, have set the tone for all constituents in the U.S. mobile marketing industry. These best practices have been incorporated into contractual agreements at the wireless operators that will encourage not only adoption, but compliance as well. The MMA will continue to publish these standard-setting guidelines to help grow the sustainable development of mobile marketing worldwide.

Guidelines and best practices help ensure a level playing field and consistent industry expectations in all mobile data services. Best practices are important not only to grow the industry but to ensure a positive consumer experience. Understanding and adhering to industry best practices is key to our industry's success. Make sure you understand the rules by which we play so that we can collectively ensure a consistent consumer experience and ease of entry for brands and media buyers worldwide.

THE FUTURE OF ADVERTISING IS IN THE CONSUMERS' POCKETS

Marco Boerries, Executive Vice President, Connected Life, Yahoo!

For many years, advertising has dominated television and Internet screens, so extending ads to the so-called third screen on mobile phones is a natural next step. This is particularly true because the time consumers spend watching television or reading newspapers is steadily declining and the number of global cell phones is skyrocketing.

There are more than 2.4 billion global cell phone subscribers today compared with roughly 1.2 billion Internet users. And recent technical improvements to both handsets and networks have made it easier to use cell phones for more than making calls. Advertisers want to make sure that their brand is seen where consumers are spending time, and as more consumers rely on sophisticated handsets to surf the Web, check their e-mail, and download media content, advertisers are looking to mobile to attract this particular audience. Many analysts and industry insiders believe that mobile marketing and advertising is beginning its growth trajectory and has the potential to be a multibillion-dollar market.

Consumer research confirms cell phones have become the one thing consumers never leave home without. They are highly personal items that are always with you and always on. That kind of loyalty and constant connection offers distinct advantages over all other forms of media in terms of consumer engagement and the ability to incent immediate action. This is especially true as you get into the ability to target consumers by location and the handsets are equipped with payment applications that enable you to find and purchase local items quickly and easily.

Mobile devices also come with distinct challenges. Whereas consumers will spend hours surfing the Web on home PCs, when they are using their cell phone, their interests are usually much narrower. They are either looking for immediate information, (e.g., weather or sports scores), searching for a local service, or killing time between other activities. To successfully reach mobile consumers, ads need to be both contextually relevant and optimized for the small screen. With the limited room on a cell phone screen, ads and search results have to be highly targeted to individual user needs. And there is the always the expectation that the ads will be served in a way that doesn't disrupt calls or other communications activities. Given these challenges, mobile advertisers are challenged to deliver a highly relevant and compelling user experience across a wide range of devices.

For several years, mobile advertising has matured along the same trajectory as online advertising. Both mediums provide vast improvements in audience targeting and results tracking over more traditional advertising vehicles; but mobile advertising can take marketing campaigns to new levels with immediate interactivity, location awareness and click-to-act content. Given the immediacy of the medium and the fact that the phone is always in the user's purse or pocket, the ability to reach and engage consumers goes far beyond any advertising opportunity out there today.

What needs to happen to turn potential into reality is that the ads and mobile applications have to be easy and fun to use while delivering valuable content to consumers. Concerns over what kinds of content consumers are willing to accept are valid, but if the advertising content they receive is targeted, easy to consume on a small screen, and provides value to them that becomes a moot point.

The way to drive usage is to ensure each and every communication is meaningful, and that requires the technology to effectively track and manage behavioral information and the applications to seamlessly deliver targeted content. Despite the obvious challenges of translating content to a mobile screen, the winners in this battle will likely be the companies with the technology and behavioral data necessary to effectively connect marketers with diverse groups of potential buyers.

Mobile advertising has experienced a watershed year in 2007. There is more inventory available, more money is being spent, and we now have case studies showcasing success including click-through rates that are as high as 10 times higher than online advertising.

The challenges in 2008 revolve around getting easy-to-use applications into consumer's hands and solidifying the partnerships necessary to create, target, and deliver compelling content.

There has been a lot of noise in the industry about the barriers erected by the wireless providers wanting to maintain complete control over their customer's online habits. While opening that walled garden is one imperative, it really is up to the entire industry to create the infrastructure, revenue sharing, and value propositions that will make mobile advertising compelling for consumers and a source of revenue for industry players.

Mobile advertising has the potential to provide consumers and marketers with unprecedented opportunities to connect with content that provides value to consumers and drives increased revenue for marketers. The immediacy and advanced targeting capabilities offered by the medium provide both a tremendous challenge and a way to connect with consumers in more engaging and relevant ways than ever before. As the industry works to grow the mobile advertising business, it is in everyone's best interest to work together to balance the needs of advertisers with the overall consumer experience. Smart marketers realize that in the mobile world they can't just deliver static content and expect it to be seen. Success will be driven by applications and content that can engage and build loyalty with a highly mobile audience.

REACHING CONSUMERS WITH HIGHLY TARGETED, INTERACTIVE MOBILE ADVERTISING

Omar Javaid, Vice President, Business Development, QUALCOMM/MediaFLO Technologies

QUALCOMM has a rich history of enabling content delivery to mobile devices, most recently through its BREW™ development platform and MediaFLO™ mobile broadcast platform for delivery of mobile television and other services. New mobile broadcast services supporting mobile video, television, and data will be in high demand by consumers, and advertisers can also use these new services for targeted, interactive, and personalized advertising.

What Are Mobile Broadcast Services?

Mobile broadcast services include applications such as live, streaming television, Clipcasting™ for delivery of nonreal-time video content, and IP datacast services for delivery of real-time data such as sports scores, stock market quotes, and news services. These applications transform the mobile device from primarily a voice-centric communication tool to a converged device that is optimized for entertainment, information, and interactive communications.

Television and video content is rapidly transforming from a traditional broadcast model with commercial content and set delivery schedules, to one with vast content created by traditional providers as well as end users. Delivery of that content is sent across a wide array of broadcast, satellite, and terrestrial networks, and increasingly, over the Internet and mobile networks. This transformation is perhaps best evidenced by YouTube and its ability to share user-generated content on a wide scale, and also create communities of interest around content.

Mobile broadcast technologies like MediaFLO enable cost-effective and intelligent delivery for all media types and associated meta data, allowing content providers to selectively distribute their assets through a high performance, dedicated broadcast network while creating a seamless, intuitive user experience. The ability of these mobile devices to receive a wide array of simultaneous content (e.g., live television for a sporting event, while also receiving box-office scores) creates a rich media experience for the user on the go.

In addition, mobile broadcast enables the delivery and storage of content on the device in advance of the user requesting and consuming it. The ability to receive sports video highlights in the background to view at leisure is possible through Clipcasting. This decoupling of demand and content allows a user's needs to be anticipated based on past or predicted behavior, and increases the potential for the wireless operator, content owner, and advertiser, to tailor the delivery and timing of content based on the user's desires, location, and past viewing history.

Finally, mobile broadcast services offer the promise of truly interactive capabilities, leveraging the 3G wireless networks. While the concept of interactive television has been discussed for years, the lack of a sustainable business model has slowed adoption. Now through the ability of mobile broadcast services to deliver integrated video, rich media, and data to a personal, always-carried mobile device—with a monetizable and immediate return path for interactive responses—interactive television, gaming, movies, and other unique multimedia experiences will become reality.

How Do These New Services Impact Mobile Advertising?

For advertisers wishing to reach mobile consumers, these applications open new avenues, especially as mobile services mature and consume larger portions of users' time and attention. The use of mobile broadcast systems will be a cost-effective means of delivering creative advertising that can be rendered on mobile phones and other devices that are personal, location aware, and nearly ubiquitous.

Mobile broadcast ads will likely be a mix of brand advertising as well as promotional advertising used to drive planned and impulse sales including location-based ads that factor the geographic location of the user to improve sales conversion. Additionally, we envision that mobile ads will support social networks and communities whereby users can distribute and share ads much like they do with user-generated content on YouTube and other video networks today, thus creating viral ad campaigns over the mobile broadcast network.

For the mobile advertiser, using this new and rapidly evolving medium is a paradigm shift from interrupting programming to serve ads to the user (as in traditional broadcast advertising), to integrating ads within broadcast content, thus creating an entirely new interactive means of communicating with the consumer.

QUALCOMM is enhancing its MediaFLO technology to support anonymous but personalized delivery of advertising as well as the ability to closely monitor and report on 100 percent of ad impressions.

The market will readily accept these new forms of advertising. M:Metrics and others have shown that consumers will accept advertising around mobile television, and when the ads are interactive with television programming, click through rates are above 10 percent, and average viewing times actually increase as consumers engage more with the media.

Summary

QUALCOMM believes reaching the mobile consumer is the path forward for advertisers, especially as today there are already more mobile devices used by consumers globally than television sets. This trend of global connectivity for virtually all consumers is irreversible, and we believe new methods of delivering mobile broadcast services for television, video, and rich media is the most cost-effective means to reach these consumers. We further believe this opens up the enormous potential outlined here for highly personalized advertising that users will accept. Mobile broadcast services are changing content delivery, and will simultaneously drive the mobile advertising market.

THE COMING AGE OF MOBILE INNOVATION

Harry Santamaki, Vice President, Multimedia, Media Industry, NOKIA

We are investing heavily in the future of mobile advertising at Nokia. Eventually there will be a single digital advertising market including both online and mobile advertising. Some players in digital marketing even claim that mobile advertising actually has the potential of being bigger than online.

Why do we believe this? Well, this is almost a cliché, but it's true: Today's mobile device is ubiquitous and highly personal. Lots of targeting information can be captured on the device. And "location" itself creates a new level of targeting that's useful and unique.

Further, mobile devices are always on, and that's how people want to consume their media. Compared with other media, like print or television, it's also closer to the consumer decision point and potential transaction. You can think of newspapers as the first mobile (or at least portable) media, but its content is static and less personalized. And people also often do research online and then walk into a store. In contrast, the mobile device is with you all the time.

This combination of ubiquity (massive exposure) and targeting capabilities, at the point of consumer decision making, is what makes mobile advertising so attractive. So, how do we see it unfolding and what's Nokia's possible role in this vision?

While at this early stage, we are seeing basic advertising formats like banners and text messages, most of the advertising opportunity will be driven from mobile search. And we think of that more as *Mobile Find*, not search in the PC sense. PC activity is more research queries, and only around 35 percent of it is related to buying, a context which made search so successful commercially.

Mobile Find is more about getting what you want—answers. It's definitely *not* a browsing experience. It is application-specific related to consumers accomplishing daily tasks. You can imagine ads contextually overlaid onto a map—things like that. But we believe it will all hang off the Mobile Find experience. That's what interests us.

In the U.S. market, operators are in a strong position. They have a unique identity, billing information, and other user information—so they have opportunities. This opportunity is there for operators around the world. Yahoo and Google don't have phone usage user data.

We think one of our strengths is a *horizontal* strategy. We've developed innovative software to capture and store user activity on the mobile device and the software to place the ads in the application. We have also developed client applications on these capabilities and have learned a lot through two commercial pilot projects in Europe.

While we assume the market will take time, we don't think there are any fundamental barriers to its development.

Until recently, the lack of critical mass of smart phones was holding back mobile advertising. People want applications on their mobile devices. All mobile phones will become increasingly capable.

Although many question whether people will accept mobile advertisements, this will not constitute a real problem either. We did a study in Finland where we asked people if they wanted ads on their devices: 100 percent said no. But we also asked if sports fans would like to receive commercial information about ice hockey, and 91 percent said yes. It's all about relevance.

The U.S. consumer is still getting used to the idea of a multifunction mobile device, but we've seen a lot of movement in 2007. The trends suggest that 2008 will be the year of the multifunction mobile device in the United States, too.

Overall, I don't see any critical or fundamental barriers. It will just take time and we've developed our business and investment strategies with this assumption in mind.

Mato Valtonen, a Finnish rock star and mobile entrepreneur, offered a great observation to me about pizza. No one in Finland knew what pizza was when it appeared in the 1970s, and it took 10 years to establish itself. Today, there's pizza everywhere in Finland and we do know now what "Mato's Pizza Constant" which equals 10 years, means to new businesses.

Similarly, we believe mobile advertising will become so common that we will one day take it for granted, forgetting how long it took to establish.

MOBILE—ADVERTISING'S FIRST SCREEN

Maria Mandel, Senior Partner, Executive Director Digital Innovation, Ogilvy

Of all marketing channels, mobile has the fastest expected growth and greatest reach. As of 2007, there are twice as many mobile phones as Internet connections—around 3.3 billion mobile phones versus 1.5 billion Internet connections.

By 2011, analysts expect there will be over 4 billion mobile subscribers, up 21 percent from 2007.

As for the mobile web, usage has been low as of mid-2007 and similarly varies by region. Usage ranges from 5 percent in Germany, to 15 percent in the United States to 20 percent in the United Kingdom. While small today, it is bigger than the World Wide Web was at the equivalent stage of its development. And many expect it to grow rapidly (54 percent year over year). These aggressive growth projections are contingent on the (1) decline of mobile data costs; (2) the growth of mobile search; (3) increase in 3G penetration; (4) improvement of handset capability (with SmartPhones, mobile Internet usage grows four to eight times).

There is tremendous potential for mobile but it is going to take some time and experimenting to develop it as an advertising channel.

Prospect of Mobile Advertising and Marketing

Advertisers are wondering what role mobile marketing will play in the media landscape. We think there is going to be rapid progress in the mobile space. Not only has consumer adoption of nonvoice features such as text messaging and surfing the mobile Internet increased, but new advertising formats and marketing opportunities are building client interest in this space. A lot of people compare mobile to the way that the Internet developed. We believe mobile will develop and mature faster than the Internet did for a number of reasons (including key lessons learned from the rise of the Internet). However, there are still key challenges specific to mobile that must be overcome to make this a viable marketing channel.

With over 250 million U.S. mobile subscribers in 2007 and over half of them using nonvoice features, the eyeballs are there, but we still need to figure out ad standards and ad models, competing cross-carrier and platform technologies, as well as consumer tolerance and acceptance of marketing tactics on their most personal device.

We see mobile's evolution via the three Cs (communications, content, commerce). With rapid growth and 95 percent penetration of ages 18 to 65 in the United States alone, we think mobile represents a critical must-win battlefront in the future mix of communication media from branding to promotion and CRM.

We think that analysts' estimates of mobile marketing spend today ($1.2 billion in 2006) and its expected growth ($10.5 billion in 2011) are overstated. While the hype overstates the short-term impact, it also may understate the longer-term impact as the number of mobile devices proliferate, marketers figure out how to leverage this new, highly personal channel; and consumer and carriers become more open to advertising supported mobile content and services.

According to Telephia and M:Metrics, as of 2007, 38 percent of the U.S. audience currently SMS text messages, 14 percent use the mobile Internet, 10 percent download content, and 2 percent stream video. Text messaging is most common mobile campaign tool at the moment. An SMS text message sent to a short code (a five- or six-digit code to which subscribers can SMS a message) can be used to trigger alerts, contests, voting, WAP site, or even the download of a game, application, ring tone, coupon, or wallpaper.

Ogilvy created a two-part SMS campaign for DHL in the San Francisco area (June/July 2007). The first part featured a five-day weather text message alert delivered by DHL to consumers' cell phones. The weather report feature was being promoted on customized bus shelters that showcased an outsized umbrella that hung over the end of the shelter offering riders additional coverage. The second part offered a free game consumers could download from DHL via their cell phone. The Stack-It game allowed users to shift DHL boxes into open slots as players do in Tetris. The game could be shared or played on a community network and was promoted on bus shelters and taxicab flip seats throughout San Francisco.

We have also used SMS text messaging for voting polls. We created the first widespread TV/mobile interaction with *American Idol*'s AT&T Wireless sponsorship, having people text-in their vote. And for Dove's *Campaign for Real Beauty,* we created a billboard asking people to text-in whether they thought the 96-year-old woman featured was "Wrinkled" or "Wonderful." We also created SMS integration at events. With American Express, we created a text-in promotion at the Australian Tennis Open where people were asked to text-in who they thought would win the match (for a chance to win tickets to Wimbledon).

We have also done several mobile advertising campaigns placing mobile banner ads on publisher WAP sites. We have measured programs for Lenovo and Cisco that have shown substantial increases to brand awareness, message association, and even purchase intent.

Our clients are also experimenting with mobile video. A recent M:Metrics study (Q4 2006) on advertising and mobile video found that over 41 percent of current mobile subscribers are keen for ad-subsidized video. We have been test piloting mobile spot ads, pre/postroll units as well as user-initiated video units for clients such as IBM.

World Market for Mobile Marketing and Advertising

The world market for mobile marketing and advertising was close to $3 billion by the end of 2007, according to a recent study from ABI Research. By 2011, the value of this market will reach $19 billion, including mobile search and video advertising.

A study featured in the Yahoo! Summit series indicated that 30 percent of youth in India, 23 percent in China and 9 percent in the United States were positive toward mobile phone advertising, especially if it subsidized relevant content and useful services.

In Asia, applications to read quick response (QR) codes have been used effectively to distribute content to phones (preinstalled mobile application that allows camera phone users to snap photo of code to have content send directly to their device). Mobile video-on-demand and mobile TV are widespread as well as growth in mobile commerce. In Europe, clients are using mobile content, location-based targeting through Bluetooth and GPS targeting technologies in addition to mainstream text messaging and mobile web campaigns.

Asia is leading the world in mobile followed by Europe. This is in part due to technical infrastructure and part due to consumer adoption. Widespread adoption of 3G devices and mobile content has stimulated growth in mobile for these markets. The United States is playing catch-up with 3G just starting to build adoption. As advanced as some of the rest of the markets are in mobile content and technology, no clear-cut advertising and marketing standards have been developed as yet in the United States.

Key Tips for Developing a Mobile Advertising Campaign

- *Integrated:* Leverage all forms of media to support campaign Stand-alone mobile campaigns don't work.
- *Clear call to action:* This marketing standard sometimes gets lost in the "cool" factor of mobile.
- *Exhaustive technical and usability testing:* It is very important in this nascent market to make sure it works and is not over the target market's heads.
- *Measure response:* Mobile provides many of the analytics that the desktop does and sometimes more intimate knowledge.
- *Build the list:* Mobile lists are precious and often go wasted.
- *Consider viral elements:* Incorporate ability for user to pass along campaign/content to others.

Summary

Regardless of the challenges that exist, the opportunity for mobile is enormous. According to *eMarketer* (January 2007), mobile marketing is expected to grow spend sixfold by 2010 in all its forms: SMS, MMS, mobile Internet display ads, content sponsorships, ring tones, screensavers, and so on.

In 2007, there were 1 billion televisions, 136 million PC/broadband homes and 71 million 3G mobile subscribers worldwide. By 2010, there will be 800 million 3G mobile subscribers and 421 million PC/broadband. By 2015, there will be almost double the number of 3G mobile subscribers than household's with televisions.

Many people refer to mobile as the third screen. But with mobile phone penetration outnumbering other devices and content consumption in the near future and mobile being the only device people carry with them all the time, mobile may soon become the first screen.

BRAND ADVERTISING IS LIKELY TO DOMINATE MOBILE ADVERTISING

Ujjal Kohli, CEO, Rhythm NewMedia

As we stand at the dawn of mobile advertising in 2008, it is fun to contemplate how this exciting new media will play out. It is similar to the way we wondered about online advertising back in 1997. How large will the market be? How quickly will it spread? What forms of advertising will dominate and more specifically will ads on mobiles be more like TV ads or Internet ads? Perhaps a whole new model will emerge that is entirely different from today's media. At this stage, no one can make an exact prediction, but what follows is one perspective.

To address which form of advertising will dominate mobile advertising, it's helpful to quickly recap some advertising basics.

The worldwide advertising ecosystem exceeds $450 billion, which includes television, radio, print, outdoor, and sponsorships. All advertising can be thought of as either brand advertising or transactional advertising. Ads can be one or the other depending on the main goal of the advertiser. In brand ads, the advertiser is hoping to simply make a positive impression on desired consumers. In transactional ads, the advertiser is seeking an immediate or near-term transaction. Sometimes, an ad can have both aspects. The total ad ecosystem is composed of roughly half brand ads and half transactional ads.

Brand ads work best around "lean back" consumer experiences such as immersive entertainment, like watching television. Transactional ads work best in "lean forward" consumer settings such as Internet search. Previous attempts to do brand advertising in lean forward settings have failed as have attempts to get consumers to transact in lean back settings. Further, brand and transactional ads are targeted quite differently. Demographics is the primary targeting mechanism for brand ads, while knowledge of what a consumer might be looking to buy in the near term works best for transactions.

Different media have turned out to be either optimal for brand or transactional ads. Television is used for both, but the majority of ads on television are brand. The Internet is largely transaction oriented. The bulk of newspaper advertising is transactional, which explains why the Internet ad boom has hurt newspapers the most.

Now to the main question: What type of advertising will ultimately dominate mobile advertising—brand or transactional?

Mobiles can be used effectively for both transactional and brand advertising because mobiles create both lean back and lean forward consumer experiences. Moreover, extensive targeting suitable for both brand and transactional ads is feasible with mobiles. Early forays into both forms of advertising have been successful on this new media.

However, transactional advertising opportunities on mobiles may be more limited than brand. Transactional advertising must be justified by measurable revenue generated. On the Internet, there are both high-ticket items as well as a long tail of smaller ticket items that aggregate into a lot of transactional revenue adding up to over one trillion dollars. Thus far, transactions on mobiles seem to be first and foremost for mobile-related items such as ring tones. Beyond the ring tones and mobile content, there seem to be only a few small ticket items like pizza, coffee, flowers, a haircut, or movies. In contrast to the Internet, both the long tail of many categories and big ticket items, like mortgages and electronics, are missing on mobiles. Therefore, the aggregate transactional ad driven revenue opportunity for mobiles may be very limited compared with the Internet.

Now on to the brand-advertising opportunity for mobiles: The fastest growing mobile content category is mobile video snacking (not mobile TV). This classic immersive entertainment experience is ideal for TV style brand ads. There are some large issues with brand advertising on television that the mobile media can address:

- Rough targeting and frequency management
- Too much clutter
- Ad skipping through DVRs and comfort breaks
- Declining youth audiences

Video ads on mobiles can address all four of the preceding issues. Mobile brand ads can be finely targeted by age, gender, and zip code, to youth audiences, with precise frequency control in an uncluttered setting and little, if any, ad skipping.

This model for video brand advertising on mobiles has seen some great early success. My company, Rhythm NewMedia, launched this pioneering model with three mobile operators (as of September 2007). Advertisers have included brands like Microsoft, Cisco, Axe, Nivea, Toyota, and others. Proving the model's effectiveness, ad message recall rates are far exceeding TV benchmarks. In addition, a recent study strengthened this point as 62 percent of all consumers researched correctly attributed the advertisers' brand messages, and 52 percent recalled prompted brand massages. Customer satisfaction with the service is also very high, as measured regularly with surveys, with steep adoption rates and practically zero complaints received. A recent study (based on Rhythm's user surveys) showed that 85 percent of all consumers researched said that they were satisfied with the Rhythm video service. Further, mobile operators like Sprint and Verizon have launched brand banner ads that are selling for high CPMs and attracting top-tier brand advertisers.

Given the enormous size of brand budgets, the potential for this form of mobile advertising is very large. Brand ads will likely far exceed transactional ads for mobiles because brand ads address key challenges facing the advertising industry and can accurately target by age, gender, and zip code, with precise frequency control in an uncluttered setting with little ad skipping.

MOBILE ADVERTISING MEASUREMENT—ONE SPORT AT A TIME

Kanishka Agarwal, Vice President, Mobile Media, Nielsen Mobile

In mobile, there will be no single, universal measure of the mobile eyeball for advertisers. There, I've said it. Mobile is a composite medium of multiple media, and expecting a universal "eyeball" metric in mobile is like asking for a universal sports scoring system, where football, basketball, soccer, poker, cricket, and badminton games are all scored the same way?

Don't get me wrong—reliable and independent measurement is critical to the success of any advertising medium, including mobile. Independent, third-party measurement gives advertisers the confidence to spend and allocate dollars in the medium. It is the currency by which advertisers and publishers transact, and it tells advertisers what they got for their spend.

Mobile—A Medium of Many Media
Mobile medium is a misnomer. Mobile is not one medium. It is a composite of relatively independent and very different advertising media vehicles that come together on one consumer device—the mobile phone. These include messaging (SMS, MMS); mobile Internet; mobile video (broadcast, video-on-demand); mobile search; mobile games and music; mobile personalization (wallpapers and ring tones).

Advertisers need to approach each of these media differently. First, each has its own unique ecosystem and hence the advertiser must work through different players for each medium. Mobile Internet ad inventory is sold directly by publishers like ESPN ; by ad networks like Third Screen Media and AdMob; and directly by carriers. In the case of mobile videos, technology enablers like mobiTV and media-FLO aggregate the ad inventory. And in the case of mobile search, there are the traditional players like Google and Yahoo and new mobile-specific search engines like Jumptap and Medio. The only common denominator here is the carrier, who is the gatekeeper to the subscriber, controlling what content the user sees and how they see it—a very different role from that of conventional ISPs.

Second, each mobile media vehicle has vastly different market penetration, and attracts different consumer segments. Therefore, media planners need to identify their media mix within mobile in addition to the allocation they must make between traditional, digital, and mobile media. According to Telephia, a division of the Nielsen Company, mobile video penetration is small, but still represents about 8.4 million subscribers in the United States (Telephia, Q1-07) and delivers a predominantly young, affluent, male audience. In contrast, mobile games have an audience of 19 million U.S. subscribers, and have a mainly female, casual-gamer audience.

Third, all mobile media vehicles are not equally relevant or effective for every campaign. Mobile messaging is well suited for call-to-action, transactional advertising, while mobile video and sponsored games, ring tones, and wallpaper are more suited for brand awareness and positioning. Mobile Internet is probably equally suitable for both brand and transactional advertising since banner ads can be both an awareness vehicle and a click-to-call link.

One Eyeball Does Not Fit All

This composite nature of mobile makes it unlikely that there will be a single, integrated measure of eyeballs across all mobile media vehicles.

Creating a universal metric is impractical because there is no common way to count eyeballs across mobile media vehicles and roll them together to give an integrated view. Even in well-established media that have extended into mobile, like television and the Internet, there is as yet no unifying metric that gives an integrated eyeball view across television and online audiences.

Even if there were such a common metric, it would require a variety of ecosystems and distributors to come together and agree to a common approach. To take my sports analogy a bit further, can you imagine the NBA, the NFL, and the USBA (U.S. Badminton Association) coming together on a common scoring system?

All-Screen Measurement, Not All-Mobile Measurement

There *is*, however, opportunity for integrated measurement *across* the three consumer screens—TV, PC, mobile phone—for equivalent media vehicles. There is potential for integrated measurement across traditional television, online video, and mobile video; across wired Internet and mobile Internet; across console games, online games and mobile games; and across traditional music, online music and mobile music. Although measurement technologies are likely to be specific to each screen, the reporting of the metrics will be integrated across the screens (Figure 10.1). Nielsen's recent acquisition of the mobile measurement company, Telephia, is based on such a vision of integrated, all-screen measurement, and an indicator of things to come.

Advertisers are already asking for such all-screen audience and advertising measurement. They do not look at mobile advertising in a vacuum, but see it as another reach mechanism in the context of existing, well-established channels. Television advertisers cannot sit on the sidelines as new distribution channels for video programming—like mobile video and video-on-demand—evolve. Their audiences are fragmenting across the various distribution channels, but the need to reach these audiences remains. Consequently, it is becoming increasingly important for television advertisers

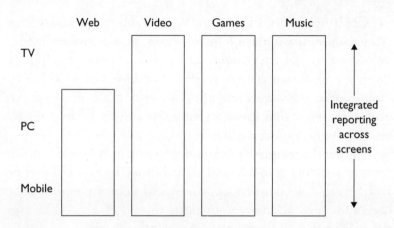

Figure 10.1   All-screen integrated reporting.

(and publishers) to measure their viewership regardless of the distribution channel. Without this, they stand to lose reach (and revenue) even if their overall viewership remains the same.

"Early Days" Sketch of Mobile Advertising Metrics

If you believe in all-screen integrated measurement, a framework for mobile advertising metrics falls out quite nicely. In fact, it is approachable and familiar to advertisers and publishers because it is essentially what they already use in traditional media.

First there are the *planning* metrics—reach, frequency, and audience composition—that media planners and buyers use to determine media mix and to achieve the desired reach and targeting when designing a campaign. In the case of mobile Internet, just as in the wired Internet, advertisers want to know who visits a mobile web site and how much time they spend on it. In fact, it is interesting to compare how audiences differ for Internet between mobile and wired. Telephia and Nielsen//NetRatings are working together to bring such all-screen Internet measurement to the marketplace.

Second, there are *currency* metrics—CPM, CPC—that determine the value and hence the price of an ad buy. For the mobile Internet, things again resemble the wired Internet with CPM and CPC measurement. In the mobile video world, Telephia is already doing early measurement of channel and program level viewership by daypart.

Finally, there are *performance* metrics—share-of-voice, share-of-spend, ad effectiveness—that help advertisers evaluate the bang from their advertising buck.

As with all other media, independent, third-party measurement is absolutely crucial for the growth of the mobile advertising market. Only then will advertisers develop the confidence and trust to spend beyond experimental dollars.

Summary

In mobile advertising measurement, we need to take one sport at a time. It is okay to integrate Roger Federer's performance across clay courts, hard courts, and grass, but let's not try to determine whether he is a better sportsman than Tiger Woods. Let's leave them where they are—good friends.

11

Conclusion and Recommendations

A few years ago, CMOs didn't know what mobile advertising was, other than something their New Media groups were looking into. Today, it has gained awareness throughout marketing organizations as an interesting piece of the overall media mix.

In 2001, ipsh! ran its first campaign for Giant Step Records for $1,000. After their acquisition by Omnicom in 2005, in 2007, ipsh! put together a campaign for Bank of America for $1,000,000.[1] Now, they have a seat at the table where mobile is considered part of the advertising strategy versus something to test. The six-year journey of this small outfit tells the story of the growth of this industry. We certainly have come a long way.

Nearly every media throughout history has embraced advertising, and increasingly so. Mobile media and entertainment will be no different. The question is how long it will take to work out the kinks, what the user experience will be, and who will dominate the ecosystem. We have to be careful reading too much into the forecasts. However, one thing is clear—there are a lot of opportunities and there are a lot of hurdles ahead of us. In this final chapter, we summarize our discussions and leave you with some recommendations.

It is silly not to learn from the lessons of the past. Advertising has been around for a long time and it has evolved systematically. Each new medium comes with the hype of making the previous generations irrelevant. A prominent industry figure and friend once said to us that he was out to destroy Madison Avenue; that the days of nonmeasurable image ads were over. Our response: Try telling that to Nike. Many brands today *are* images versus products in the traditional sense. And it's all about distributing content to support that image. Like it or not, image advertising has a meaningful and permanent role in the media mix.

Every new medium eventually finds its unique value as part of the larger whole. Though inefficiencies plague radio, TV, and print, they are not going away—and they shouldn't! Yes, one of the key trends shaping advertising is the shift from analog to digital, and mobile makes the transformation even more compelling. But instead of counting the days to the demise of these traditional mediums and channels, we should be focusing on how to enhance their value using mobile as part of the media mix.

It is a mistake to look at advertising only from the technology perspective. You must always look at it from the objectives of the brands and creative agencies and figure out which tools and mediums work best to meet and exceed those goals. Find a friend who has a friend that works as a media buyer. Call and have a chat with them; learn what they do and how they think.

The glamour of mobile is seductive. The promise of massive reach is too big to pass up. And it's not just reach—mobile also provides purity. The targeting capability of mobile is immense.

Mobile also makes every medium accountable. No longer will the wishy-washy gut feel or irrelevant surveys or diaries be sufficient; brands will demand that their agencies provide answers: "Show me the ROI, show me how consumers engaged with this campaign, and show me how it impacted my sales." Every year billions of dollars are wasted on measuring impact, understanding consumer behavior, and designing new campaigns. Marketing agencies measure their own performance. The "let's see what sticks" approach has no place in the digital world.

Instead of guesswork, let the data speak to you about what consumers are doing—their desires and needs, their subconscious and conscious behaviors, the social ecosystem in which they thrive. The need for creative talent will not go away, in fact, the digitization process will only open up new opportunities, but it does make everyone and everything accountable for every dollar spent.

Mobile becomes especially important for reaching the youth demographics, who are already attached (perhaps literally!) to their mobile phones. They are not shackled by preconceived notions of this new medium and want to proactively engage and communicate with any compelling piece of content they can lay their hands on. For them, an advertisement is information, yes, but it is more importantly a social currency that enables them to have meaningful water cooler conversations with their friends. The targeting capability in mobile can help make every interaction contextual, every query-response relevant, and every second spent engaging. This is what the young consumer wants.

Mobile can also tie the media experiences across all channels. Like a remote control, it can manage how an individual goes about interacting with media, content, and information throughout the day—only engaging in what's important and relevant.

Yet, with all these benefits, carriers don't realize the value of the assets, and advertisers need significant education to figure out how to use this uniquely compelling medium to supercharge their brands. It is potentially revolutionary but realizing that potential will rely on the ability of technology players to reach across the aisle and articulate the business case to advertisers on their own terms.

There are inherent benefits for all participants in the value chain. And that's the basic requirement for any market to thrive.

For the user, relevant (opt-in) and targeted advertising and promotions deliver value. In all recent surveys, the number of users willing to pay for the mobile TV service is a very small fraction of the number of users who want to use the service. With a business model that supports advertising, more consumers can afford to enjoy the full capabilities of their handsets. And they can filter incoming content, promotions, and advertisements to their taste and needs. So the ads become more than something to tolerate but are valuable in and of themselves. If you were on a road trip and the kids were hungry, you'd likely be happy to find a good restaurant and happier still if you walked in with a 10 percent off mobile coupon.

From an advertiser's point of view, mobile provides unparalleled reach, targetability, and a reliable and fairly accurate measurement tool. It also helps them make other mediums interactive and measurable. It would be great if a consumer driving past a billboard could request more information about a product offer—or better yet, sample and buy.

For content providers, both big and small, mobile offers an ability to go direct to the consumer in addition to working with carriers on revenue-sharing arrangements. And if you're a content provider with traction and user profile data for a few million loyal subscribers, advertisers would love to talk to you.

For the carrier, it is an excellent way to build loyalty and "stickiness." It is also a way to expand the number of data users by subsidizing premium content and even transport costs through advertising, thus lowering the barrier to usage. There's a big gap between the United States and data usage in Europe and Japan, and that gap can be filled.

The promise of mobile as an advertising medium is unprecedented. Given all the potential, the Advertising Yoda might ask—why has it not happened yet? The ecosystem is too complex is the answer—too much fragmentation, too many players looking to chop the advertising spend, too few standards and measurement metrics, and insufficient inventory and audience to interest advertisers. So far, advertisers have been dabbling with R&D budgets and not campaign dollars, though it started to change quite a bit in 2007.

The biggest problem with mobile is the fragmentation of reach. Advertisers who run a national campaign have to think about multiple carriers and the permissions they have to obtain; they have to worry about the different types of devices in the market and their capabilities and limitations; they have to consider different types of network that might control the creative element of the campaigns. Some agencies and brands are brave enough to power through the complexities; some are not.

While the potential is immense, significant risks and potential challenges need to be tackled before the medium evolves into a vibrant advertising industry. The most prominent among them are privacy and data security. Once you start mining user data, significant profile information can be developed. But how that information is used and by whom becomes a significant legal minefield. And if the industry doesn't want regulators to get involved, the security policies and procedures need to be in place to protect the data from theft or misuse.

Next, the advertising ecosystem needs to be fostered so that everyone in the value chain benefits relative to their contribution. As we have seen time and time again, if the ecosystem is equitable, a segment thrives. If not, it is relegated and growth slows or the interest of participants dissipates altogether. There needs to be a good balance of power between advertisers, content providers, carriers, and consumers. Remember, markets need to be *made*, and this one may be a textbook case for the value of industry cooperation.

The next big hurdle is the lack of standards and common measurement metrics. It wasn't until Nielsen and Comscore became established in the digital world that online advertising started to take off. While we have the experience of online with us, the expediency with which industry can establish these standards and metrics with third party auditing capability is going to determine how soon the mobile advertising industry becomes a vibrant and sustainable business. Unless and until the mobile industry can present a unified front to the media industry, it will not earn its rightful share of the budget.

THE PILGRIMAGE TO CONTEXTUAL NIRVANA

This book has been about how you go from the mobile advertising's state of *cautious optimism* to the transcendental state of *contextual nirvana*. Technology plays a key role in this journey. The opportunity to do one-on-one advertising, anytime-anywhere, in any spatiotemporal context is simply too attractive to ignore. As players beef up their data- warehousing initiatives to mine the capability of microsegmentation and analytics-driven campaigns, advertisers will be able to get a single view of the customers across mediums and can optimize campaigns in real time. This can be only attained if due attention is paid to and substantive investments are made in the unified technical architecture discussed in Chapter 8.

Mobile bandwidth will increase to more than 1Gbps within five years. We will care less about the network we are on as the device will use the best available connection without worrying about carriers, networks, and price points. Device processor speeds will increase to 1GHz, more than multi-GB of memory will be standard, with over 100GB hard drives. Screen resolutions will be far clearer and work in sunlight and the with batteries will last far longer. Perhaps more importantly, the next 5 to 10 years will see unprecedented integration of technology into the social fabric of communities and nations. Broadband networks, sensors, digital content and multipurpose devices will become so ingrained in our daily lives that we will look back and ponder at the relatively primordial mobile age we are in today.

By the time this book reaches the market, Japan would have crossed 80 percent in 3G penetration, South Korea 70 percent, and most of Western Europe and North America will be past their inflection range of 20 percent to 25 percent 3G penetration. Each region has its own growth patterns, its own intricacies, and its own ecosystem and regulatory environment, but trends across geographies are unquestionably similar. Some are ahead in their digital sojourn, whereas others are just getting started. Advances in technology will lead to adaptation in consumer's behavior and in their engagement with information and the social fabric. The device will become the broker to the outside world that understands users and manages their lives.

Tectonic shifts in the advertising industry won't happen overnight. However, the future will belong to those who have an early start in understanding the medium and those who participate in working out the details of the emerging marketplace. Others will invariably be caught napping in the middle of this paradigm-changing environment.

As discussed in Chapter 8, analytics will play a critical role in delivering contextual relevance. Operators' leverage will be defined by how they monetize the profile data; mobile industry's strength will be determined by how unified it is in providing solutions to the media industry. Unless service providers embrace mobile advertising in all its glory, operators will never become media-focused companies and their fear of becoming dumb pipes will become a self-fulfilling prophecy.

Mobile affords the opportunity to understand the complex user-behavior based on real data (as opposed to surveys, gut-feel, and holy sermons). It can use this to fine-tune the ad fire hose, and deliver only the relevant, the necessary, and the timely. Like a trusted lifelong secretary, analytics will help protect us from unwanted phone calls.

Accountability and ROI is the great promise of the mobile medium. The rate at which the industry can come together for form standards, accepted best practices, case studies for education, standard pricing models, and third party audit compliance will dictate how fast it grows into a multibillion segment of the advertising industry. The mobile advertising industry should also demonstrate the discipline to self-regulate on an ongoing basis. Instead of taking years to pass industry guidelines and code of conduct, such matters should be dealt with expeditiously. If not, we might as well invite regulators to slow down growth.

Each player in the value chain plays an important part—start-ups and entrepreneurs in challenging the status quo and bringing fresh technology and business ideas to the table; carriers in providing the infrastructure to be effective; agencies in flexing their creative muscles to come up with innovative and engaging campaigns. Competition is going to be fierce. So what are our recommendations?

KEEP THINGS IN PERSPECTIVE

Telecom is a four-trillion-dollar global industry. While advertising represents a new source of revenue for U.S. operators, it isn't being managed as a top priority. But keep an eye on the income statements of operators like Vodafone, NTT DoCoMo, China Mobile, and Reliance Infocomm. Once you start seeing operators breaking out advertising revenue numbers, it will be a clear indicator that something significant is happening. Remember, most of the operators' data revenues were below 5 percent to 10 percent of their overall average revenue per user (ARPU) 10 years ago, and the United States didn't even start registering its data revenues until 2003. Now most operators are reporting between 20 percent to 30 percent data contribution to ARPU. That's significant.

Global advertising expenditures at the end of 2007 were approximately 450 billion dollars. And while Internet advertising is the new gold rush, it is still only 7 percent of the pie. Newspapers, magazines, and TV still accounted for a whopping 79 percent of the advertising spend. Mobile won't even start registering as a separate category in PricewaterhouseCoopers' and ZenithOptimedia's numbers until at least 2010. The most experienced market of Japan got only 0.65 percent of its revenues from mobile advertising in 2006 (see Chapter 4).

This reminds us of the long road ahead and underscores the real competition for mobile advertising. As Richard Saggers of Vodafone noted (see Chapter 10), the real competitor to mobile advertising is not the other operators or even the Internet brands but the other mediums that have a good grasp on the advertising spends, the needs of agencies, and the metrics to validate it all. The mobile advertising industry has to prove to brands and agencies that it is a uniquely compelling medium worthy of its share of the spend. Until then, the shifts in ad budgets to mobile advertising will be trivial.

Understand the Business, Not Just the Technology

Technologists play an important role in the future development of mobile advertising, to be sure. However, we believe the most successful will be those who understand that technology is a *means to an end*. Mobile advertising technology exists to serve the needs of the advertising industry, which has been around a lot longer than all of us.

The brief historical perspective in Chapter 1 intended to help us realize that mobile advertising is part of a long evolution of media, all of which share the same advertising objectives. The emerging mobile advertising industry and its players need to fully understand those objectives as well as the fact that advertisers have choices. The industry then needs to be very clear about how it meets those objectives in a distinctive way relative to other media.

Go to conferences; read a book; take a class. Understand the business of advertising as well as you understand your technology.

At the end of the day, it boils down to the basic wisdom of understanding your customer. It will likely prove more effective to target a fair share of the vast global advertising market based on our value proposition versus thinking mobile is going to antiquate all other advertising media.

CHANT THE USER EXPERIENCE MANTRA

Networks are becoming capable of delivering higher bandwidths; new devices have very fast processors and rich multimedia capabilities; digital content is becoming more pervasive. It feels as if we're at the cusp of hockey stick growth.

Yet with all these improvements, digital multimedia content will only proliferate if we provide a usable interface. This is painfully clear. And beyond basic navigation, the user experience needs to be personalized based on needs, preferences, and device capabilities. It needs to be *super simple* and elegant to use. The horribly confusing consumer silos between WAP, video, and downloadables need to disappear forever. Only then can the true potential of digital media be unleashed. As such, all in the value chain need to focus on the single most important aspect of any service—*consistent and immersive user experiences.*

Give Consumers Control

Users are demanding control in every media they consume, whether it is interactive television or the Internet. Remember: *Content is what content does!* It's all about access, flexibility, control, and shareability.

Mobile media is not immune to these macro market trends. In 2008, more users will be accessing the Web from mobile phones than from PCs. The most critical consumer on-ramp to mobile media and the foundational glue of mobile search is fragmented, but it will radically improve over the next few years. Some aspects of the interactive web phenomena are not impacting mobile media yet, but that will eventually change. For all the hype in mobile interactivity, users still can't cut and paste or cross-link mobile sites!

Respect Consumer Privacy

Experience shows that unless privacy concerns are taken into consideration at the design stage—in the crafting of technology and policy—they will certainly come back to haunt you. In the wireless world, privacy is less about legislative compliance and more about basic good business practices.

Remember the rules of the agra: If you can't satisfy the basic contract between buyers and sellers, don't even bother inviting advertising to join the market. Privacy should be front and center of any mobile advertising strategy for the carriers, advertisers, technology enablers, industry bodies, and the regulators. Unless we can make consumers comfortable with our policies and procedures, the growth of this nascent industry will be slow.

Also, frequency capping needs to be addressed at an individual level, not just at a channel or market-level basis. It is obvious from user trials that it is annoying to receive multiple advertisements in a single session. If the objective of advertising is to influence consumers, you likely don't want to message them when they're pissed off!

Our focus should be to turn privacy into a competitive advantage, not a barrier. By being absolutely transparent and inclusive of customer's concerns, we will be in a much better position to engage them. Perhaps every major player in this business (mobile advertising) should have a Chief Privacy Officer who looks out for the consumers every step of the way.

Remove Consumer Friction

For mobile advertising to scale to massive proportions, the use of mobile media has to increase. And it is Generation C, the younger consumer, that can make or break new media almost overnight with viral adoption or immediate rejection. Right now, mobile media is simply too expensive for them. The industry needs flat-rate pricing and all-you-can-eat models to free up major consumer volumes, especially for younger demographics. This needs to be the rule, not the exception, as it currently is.

And it is just too complex to discover and share content. The encouragement of a viral component to mobile media is critical for the growth of mobile advertising and also for the measurement of engagement.

Models are forming around the three basic advertising types, interactive campaigns, brand campaigns, and mobile search. What we see today is very different from what we will see five years out. We will see more clarity, more transparency on pricing, and more measurability. All of these are necessary for mobile advertising to attract significant dollars.

The industry should also work together to simplify and integrate ad planning and purchasing processes to maximize efficiency in a multichannel, a multiplatform, and a multivendor environment.

Focus on the Most Critical 1 Percent in the Market

Usage research on sites like MySpace, Facebook, YouTube, and Wikipedia shows that only one percent or fewer consumers contribute to community sites by uploading or creating new content. Research also shows that 10 percent provided comments while 90 percent were happy to just watch, click, and consume. As we eluded to earlier, content is what content does. This is a fundamental difference from the old guard media world of top-down editorial power and control—the days of programmed content are surely numbered.

The role of media in lives of the new consumer has become a sort of social currency in the market for expressing individual and social identity. Media, or more specifically, digital media has taken on new values in this youth culture of cross-linking, forwarding, and sharing. It has become a means of social interaction around the globe. If it isn't worth sharing, is it worth anything at all?

Digital media has taken on a new value for this forwarding culture generation. It has also become a popularity currency of sorts. Far more popular than posting content are the interactive features that let people send shout-outs, messages, links, and virally communicate what they think is hot at the moment. Mobile community participation will drive mobile TV and video—not user-generated content. That content will no doubt be important in mobile, especially with camera phones, but it is secondary to the viral communications required to link and share.

But the current mobile media pricing models are excluding the massive participation necessary for this linking and sharing to really happen. Social networking usage in mobile has the potential to be massive, but the costs are simply too high for the most likely heavy users. The industry needs to carve social networking data usage out of the normal data plan and offer it a very low rate, subsidized by mobile advertising. This would significantly lower the total consumer cost and potentially could dramatically increase the addressable market of mobile youths. It would also create a new, highly visible and highly marketable mobile media service at the retail point-of-sale. Combined with the technical ability for users to paste a link in a mobile application, the new low-cost viral impacts could be phenomenal. Stated simply, the mobile requirement to become viral is to make everything sufficiently contagious. Don't launch anything on mobile that is not sufficiently contagious. If everyone in the target audience sends it to one other person they know—that is sufficiently contagious. Take advantage of the alpha users; if they love your advertisement or product, they will spread it and tell their friends about it.

So far, the industry has not achieved a magical balance between viral enablers and low costs to the consumer to leverage this powerful 1 percent for major scale. If the key prerequisites of consumer pricing and a sufficient measure of mobile exclusivity can be addressed without strangling web interactivity, the chances of that sneaky little exponential catching on might improve.

AGENCIES: EMBRACE DIGITAL

Together with the changing consumer psychographic, convergence is blurring the lines between content and advertising. The mobile phone is bringing disparate industries together to form a powerful fabric of conversations. Just as many legacy executives didn't "get" mobile data, many of the dominant agencies didn't completely understand the impact of digital advertising. Only after big spenders like Ford,

Procter & Gamble, American Express, and McDonald's starting shifting their advertising spend to digital did many agencies start seriously learning about CPMs, CPCs, and PPCs.[2] The initial foray was through acquisitions before Internet advertising became ingrained into their overall campaign strategy. With mobile, history is repeating itself, but the impact is likely to be more profound. Not only is it a new medium for engaging users but it also helps in making other advertising mediums interactive and measurable. Agencies and advertisers will have to respond more quickly than they do today. Like ipsh! At Omnicom, mobile personnel should be given seats at the table to discuss how mobile can enhance the campaign and consumer relationship.

Advertisers will reward media partners who can deliver reach, engagement, targeted relationships, something to viral about and finally transactions. Technology helps glue all these together. Understanding the interrelationships of the three screens and the impact of these mediums on each other is going to be critical.

OPEN UP, STANDARDIZE, AND CREATE AN INDUSTRY

Although there are profound positive aspects of mobile media and advertising, that potential is currently untapped. In the online world, Google, Yahoo, and Microsoft are the three major players for search, contextual ads, and banner ads, consolidating the reach of all those types of ads for the Web. There is no parallel to that today in mobile. Mobile carriers receive tiny revenue streams because they are still too fractured to offer a scalable, high-volume, highly targeted ad campaign value. The off-deck mobile ad networks are starting to appear, but they are missing the quality targeting value they need. And the mobile advertising value chains and models are all over the map, creating vendor opportunities but also stirring up clouds of confusion for the ad agencies and brand marketers.

Mobile operators need to adopt advertising as a core part of their business and not as a peripheral or fringe effort, as is the case today. There are significant issues around the various business models, or worse, no business models, that need to be created and standardized. They need coherent business models to deliver value for advertising customers that may want different models and value-adds. And this must all be blended into voice, messaging, and media services so that it adds value, to the customer's transaction, whether that is communications or media grazing.

Present a Unified Front

Mobile operators (or someone!) needs to standardize and present a unified data and metric front to the world of agencies and brand marketers. Until this happens, the industry risks stalling out in early takeoff, or worse, in midair. The future will be incredibly bright when standards are in place for planning, buying, and measuring mobile advertising campaigns.

We need common interfaces into agencies, similar to Atlas Solutions on the Web and interactive television, to enable collaborations and campaign modifications on a rapid-fire, focused basis. The results will be an easy-to-work-with industry that scales very fast—perhaps the fastest scale of revenues of any medium in history. The really massive mobile advertising opportunities may reside in a whole new world of targeted advertising enabled by new web services that expose internal data profiles and segmentation targets to mobile advertising networks.

Mobile operators will create significant new value to the world of mobile advertising by aggressively supporting the Web's "software as a service" paradigms, to extend their in-house capabilities for third party consumption enabling targeted advertising. Also, anonymous user profiles, user segmentation data, device data, network location data, presence information, and more could all be shared far more cohesively and aggressively with mobile advertising platforms to increase advertising rates and returns on campaigns. In addition, *verifiable* campaign performance data could be accessed cross-operator, with cohesive operator-defined, standard-access methods through these web services.

In theory, this model would give the mobile carriers a powerful network effect in attracting major campaigns. It would make campaign management and ROI analysis far more transparent. Their arguments about not wanting to be "dumb pipes" would literally evaporate if they built a robust media and advertising ecosystem with web services-based access to support third parties. It would be the missing building block enabling mobile to compete with other industries for advertising dollars, and the key to an incredibly bright, scaleable future.

Visualize Three Screens

The future of convergence is very exciting for advertising. By tying the user experience across the three interactive mediums of Internet, interactive television, and mobile, advertisers can make advertisement much more compelling than the current state of art, and make each dollar spent *count*. The new advertisement ecosystem will only be successful if users are put into control of decisions relating to what ads are pushed to the users when. By providing the configuration capability to the subscriber, ads become much more context-driven as well as relevant, thus maximizing their impact. Invest in segmentation; invest in data warehousing. And invest in delivering *experiences*, not just content.

Some of the emerging business models will not be favorable to the operators, especially around user-generated content. Instead of fighting it, operators should think about enhancing the experience by adding value and monetizing through network elements (in addition to collecting revenue from the transport). If operators are smart about it, they can abstract out network elements such as location, presence, and user profile, and make it available to third-party developers.

This will be a great win-win for the ecosystem as it will enable everyone in the value chain to provide the best possible user experience. Then, the business model will take care of itself. Yield management systems take years to optimize, so start collecting data so that you can learn from it and use it as an unfair competitive advantage.

Telecom operators are one of the biggest advertising spenders. In the United States, in 2006, they were third behind the Automotive and Retail with AT&T second behind P&G in national marketing spend at $3.3 billion.[3] The best vehicle for operators to advertise is mobile itself. It is also the best medium to educate users on new plans, services, applications, and compelling content offerings. This medium hasn't been tapped effectively thus far. This will require not only technology investments but organizational restructuring to integrate advertising into services.

Operators and publishers who can provide an integrated three-screen platform to advertisers will be at a significant advantage. The road to connect these three platforms with a single user profile will be like a tough mountain trek; it will require lots of preparation while dealing with uncertainty and limited resources, but reaching the top will be exhilarating.

Educate, Evangelize, and Standardize

Did we mention standardize twice in this section? We can't emphasize it enough! Brands and agencies are eager to embrace new mediums to test their effectiveness and potential. While the possibilities excite them, the complexities scare them. What this nascent industry needs is education, the sharing of best practices, lessons from campaigns that went right and from the ones that didn't, the metrics around cause-and-effect, and tools to understand and execute campaigns. This book will play a role in the process. Organizations like the Mobile Marketing Association (MMA) have done a good job of bringing parties to the table to collaborate and roll out best practices and case studies but more needs to be done (see Laura Marriott's opinion piece in Chapter 10).

Without standards in media formats and *independent* audit capability of measurement metrics, the growth of mobile advertising industry will be slow. Competing industry organizations and players should come together to define standards, guidelines, and best practices; otherwise legislators might end up defining it for them.

Prepare for Data Everywhere—From Gigabytes to Yottabytes[4]

The Internet advertising business has forever shifted the power of the advertising industry to digital. Analytics types are now the new rock stars—sitting center stage in the spotlight with the creative types. Twenty years ago, this scenario could have never have been dreamed up. With this massive market shift, the power and importance of analytics will only accelerate further.

IBM estimates that by 2010, the size of world's information base will be doubling every 11 hours.[5] In the telco world, the information explosion has already started. With the migration from 2G to 3G, bytes of data per customer has grown manifold with the operators struggling to store, let alone analyze, this splurge in data. Companies who lay the groundwork of a solid analytics foundation for their future campaigns, analysis, and CRM systems will lead the industry by breaking new ground to understand consumer behavior and designing creative advertising implementations to leverage it. The key performance indicators (KPIs) should be established early on in the process and aggressively updated to reflect a rapidly evolving marketplace. The variables in the five-points framework are a solid start. Data should be *revered!* It should not just be collected, collated, stored, and put into a data warehouse for further analytics and analysis against the key performance indicators. The resulting metrics should also be massaged, loved, and become the heartbeat of change in new campaign variations.

Only by absorbing data can one truly understand consumer behavior and spot microtrends before they come mainstream. Understanding microtrends helps in microsegmenting the subscriber base that can lead to a more one-on-one engagement with the user that fosters trust, loyalty, and longetivity, which translates into healthier return on customer.

Standardize around Mobile Metrics

Mobile advertising campaign data, metrics and analytics will be the most important new mobile back-end capabilities in the market. They will drive the performance of any new ad campaign and separate the leaders in this new market from the losers.

In Chapter 3, we introduced the five-points framework to help guide our thinking around mobile advertising. The variables of reach, engagement, targeting, viral effects, and transactions help us get our mind around the opportunity, benefits, complexity, the competition, and execution of a mobile advertising strategy. By mastering these five elements, any advertising organization will have an unfair competitive advantage and every campaign will be successful beyond expectations. The five-points framework enables an effective starting point in framing a mobile campaign. It is also useful in comparing and contrasting the five points across other media for the best views across complicated variables. When the mobile industry solves the issues related to device management, massive silos of distinct media, and complex campaign management, it will result in tremendous value in this fragmented consumer universe. Best targeting will lead to best engagement metrics, and this will promote new forms of mobile media. The best targeting for engagement will win. The world of mobile media will be attractive to advertisers once the basics have been put in place. It will scale faster than anticipated when all the pieces come together. If critical mass can be reached, along with a high degree of accurate targeting that leads to measurable engagement, mobile may play a key role in this new advertising world of highly fragmented audiences.

Let's revisit our five-points framework in the context of some notable campaigns discussed in the book (see Figure 11.1). We found campaigns doing rather well in one or two, maybe three areas but rarely any that excelled in all the categories. For reach, off-deck campaigns do rather well due to the ability to go cross-carrier and cross-country very quickly by using the simplicity of the browser to bypass the fragmentation. The pricing is very favorable to the advertisers in number of impressions served to click-through rates, if brands are interested in just creating lot of awareness fairly quickly—especially for goods that have a low price-point. Reliance's Cadbury campaign was a good example of tremendous reach within a carrier subscriber base. They could tap into the local culture and curiosity of checking the exam results (and being the second largest carrier in India) and deliver the goods for Cadbury.

Engagement requires lot of creative thinking. How does one roll-out a campaign where people spend lot of time

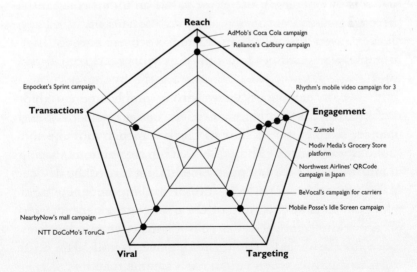

Figure 11.1   Using the five-points framework to maximize ROI of mobile advertising campaigns.

interacting with the ad content? Zumobi does it by focusing on the user experience, while Rhythm did it by rolling out pre/post roll video ads with content that increased the value and usage tremendously. Consumers provided feedback without prompting and engaged with the media and the medium, driving ROI for the brands; they kept coming back for more and started investing campaign dollars with operator 3. Northwest's QR Code campaign in Japan invited users to point, click, and download information related to Northwest specials and schedules, putting the new technology to good use. ModivMedia's grocery store platform turns a mundane shopping experience into an engaging one that benefits both the customer and the brands that are trying to get in front of the customer at the right time. And it has direct impact on Transactions or sales for the store as well as the likes of P&G and Unilever.

Targeting capability is just starting to be used, though primarily within carrier environments, indicating the power carriers have in this ecosystem if they are smart about execution and strategy. Mobile Posse's idle screen application with a small regional carrier showed that by targeting contextual ads and engaging the users based on their preferences, the engagement rate was as high as 45 percent. Similarly, Bevocal used the idle time during customer care calls to promote plans and content offerings with good conversion rates.

Not many campaigns have a strong viral component built in. As we discussed at length, carriers, content providers, and handset manufacturers should work together to make this capability a priority. Make the communication and sharing of information and content an essential feature of the device. NTT DoCoMo's ToruCa feature of sharing digital coupons with friends is an example of the use of an advanced technology while NearbyNow used TXT messaging to let users share latest sale information with their friends. The ROI starts to multiply when you make it simple.

Finally, transaction capabilities are where mobile excels strategically. No other platform or medium provides the benefit of carrying the campaign all the way to closure—*a sale*. Advertising is all about sales and if you can't weave this critical component into your campaign, you are missing out. As Enpocket's campaign for promoting Sprint's content showed, carriers should first use this channel to promote the services and goods they already have.

CHOOSE YOUR MARKET WISELY

Rhythm New Media initially entered the market with a mobile video advertising solution. For it to get traction, it needed an operator with good 3G penetration; it also needed a country where consumers are open to trying out new advertising media and business models. Despite being based in the United States, it targeted the U.K. market and started working with operator 3. The U.K. market is one of the few markets (other markets included Sweden and Norway) where digital market share of the advertising spend exceeded 10 percent in 2006 and is expected to cross 20 percent by 2009.[6] Operator 3 has 100 percent of its subscribers on 3G and has been aggressive in launching new video-related applications. As a result, the very first trial turned into an ongoing business with brands moving from spending R&D budgets to actual campaign dollars (see case study in Chapter 7).

Similarly, Geovector Corporation with its advanced local search technology went to work with NTT DoCoMo in Japan to find home for its technology first instead of trying to woo U.S. operators at home. Depending on the infrastructure required for a given channel to succeed, you should choose markets and partners carefully or you will left with meaningless reach and negative ROI.

Operators, agencies, and technology providers with local presence benefit immensely by being on the ground. Companies like Vodafone, Orange, Telefonica, and T-Mobile can offer advertisers a common buying-selling process, a single platform to launch campaigns, and a unified view of analytics across regions. Similarly, large agencies like Omnicom, WPP,

Interpublic, Publicis, Dentsu, and Havas with local presence in multiple countries are can better coordinate and compete for multiregion launches for large brands like Nike, Coke, and Unilever.

Each market is different with its own set of unique characteristics for mobile and advertising industries. These differences should be carefully studied during the strategy phase of building technology, practices, teams, and campaigns. While NTT DoCoMo succeeded with i-mode in Japan, it failed everywhere else (including their disastrous AT&T Wireless investment). While Vodafone created dominant positions in Europe, their Japanese venture had to be sold to Softbank, who turned the business around in no time. All the failed ventures didn't take into account the local ecosystem, assumed too much, and didn't have the right people on the ground running the show. This story has nothing specifically to do with wireless but rather business 101; too often we forget and rush to capture the pot of gold at the end of the rainbow.

WATCH YOUR KIDS: THEY ARE THE MARKET

Audiences of today are increasingly complex and sophisticated. Their views of tomorrow's media, content, interaction, community, creation, distribution, limitations, and devices is very different from the "established" market wisdom.

Two of us have four-year-old daughters. Just observing them interact with digital media has been a fascinating learning experience while writing this book. They want to use daddy's phone to chat with their grandparents irrespective of their global location. Distant locations around the world have literally melted away as a communication paradigm. They want to watch the Disney cartoon videos on-demand on the phone. One of them has taught her younger brother that the phone is a video camera—when he comes running around the corner, he points it like a camera, he doesn't put it his ear like a phone. Another wants to take pictures when she wears a new dress and instantly share it with her favorite uncles around the globe so that they can talk about it in a few minutes. All of them have taken videos from a mobile phone already. From a digital pacifier in their infant years, the mobile phone has already turned into a digital utility for them—*and it all began before they turned four.*

As Ian Stewart of MTV says in Chapter 10, "This generation doesn't notice technology around them. [They] have grown up with . . . digital. This is their world. They know no other paradigm." This paradigm is going to affect the market more than any technology can.

THE FINAL WORD

> *Advertising, once a gamble, has become under able direction, one of the safest of business ventures. Certainly no other enterprise with comparable possibilities need involve so little risk.*
>
> —Claude Hopkins, *Scientific Advertising*, 1923

We began our discussion with a review of the basic agra and how it supported the objectives of advertisers. Fast forward a few centuries and here we are at the cusp of a digital transformation, the age of an engaged and empowered consumer. And the era of ferocious change. Digital advertising, as a new medium, is ripe with opportunities and challenges. Mobile will play a critical role in connecting buyers and sellers.

Sound, graphics, video, and even text. Communicating, discovering, sharing. Cutting-edge voice interfaces, bar coding, and screens that you not only can see outside but also can project onto your wall! Consumers who have become addicted to accessing, discovering, and sharing all kinds of stuff and want to do the same when they're mobile. Devices measured in the billions driving immeasurable exposures. Precision targeting based on intent and location.

Is mobile media an advertisers dream or what? We'd argue it's not only a dream but a necessity. Advertisers want to capture consumer attention and the mobile phone certainly has it. If this is where eyeballs are, this is where advertisers need to be. This emerging medium has the capability of supercharging the brand.

Yes, there are lots of obstacles. But that's just work. There's nothing fundamentally in the way. A few years ago, the three of us were rightfully skeptical about the future for mobile advertising. But, while we have spent a lot of time quantifying the problems and risks here, we hope we have convinced you that there's light at the end of the tunnel and that it's blinding!

For us it has been a great journey exploring the subject. We hope this book has been useful to you. We've almost convinced ourselves to stick with this emerging opportunity!

We would like to hear from you. We look forward to your feedback and input and want to carry the conversation forward.

Please feel free to get in touch with us at chetan@chetansharma.com, joeherzog@gmail.com, and melfivjm@aol.com or at www.chetansharma.com/blog.

NOTES

1. Interview with Nihal Mehta, founder of ipsh!, June 2007.
2. In 2006, American Express cut TV advertising spending from 80 percent in 2004 to 35 percent, Ford committed 15 percent to Internet advertising, and McDonald's reduced network TV advertising from 66 percent to 33 percent (Parks Associates).
3. *Advertising Age* 2007 yearbook.
4. 1 Yottabyte = 10^{24}.
5. "Your Guide to Profits: Insights through Business Analytics," Balasubramanium Venkitachalam, WPP, accessed from www.wpp.com/WPP/Marketing/ReportsStudies/YourGuidetoProfits.htm, accessed December 11, 2007.
6. ZenithOptimedia, January 2007.

Index